Applied Econometrics Association Series

General Editors: **Jean H. P. Paelinck**, Emeritus Professor, Erasmus University, Rotterdam; and **Henri Serbat**, University of Paris 2

The vital importance of econometrics for understanding economic phenomena is increasingly recognized in every field of economics.

The discipline is based on 'scientific processes which aim to identify, explain and forecast economic phenomena using formalised tools to produce, measure, structure and model the information' (Gérard Duru and Henri Serbat, 1991).

The Applied Econometrics Association, established in 1974, seeks to develop the use of econometric tools by producing regular updates on the state of the art and the progress made in each specific field, and so to further the transformation of unconnected facts into pertinent information for use in analysis and decision-making.

The series was conceived to form a set of working references for advanced students and researchers in each specific field, as well as a guide to development across the discipline more broadly.

This exchange of knowledge will be continued permanently by the opening of a debate site on the Internet [http://www.aea.fed-eco.org].

Titles include:

Françoise Bourdon and Jean Bourdon (*editors*)
WAGE ECONOMETRICS AND MODELLING

Fabrizio Carlevaro and Jean-Baptiste Lesourt (editors)
MEASURING AND ACCOUNTING ENVIRONMENTAL NUISANCES AND SERVICES

Arthur Getis, Jesús Mur and Henry G. Zoller (*editors*)
SPATIAL ECONOMETRICS AND SPATIAL STATISTICS

Siv S. Gustafsson and Danièle E. Meulders (*editors*)
GENDER AND THE LABOUR MARKET
Econometric Evidence of Obstacles to Achieving Gender Equality

Hans Heijke and Joan Muysken (*editors*)
EDUCATION AND TRAINING IN A KNOWLEDGE-BASED ECONOMY

Pavlos Karadeloglou (*editor*)
EXCHANGE-RATE POLICY IN EUROPE

Pavlos Karadeloglou and Virginie Terraza (*editors*)
EXCHANGE RATES AND MACROECONOMIC DYNAMICS

Sandrine Lardic and Valérie Mignon (*editors*)
RECENT DEVELOPMENTS ON EXCHANGE RATES

Benoît Mahy, Robert Plasman and François Rycx (*editors*)
GENDER PAY DIFFERENTIALS
Cross-National Evidence from Micro-Data

Applied Econometrics Association
Series Standing Order ISBN 0–333–71460–1
(*outside North America only*)

You can receive future titles in this series as they are published by placing a standing order. Please contact your bookseller or, in case of difficulty, write to us at the address below with your name and address, the title of the series and the ISBN quoted above.

Customer Services Department, Macmillan Distribution Ltd, Houndmills, Basingstoke, Hampshire RG21 6XS, England

---

Exchange Rates and Macroeconomic Dynamics

Edited by

Pavlos Karadeloglou

and

Virginie Terraza

palgrave
macmillan

First published in 2008 by
PALGRAVE MACMILLAN
Houndmills, Basingstoke, Hampshire RG21 6XS and
175 Fifth Avenue, New York, N.Y. 10010
Companies and representatives throughout the world.

PALGRAVE MACMILLAN is the global academic imprint of the Palgrave Macmillan division of St. Martin's Press, LLC and of Palgrave Macmillan Ltd. Macmillan® is a registered trademark in the United States, United Kingdom and other countries. Palgrave is a registered trademark in the European Union and other countries.

ISBN-13: 978–0–230–50062–4 hardback
ISBN-10: 0–230–50062–5 hardback

This book is printed on paper suitable for recycling and made from fully managed and sustained forest sources. Logging, pulping and manufacturing processes are expected to conform to the environmental regulations of the country of origin.

A catalogue record for this book is available from the British Library.

A catalog record for this book is available from the Library of Congress.

10 9 8 7 6 5 4 3 2 1
17 16 15 14 13 12 11 10 09 08

Printed and bound in Great Britain by
CPI Antony Rowe, Chippenham and Eastbourne

Contents

List of Tables

List of Figures

Notes on the Contributors

Virginie Coudert is economic advisor at the Banque de France in the Financial Stability Coordination Department. Her areas of expertise concern Financial Macroeconomics and exchange rates.

Cécile Couharde is Lecturer at the University of Paris 13. Her researches focus on equilibrium exchange rates and exchange rate regimes.

Victoria Dobrynskaya is Senior Lecturer at Department of Theory of Money and Credit, State University – Higher School of Economics, Moscow, Russia. Her main fields of research are international macroeconomics and finance, monetary policy, macrofinance, asset pricing, behavioral economics.

Jan Frait is Professor of Economics at the Technical University, Faculty of Economics in Ostrava (Czech Republic). Jan Frait is currently Board Member of the Czech National Bank and Editor in Chief of the Czech Journal of Economics and Finance. His research is mainly oriented to the equilibrium exchange rate, inflation, economic growth.

Pavlos Karadeloglou is Head of the Global Economy Section in the European Central Bank. His areas of expertise focus on macroeconomics with emphasis on international issues as well as macroeconomic modelling.

Luboš Komárek is currently an advisor to the Bank Board Member at the Czech National Bank, Associate Professor at the Prague School of Economics and Vice-President of the Czech Economic Society. His research is mainly oriented to the equilibrium exchange rate, currency substitution, FX interventions, monetary policy transmission mechanisms and estimation of financial integration.

Dmitry Levando is Assistant Professor at Department of Macroeconomics, State University – Higher School of Economics, Moscow, Russia. His main research interests are international finance, choice under uncertainty, theory of contracts and exchange.

Ronald MacDonald is the Adam Smith Professor of Political Economy at the University of Glasgow. He has published widely in the areas of Macroeconomics and International Finance and has a special interest in the Economics of Exchange Rates. He has acted as a consultant to various public and private sector institutions.

Martin Melecký is currently a PhD student at the University of New South Wales, Department of Economics, USA. His researches are mainly focused on modelling of equilibrium exchange rates, currency preferences, implications of imperfect credibility for central banks, the monetary policy transmission mechanism in small open economies and sovereign debt management.

Christos Papazoglou is a Senior Economist in the Economic Research Department of the Bank of Greece and Assistant Professor of Economics at the Panteion University of Athens, Greece. He has numerous publications in economic journals and collective volumes. His research interest as well as his publications focuses on the area of international economics and on issues concerning the post-communist economies of Central and South Eastern Europe.

Virginie Terraza is Assistant Professor at the University of Luxembourg. Her main researches concern econometrics methods in fields of financial risk modelling and portfolio management. Presently, her work is concerned with funds investments risks and performance in collaboration with the Lux-investment Advisors Bank, Luxembourg.

Viktor Várpalotai is Assistant Professor at the University of Budapest, Hungary and researcher at the Magyar Nemzeti Bank. His research interests are Macro modelling, Bayesian econometrics, Monetary policy.

Gregory de Walque, PhD is Economist at the National Bank of Belgium. His current researches focus on micro-founded macroeconomic models with money, dynamic stochastic general equilibrium models.

Raf Wouters is Senior Economist at the National Bank of Belgium. His research interests are monetary policy in micro-founded macroeconomic models, Bayesian estimation of dynamic stochastic general equilibrium model.

Introduction

Pavlos Karadeloglou[1] *and Virginie Terraza*[2]

The impact of exchange rate movements on prices and economic activity is in the core of international macroeconomic theory and policy. More recently, the interest in this issue has resurged following the rather strong exchange rate fluctuations, the unsustainability of the current account imbalances and the anticipated shifts in exchange rate regimes in some emerging economies. The classical international macroeconomic theory teaches that currency depreciations are expansionary while the opposite is true for domestic currency appreciations. However, factors like degree of trade openness, the market structure, the geographical composition of trade, the importance of intra-firm trade and the macroeconomic and institutional environment influence on the degree and intensity of the impacts.

Exchange rate models developed in the years following the fall of Bretton Woods were based on the assumption that exchange rate developments closely follow movements of fundamentals and that their movements matter. The price-competitiveness-channel together with import and consumer price developments are certainly obvious transmission mechanisms of the exchange rate developments to the macroeconomy, as swings in the nominal effective exchange rate affect relative costs and prices with a subsequent impact on export performance and thus activity. Recently the profession has made considerable progress, pursuing several new routes in an attempt to narrow down the still wide uncertainty about the size of the impacts. At the same time, one of the main directions in the empirical research in economics was to quantify the role of exchange rates in moderating the impact of economic disturbances.

When considering the factors determining exchange rate movements a familiar starting point is the theory of (relative) purchasing power parity (PPP), according to which the inflation differential at home and abroad is reflected in a corresponding change in the nominal exchange rate. Following the provocative paper by Obstfeld and Rogoff in 2000 about 'Risk and Exchange Rates' published in the NBER Working Paper No. 6694, where six key puzzles in International Finance related to transaction costs were identified, a large and vibrant literature seeking to establish if indeed transaction costs explain the puzzles was generated.

The first part of the book, deals with the PPP persistence puzzle, with econometric aspects of the exchange rates dynamics and its implications and the misalignment on equilibrium exchange rates. In chapter 1, **R. MacDonald** examines two of the puzzles addressed in Obstfeld and Rogoff, namely the PPP puzzle and the exchange rate disconnect. He argues that the latter actually has two puzzles subsumed within it, what he refers to as the levels and volatility puzzles. Hence, in total, he explores three puzzles in this paper, namely the PPP puzzle, and what we have referred to as the levels and volatility puzzles, and seeks to provide an explanation for these puzzles. He argues that the PPP Puzzle – the combination of a high volatility of real and nominal exchange rates with the slow mean reversion of real exchange rates – can be explained in a number of ways, from product and time aggregation biases to pricing to market, non-linear adjustment, real factors and imperfectly substitutable goods, with the preferred explanation for the PPP puzzle being a combination of pricing to market and real factors, such as the effects of productivity differentials on exchange rates. This conclusion has clear implications for the measurement of equilibrium values of currencies. The levels puzzle concerns the supposed poor out-of-sample forecasting properties of exchange rate models and, in particular, the findings of Meese and Rogoff (1983) that fundamentals-based models cannot outperform a random walk. He argues in this paper that the random walk paradigm can be convincingly overturned at horizons as short as two months, and this seems a robust result. The key to overturning this result is the use of econometric methods, which capture the underlying data dynamics and the long-run relationships. The volatility puzzle concerns the apparent excessive volatility of exchange rates in flexible rate regimes – intra regime volatility – and the sharp rise in both real and nominal exchange rate volatility in the move from fixed to floating exchange rates – inter-regime volatility. In this paper he argues that excessive exchange rate volatility is entirely consistent with a number of forward-looking exchange rate models and in fact the empirical evidence suggests that intra-regime volatility may be something of a chimera. He also claims that the issue of inter regime volatility may also be overplayed since once the role of distortions are recognised in fixed rate regimes fundamentals become more volatile. He concludes that although there are still a number of puzzles in the exchange rate literature the three key puzzles considered in this paper have been resolved.

To determine whether the real exchange rate is misaligned with respect to its long-run equilibrium is an important issue for policy makers. In particular, the potential misalignment (which is the difference between the 'equilibrium exchange rate' consistent with macroeconomic fundamentals and the observed exchange rates) is one of the most important policy issues faced by the new EU Member States in view of their future adoption of the euro and with the big challenge being the participation in the exchange rate mechanism. In chapter 2, **Jan Frait, Luboš Komárek and Martin Melecký** focus on the development of real exchange rates and its determinants in five new EU Member States namely the Czech Republic, Hungary, Poland, Slovakia, and Slovenia. They provide the long-term trends leading to real exchange rate appreciation, pointing to the differences in the individual countries as well as a survey of existing empirical literature on the real exchange rates in transitional countries. Using the purely statistical (Hodrick-Prescott and Band-Pass filter) as well as the BEER-like approaches, which were estimated by two single equation techniques (Engle-Granger and ARDL), they conclude that the real exchange rates have generally evolved in line with the determinants that are believed to be fundamental. The differences among the individual countries can sometimes be explained by different development of their fundamentals.

The question related to the misalignment or not of the Chinese exchange rate has been a topical issue in the discussion of international fora as many analysts argue that this may be a solution for the correction of global imbalances. **Virginie Coudert and Cécile Couharde** (Chapter 3) investigate the size of a possible misalignment in the Chinese real exchange rate. To do so they investigate the trend of several economic indicators that show some signs of undervaluation of the real exchange rate of the renminbi during the recent years: real effective exchange rate depreciation, surging foreign exchange reserves, current account surpluses. Second, they use cross-section regressions relating the real exchange rate to a 'Balassa effect', on different samples of countries. Third they address the issue of the 'Balassa effect' in the framework of a BEER approach using panel-data estimations. The econometric estimates confirm the trend of the stylised facts about the undervaluation for the Chinese renminbi.

In the second part of the book the importance of exchange rates dynamics in the pass-through effects (PTE) is examined. In chapter 4, **Victoria V. Dobrynskaya and Dmitry V. Levando** propose an analysis of PTE on consumer prices of different categories of goods and producer prices in different industries in Russia taking into account links between monetary policy and exchange rate regimes. They address the question whether the monetary policy in Russia counteracts exchange rate changes and reduces pass-through. Using an empirical approach, they test if PTE: 1) is incomplete in the short run and long run; 2) is different for consumer and producer prices; 3) is different for the components of CPI (food, goods and services) and the components of PPI (export- and domestic market-oriented industries) and if monetary policy decreases PTE. They conclude that PTE on all prices is incomplete even in the long run and that PTE on consumer prices is higher than PTE in developed countries. Furthermore, prices of food and goods are highly exchange rate elastic while prices of services do not react to exchange rate changes. This characterises Russia as a small economy, which is highly dependent on shocks in the world markets.

In chapter 5, the importance of exchange rate analysis and its impact on the economy is demonstrated in an inflation-targeting context adopted by the Hungarian Central Bank since June 2001. The main important issue in such a policy context is the exchange rate pass-through. This is a major focus of interest for policymakers and academics. The former are primarily interested in the extent and timing of ERPT as a key ingredient of their forecasting models of prices and of the trade balance. Along with academics, they are also interested in the role of ERPT in understanding the mechanisms of international price adjustment, e.g. in reconciling the observation that the relative stability of import prices does not reflect the high volatility of nominal exchange rates with economic theory. Evidence of 'disconnect' between exchange rates and prices would also imply a greater degree of insulation and thus greater effectiveness of monetary policy. **V. Varpalotai** presents an inflation-forecasting model using an approach which is new not only in Hungary but also in the relevant literature. This model is based on disaggregated econometric estimates with special interest on slow price adjustment which are complemented by expert assumptions in a unified framework. The model delivers forecasts of the prices of marketed goods included in the CPI basket by describing the gradual process when costs gradually pass-through to consumer prices. Actually, it is the empirical estimation of this slow cost pass-through process that provides the novelty of the model in terms of economics and econometrics. By considering wages, foreign prices, exchange rate, transportation costs and energy prices the model contributes in answering two questions: (1) How do prices change following changes in the prices of their cost factors? (2) What happens during the transitory period when changes in costs and prices separate?

The third part of the book deals with econometric aspects of the exchange rates dynamics linked to structural shocks on different economies. The contribution of the dynamic stochastic general equilibrium (DSGE) model is used by **G. de Walque and R. Wouters** to analyse the existing linkages between the United States and the euro area. They try to empirically estimate a New Open Economy Model to analyse the behaviour of the exchange rate and the current account between the two economies. They use a Bayesian full information approach to estimate the model; the latter is used to evaluate the impulse response functions for different shocks (productivity shocks domestic demand and monetary policy shocks). Their results confirm that positive productivity shocks and declining mark-ups, or the typical characteristics of the new economy, are unable to explain a major appreciation of the exchange rate. Although in its present state, the model has clearly some problems to replicate the observed international synchronisation in the cyclical output and aggregate demand components, it remains a topic for further research to analyse how much of the observed correlation between the output of the two major economies can be explained once we allow for a positive correlation between the domestic shocks that hit the two economies (which are assumed to be orthogonal in the estimation approach up to now). In particular, they can identify the major sources of exchange rate and current account developments. Finally the main findings suggest that shocks issued from the uncovered real interest parity seem to be important to explain the short run volatility in exchange rates, while fundamental shocks explain the long run swings.

In chapter 7, a dynamic macroeconomic model is used to study the impact of liberalisation on the behaviour of the real exchange rate in a representative transition economy operating under a flexible exchange rate regime. **Christos Papazoglou** identifies the role of liberalisation in the emergence of the stylised fact concerning the behaviour of the real exchange rate at the early stages of transformation of the transition economies. The analysis considers the impact of two specific shocks related to liberalisation. The first refers to an increase in the core inflation while the second analyses a shock on the financial sector, under a fall in the demand for money. The results are affected by two assumptions reflecting the particularity of transition economies: The particular shocks on domestic inflation are increased due to the observation that the private sector does not extend over the entire economy. The second concerns the underdevelopment of the domestic financial sector, which diminishes the impact of the two disturbances on the rate of exchange depreciation. As a result of these two specific features the possibility of real appreciation during the adjustment process increases. The particular disturbance impacts more on the inflation rate than on the exchange depreciation rate in the short run and generates the necessary adjustment mechanism that brings the system towards the new long run equilibrium.

Notes

1. European Central Bank.
2. LSF, University of Luxembourg.

Part I

The Purchasing Power Parity and its Implications for Equilibrium Exchanges Rates

1
Three Exchange Rate Puzzles: Fact or Fiction?

Ronald MacDonald

1.1 Introduction

In their provocative paper, Obstfeld and Rogoff (2000) advocated explaining six key puzzles in International Finance by appealing to transaction costs. Their paper has generated a large and vibrant literature which seeks to establish if indeed transaction costs explain the puzzles. In this paper we examine two of the puzzles addressed in Obstfeld and Rogoff, namely the PPP puzzle and the exchange rate disconnect. We argue that the latter actually has two puzzles subsumed within it, what we refer to as the levels and volatility puzzles. Hence, in total, we explore three puzzles in this paper. A common conclusion often expressed regarding the puzzles is that they cannot be understood in terms of a standard macroeconomic framework and therefore to understand exchange rate behaviour the profession has to move towards a market microstructure approach and effectively abandon macroeconomic fundamentals (see for example, Flood and Rose (1995)). The bottom line in this paper is, however, that macroeconomic fundamentals are useful for explaining exchange rate behaviour and indeed can be used to explain the exchange rate puzzles.

The so-called PPP puzzle (Rogoff (1995)) concerns the high volatility of real and nominal exchange rates and the slow mean reversion of real exchange rates. The ballpark figure for the latter is within a range of three – five years for CPI-based real exchange rates. The puzzle arises because the exchange rate volatility is consistent with a standard price stickiness story (i.e. liquidity effects in the presence of sticky prices), but the slow mean reversion is not consistent with price stickiness (a half-life of one year would be consistent).

The levels puzzle relates back to the seminal paper of Meese and Rogoff (1983) in which they demonstrated that a standard set of macroeconomic fundamentals are unable to beat a simple random walk at horizons of less than three years. This conclusion has apparently been reaffirmed by many researchers in the period post-1983 (see, for example, Frankel and Rose (1995) and Rogoff (1999)). In this paper we argue that the levels puzzle is not really a puzzle and can be explained when proper account is taken of the interaction between the macroeconomic fundamentals and exchange rates.

The volatility puzzle has two aspects: inter- and intra-regime volatility. For example, a standard asset-pricing framework would imply

$$Var(s_t) \leq Var(\hat{s}_t) \tag{1.1}$$

where $(\hat{s}_t)$ is some measure of the fundamental based exchange rate, but in actuality what we observe in flexible rate regimes is:

$$Var(s_t) > Var(\hat{s}_t) \tag{1.2}$$

This is the intraregime puzzle – the stylised fact that exchange rates in floating regimes seem to be excessively volatile relative to macroeconomic fundamentals. However, as we shall see in this paper, a number of macroeconomic models predict that the direction of the variance inequality in (2) is correct. The concept of intra-regime volatility (Baxter and King (1989) and Flood and Rose (1999)) is that in moving from fixed to floating rates the volatility of macroeconomic fundamentals remains unchanged but the volatility of exchange rates – both real and nominal – increases dramatically. In this paper we show that recent empirical work suggests that the intraregime puzzle can be explained if care is taken to define the macro fundamentals.

1.2 The PPP puzzle

Central to the PPP puzzle is the slow mean reversion speeds of real exchange rates. Consider the following AR process for the real exchange rate:

$$q_t = \rho q_{t-1} + \beta + \varepsilon_t, 0 < \rho < 1, \tag{1.3}$$

where q is the log of the real exchange rate, ρ is the parameter of mean reversion, ε_t is a random error term and β is a constant. If we write the log of the equilibrium exchange rate as $\bar{q}$ and if we define this as the unconditional expectation of the process in (3) then (assuming $\rho < 1$): $\bar{q} = \beta/(1 - \rho)$.

Long-run PPP is violated if $|\rho|=1$ and if ρ and/or β are not time-invariant constants (our discussion here follows Abuaf and Jorion (1990)). If long-run PPP holds, short-run PPP is violated whenever $q_t \neq \bar{q}$ and factors which would prevent a continuous equality between short- and long-run PPP would be non-zero interest differentials and foreign exchange market intervention.[1] Traditional PPP focuses on the existence of long-run PPP and, more specifically, how long it takes for a currency to settle at its long-run PPP value. In other words: how fast is mean reversion in expression (3)? To answer this question it is useful to introduce the concept of a half-life; that is, how long does it take for half of a shock to PPP to be extinguished? If a and b denote the initial and final deviations from equilibrium, respectively, the number of intervals from a to b will be given as $(\ln b\text{-}\ln a)/\ln\rho$ and therefore the formula for a half-life is given as:

$$hl = \frac{\ln (0.5)}{\ln (\hat{\rho})}. \tag{1.4}$$

In the traditional form of PPP money neutrality probably suggests hl should be around one year, and this would imply a value for ρ of 0.5, with annual data. However, and as we shall see in more detail below, estimated half-lives are much higher than one year. For example, for the post Bretton Woods period when currencies are examined on an individual basis, ρ turns out to be statistically indistinguishable from unity. However, when data from prior to the post-Bretton Woods regime, or when panel data are used for the post-Bretton Woods, there is clear evidence of statistically significant mean reversion and the half-life falls within the range of three to five years (see MacDonald (1995) and Rogoff (1996)). Rogoff (1996) has labelled such mean reversion speeds, combined with the large volatility of real exchange rates as the PPP puzzle:

> How can one reconcile the enormous short-term volatility of real exchange rates with the extremely slow rate at which shocks appear to damp out? Most explanations of short-term exchange rate volatility point to financial factors such as changes in portfolio preferences, short-term asset price bubbles and monetary shocks. Such shocks can have substantial effects on the real economy in the presence of sticky nominal prices. Consensus estimates for the rate at which PPP deviations damp, however, suggest a half-life of three to five years, seemingly far too long to be explained by nominal rigidities. It is not difficult to rationalize slow adjustment of real shocks if real shocks – shocks to tastes and technology – are predominant. But existing models based on real shocks cannot account for short-terms exchange-rate volatility. (Rogoff, 1996, pp. 647–8)

A useful way of trying to understand and explain the PPP puzzle is to decompose the overall (CPI-based) real exchange rate into two relative price components, an internal and external component. Assume that the overall price level, p, is made up of a price level for traded goods, which, in turn, is the sum of the n traded goods produced in the home and foreign country, and the price level for non-traded goods, which is the sum of the m non-traded goods produced:

$$p_t = \beta_t p_t^T + (1 - \beta_t)\, p_t^{NT},\ 0 < \beta < 1, \tag{1.5}$$

$$p_t^* = \beta_t^* p_t^{T*} + (1 - \beta_t^*)\, p_t^{NT*},\ 0 < \beta^* < 1, \tag{1.5'}$$

where P_t^T denotes the price of traded goods, P_t^{NT} denotes the price of non-traded goods the βs denote the share of traded goods in the economy and lower case letters again indicate that a log transformation has been utilised. The existence of non-traded goods can impart an important bias into the determination of the equilibrium exchange rate. This may be seen in the following way. Consider the definition of the real exchange rate, defined with respect to overall prices:

$$q_t \equiv s_t - p_t + p_t^*, \tag{1.6}$$

and define a similar relationship for the price of traded goods as:

$$q_t^T \equiv s_t - p_t^T + p_t^{T*}. \tag{1.6'}$$

By substituting (1.5), (1.5′) and (1.6′) into (1.6) we can obtain:

$$q_t = q_t^T + (\beta_t - 1)[(p_t^{NT} - p_t^T) - (p_t^{NT*} - p_t^{T*})] \tag{1.7}$$

or

$$q_t = q_t^T + q_t^{T,NT}$$

where

$$q_t^{NT,T} = (\beta_t - 1)[(p_t^{NT} - p_t^T) - (p_t^{NT*} - p_t^{T*})],$$

the relative price of non-traded to traded goods in the home country relative to the foreign country is usually referred to as the relative internal price ratio.

From the perspective of trying to unravel the sources of deviations from PPP, expression (1.7) is quite neat because it indicates that there are two potential sources of systematic movements in real exchange rates (which is another way of thinking about deviations from PPP): one is through movements in the relative price of traded goods, captured in q^T, and the other is movements in the internal price ratio, $q^{NT,T}$. In a world where all macroeconomic shocks are nominal, the existence of non-traded goods would have no impact on the real exchange rate since all prices, both traded and non-traded, would move in proportion to, say, a monetary disturbance. However, in a world where there are both real and nominal disturbances, real shocks can lead to movements in $q^{NT,T}$ which are independent of q^T, thereby producing a violation of PPP. In this regard, perhaps the best known real shock is a total factor productivity shock which occurs in the traded sector and gets transmitted into p^{NT} and, ultimately, the CPI-based real exchange rate. This is the so-called Balassa–Samuelson hypothesis, which we discuss in the next chapter. We shall return to expression (1.7) below.

As Rogoff (1996) notes, and as we will demonstrate further below, the q^T term is highly volatile and its variance innovation dominates the variance innovation of $q^{NT,T}$. Since $q^{NT,T}$ is usually taken to be driven by 'real shocks', such as taste and technology shocks, which are likely to be highly persistent, the variance behaviour of $q^{NT,T}$ makes it difficult to explain the behaviour of q in terms of $q^{NT,T}$. In sticky price models the volatility of the nominal exchange rate gets transferred on a one-to-one basis into the volatility of q^T. But how can the persistence of q^T be explained? We turn to some explanations after discussing the empirical evidence.

1.2.1 Testing PPP

Recent tests of PPP have focused on using unit root methods to determine if real exchange rates are mean-reverting and co-integration methods to test the relationship between the nominal exchange rate – relative price relationship. The latter tests of PPP focus on the following kind of relationship:

$$s_t = \beta + \alpha_0 p_t + \alpha_1 p_t^* + \varphi_t, \tag{1.8}$$

and on the properties of the residual term in (1.8). In particular, if s_t, p_t, and p_t^* are integrated of order one – I(1) – then so-called weak form PPP (MacDonald 1993) exists if the residual term from an estimated version of (1.8) is found to be stationary, or I(0). Strong-form PPP exists if, in addition to weak-form holding, homogeneity is also satisfied; that is, $\alpha_0 = 1$ and $\alpha_1 = -1$. If the estimated coefficients are equal and opposite then this implies relative prices affect the exchange rate in a symmetrical fashion; that is, $\alpha_0 = -\alpha_1$. The distinction between weak- and strong-form PPP is important because the existence of transportation costs and different price weights across countries means that 'there are no hypothesis regarding the specific values of α_0 and α_1 except that they are positive and negative' (Patel 1990).

The basic message from co-integration-based tests of (1.8) is that the estimator used matters. For example, the application of the two-step Engle–Granger method, in which symmetry is generally imposed, produces little or no evidence of co-integration – see, for example, Baillie and Selover (1987), Enders (1988), Mark (1990) and Patel (1990) for evidence for a variety of bilateral currencies from the recent floating period (see MacDonald (1995,2006)).

However, as is now well known the two-step method of Engle and Granger suffers from a number of deficiencies such as having poor small sample properties and, in the presence of endogeneity and serial correlation, the asymptotic distribution of the estimates will depend on nuisance parameters (see, for example, Banerjee et al. (1986)). Since Johansen's (1988, 1990) full information maximum likelihood method produces asymptotically optimal estimates (because it has a parametric correction for serial correlation and endogeneity) a number of researchers have applied this method to testing the PPP hypothesis. Thus, Cheung and Lai (1993), Kugler and Lenz (1993), MacDonald (1993,1995) and MacDonald and Marsh (1994) all report strong evidence of co-integration, and therefore support for weak-form PPP, but little evidence in favour of strong-form PPP when US dollar bilateral exchange rates are used, since homogeneity restrictions are usually strongly rejected. MacDonald (1993,1995) reports more evidence in favour of strong-form PPP when DM-based bilaterals are used. MacDonald and Moore (1996) use the methods of Phillips-Hansen (1990) and Hansen (1992) as an alternative (to Johansen) way of addressing issues of simultaneity and temporal dependence in the residual of (1.8). They also report strong evidence of weak-form PPP for US dollar bilaterals, while strong-form PPP holds for most DM-based bilaterals.

The superior performance of PPP when DM-based exchange rates are used is a recurring theme in the empirical literature and was first noted by Frenkel (1981) in the context of the traditional regression-based tests of PPP, discussed above. The effect may be attributed to a number of factors. First, the existence of the ERM has attenuated the volatility of DM bilaterals relative to US dollar bilaterals, thereby producing a higher signal-to-noise ratio. Second, the geographical proximity of European countries facilitates greater goods arbitrage and therefore makes it more likely that PPP will occur. Third, the openness of European countries, in terms of their trade making up a greater proportion of their collective national output than in the US, means that the arbitrage process is more likely to occur, thereby forcing the LOOP.

Pedroni (1995) has proposed panel co-integration methods as an alternative to panel unit root tests. The construction of such a test is complicated because regressors are not normally required to be exogenous, and hence off-diagonal terms are introduced into the residual asymptotic covariance matrix. Although these drop out of the asymptotic distributions in the single equation case, they are unlikely to do so in the context of a non-stationary panel because of idiosyncratic effects across individual members of the panel. A second difficulty is that generated residuals will depend on the distributional properties of the estimated coefficients and this is likely to be severe in the panel context because of the averaging that takes place. Pedroni (1995) proposes statistics which allow for heterogeneous fixed effects, deterministic trends, and both common and idiosyncratic disturbances to the underlying variables (and these, in turn, can have very general forms of temporal dependence). Applying his methods to a panel of nominal exchange rates and relative prices for the recent float, he finds evidence supportive of weak-form PPP. Pedroni (2000) confirms this panel evidence in favour of weak form PPP using group mean panel estimators.

The evidence in this section may be summarised as suggesting that on both a single currency basis, and on the basis of panel tests, for the recent floating experience, weak-form PPP holds for dollar bilateral pairings and strong-form PPP holds for many DM-based bilaterals. Although a finding in favour of weak-form PPP would now seem to be widely accepted in the literature, it is important to note that the implied mean reversion from the studies discussed in this section is often painfully slow.

Most other recent tests of the PPP proposition have involved an examination of the time series properties of the real exchange rate. In order to test if the autoregressive parameter in an estimated version of equation (1.3) is significantly different from unity, a number of researchers (see, *inter alia*, Roll (1979), Darby (1980), MacDonald (1985), Enders (1988) and Mark (1990)) have used an augmented Dickey–Fuller (ADF) statistic, or a variant of this test to test the unit root hypothesis for the recent floating period. A version of an ADF statistic for the real exchange rate is given as:

$$\Delta q_t = \gamma_0 + \gamma_1 t + \gamma_2 q_{t-1} + \sum_{j=1}^{n-1} \beta_j \Delta q_{t-j} + \nu_t, \tag{1.9}$$

where l is the lag length of the real exchange rate. As is standard in this kind of test, evidence of significant mean reversion is captured by a significantly negative value of γ_1. However, in practice the estimated value of γ_1 is insignificantly different from zero implying that the autoregressive coefficient in (1.3) is statistically indistinguishable from unity. However, as Campbell and Perron (1991), and others, have noted univariate unit root tests have relatively low power to reject the null when it is in fact false, especially when the autoregressive component in (1.3) is close to unity.

One natural way of increasing the power of unit root tests is to increase the span of the data. Intuitively, what this does is to give the real exchange rate more time to return to its mean value, thereby giving it greater opportunity to reject the null of non-stationarity. And a number of researchers (see, for example, Edison (1987), Frankel (1986, 1988), Abuaf and Jorion (1990), Grilli and Kaminski (1991) and Lothian and Taylor (1995)) have implemented a real exchange rate unit root test using approximately 100 years of annual data. In contrast to comparable tests for the recent floating period, these tests report evidence of significant mean reversion, with the average half-life across these studies being around four years. Diebold, Husted and Rush (1991), also use long time spans of annual data, ranging from 74 to 123 years, to analyse the real exchange rates of six countries. In contrast to other long time span studies, the authors use long memory models to capture fractional integration processes. They find considerable evidence that PPP holds as a long-run concept and report a typical half-life of three years.

Although studies which extend the span by increasing *T* are obviously interesting, they are not without their own specific problems since the basket used to construct the price indices is likely to be very different at the beginning and end of the sample period. This may be viewed as the temporal analogue to the spatial problem that arises in comparing price indices at a particular point in time and makes the interpretation of the results difficult. Also, such studies suffer from spanning both fixed and flexible rate regimes with the inclusion of data from the former regime making mean reversion more likely. Additionally, Froot and Rogoff (1995) raise the problem of 'survivorship', or sample selection, bias in these studies. Such bias arises because the countries for which very long spans of data are available are countries which have been wealthy for relatively long periods of time and are more likely to produce evidence in favour of PPP because their relative price of non-traded goods have not changed that much. Countries which only comparatively recently became wealthy (such as Japan) or countries which were once wealthy but are no longer (such as Argentina) have not featured in the studies mentioned above. However, such countries are more likely to produce a violation of PPP over long time spans because their relative prices of non-traded goods have changed dramatically (Froot and Rogoff (1995) have presented some empirical evidence to suggest that there is some support for this hypothesis). For these reasons attention has turned from expanding *T*, the time series dimension, to extending *N*, the cross sectional dimension.

The more recent panel exchange rate literature has involved testing for the stationarity of the residual series in (8) or reparameterising the equation into an expression for the real exchange rate and testing the panel unit root properties of real exchange rates. The first paper to test mean reversion of the real exchange rate in a panel setting was Abuaf and Jorion (1990). In particular, using a ZSURE estimator they implement a Dickey Fuller style test for 10 US dollar-based real exchange rates for the period 1973 to 1987, they are only able to reject the null hypothesis of a unit root using a ten per cent significance level. More recent tests of the panel unit properties of real exchange rates have been conducted using the test(s) proposed by Levin and Lin (1992,1994), who demonstrated that there are 'dramatic improvements in statistical power' from implementing a unit root test in a panel context, rather than performing separate tests on the individual series. The panel equivalent of the univariate ADF is:

$$\Delta q_{it} = \gamma_i + \delta_i q_{i,t-1} + \sum_{j=1}^{l-1} \beta_{ij} \Delta q_{i,t-j} + v_{it}, \tag{1.10}$$

where, as before, i denotes the cross sectional dimension.

The Levin and Lin approach involves testing the null hypothesis that each individual series is I(1) against the alternative that all of the series as a panel are stationary. Their approach allows for a range of individual-specific effects and also for cross sectional dependence by the subtraction of cross sectional time dummies. Frankel and Rose (1995), Wu (1995), Oh (1995) and MacDonald (1995b) have all implemented variants of the Levin and Lin panel unit root test on 'overall' price measures (such as WPI and CPI) and find evidence of mean reversion which is very similar to that reported in long time spans of annual data, namely half-lives of four years. Another feature of these studies, which is quite similar to the long time span studies, is the finding of price homogeneity when PPP is tested in a panel context using nominal exchange rates and relative prices. Oh (1996) and Wei and Parsley (1995) have examined the unit root properties of panel data for the Summers–Heston data set and tradable sectors, respectively, and report similar results to those based on aggregate data.

Bayoumi and MacDonald (1998) examine the panel unit root properties of inter- and intra-national exchange rates. The former are defined for a panel of CPI and WPI based real exchange rates for 20 countries, over the period 1973 to 1993, while the intra-national data sets are constructed from Canadian regional and US federal data for the same period and the same number of real rates. The argument in the paper is that, if indeed, the predominant source of international real exchange rate movements is monetary, observed mean reversion should be more rapid in international data than in intranational data because monetary shocks are transitory relative to real shocks. This is, in fact, borne out by the panel data sets: for the international data set there is clear evidence of stationarity on the basis of the Levin and Lin test, while for the intra-national panel sets real rates are non-stationary and only very slowly mean-reverting.

Goldberg and Verboven (2005) use the Levin and Lin panel unit root test to examine what they refer to as the absolute and relative forms of the LOOP.[2] Their data set comprises the prices of 150 car vehicle makes in five separate European markets over the period 1970–2000. They demonstrate that there are substantial deviations from the absolute version of the LOOP, which they explain within the framework of a structural product differentiation model, and report half-lives of approximately 8.3 years. For the relative version of the LOOP they find much less evidence of deviations and much faster half-lives, of between 1.3 to 1.6 years. Clearly the latter are much faster speeds than those found using aggregate price data.

One problem with the Levin and Lin test is that it constrains the δ parameter to be equal across cross-sectional units (although the dynamics are not constrained to be equal across the units). Im,

Pesaran Shinn (1995) propose 2 statistics which do not suffer from this constraint, namely the standardised t-bar and LR-bar statistics. Coakley and Fuertes (1997) implement these statistics for a panel date set comprising 10 countries for the post Bretton–Woods period, and they are able to 'comfortably reject the unit root null', thereby providing further evidence of the power of the panel.

Liu and Maddalla (1996) and Pappell (1997) both highlight the importance of residual correlation in panel unit root tests, a feature absent from the first set of critical values tabulated by Levin and Lin (1992) (used by Frankel and Rose (1995), Wu (1995), Oh (1995)) although not in the Levin and Lin (1994) paper (used by MacDonald (1995)). Pappell (1997) finds that for a number of different panels the null of a unit root cannot be rejected when monthly data are used, although it can be using quarterly data. O'Connell (1997) also takes the Levin and Lin test to task by noting that the power of the test relies on each new bilateral relationship added to the panel generating new information. Although each relationship added may indeed contain some new information it is unlikely that this will be one-to-one given that the currencies are bilateral rates, often defined with respect to the US dollar, and therefore will contain a common element. Correcting for this common cross correlation using a GLS estimator (although assuming that the errors are i.i.d over time), O'Connell (1997) finds that the significant evidence of mean reversion reported in earlier studies disappears. Pesaran et al. criticise the assumption that the autoregressive coefficients are the same across countries and propose.

The observation, referred to above, that PPP works better for DM-based bilaterals than US dollar bilaterals is confirmed in a panel context by Jorion and Sweeney (1996) and Pappell (1997), who both report strong rejections of the unit root null (CPI) based real exchange rates when the DM is used as the numeraire currency. This result is confirmed by Wei and Parsley (1995) and Canzoneri, Cumby and Diba (1996) using tradable prices. Pappell and Theodoridis (1997) attempt to discriminate amongst the potential reasons for the better performance of DM rates by taking the candidates referred to earlier – measures of volatility, openness and distance. Using a panel database constructed for 21 industrialised countries, over the period 1973 to 1996, they find that it is both volatility and distance which are the significant determinants of this result; openness to trade proves to be insignificant. Lothian (1997) has given another reason why US dollar bilaterals are likely to work less well in a panel context and that is because they are dominated by the dramatic appreciation and depreciation of the dollar in the 1980s (therefore the informational content of adding in extra currencies is less for a dollar-based system than a mark-based system).[3] Pappell and Theodoris have confirmed this result and, in particular, show that the evidence in favour of PPP for the dollar strengthens the more post-1985 data is included in the sample.

In a bid to gain further insight into the robustness of the panel unit root findings discussed above, Engle, Hendrickson and Rogers (1998) analyse a panel database constructed from prices in eight cities, located in four countries and in two continents. They use this panel data set to address some of the perceived deficiencies in other panel tests. For example, their panel estimator allows for heteroscedastic and contemporaneously correlated disturbances; differing adjustment speeds of real rates and the model structure used means that their results are not dependent on which currency is picked as the base currency (which, as we have seen, is an issue in some tests). In implementing this general panel structure, they are unable to reject the null of a unit root for the period September 1978 to September 1994. However, and as they recognise, it is unclear if their failure to reject the null is due to the fact that their panel is much smaller than that used in other studies and also is defined for prices in cities, rather than country-wide price measures which are used in most other studies (also, they do not allow the disturbance terms to have different serial correlation properties, which, as we have seen, may be important).

Engel (2000a) has argued that the unit root tests used to extract half-lives are likely to have serious size biases and are therefore unreliable. Using a Monte Carlo exercise Engel shows that with 100 years of annual data and a non-traded component of the real exchange rate of 42 per cent that the true size of the ADF test is 0.90 rather than the 5 per cent that is commonly used. Therefore the probability of rejecting a unit root is 90per cent when a 5 per cent critical value is used. Imbs, Mumtaz, Ravn and Rey (2002) argue that differentiated goods prices mean reverting at different rates and aggregating across goods will introduce a positive bias into aggregate half-lives. Using CPI-based real exchange rates and the sectoral disaggregate components of these prices collected from Eurostat, over a sample period 1975 to

1996, Imbs et al estimate half-lives for the CPI-based real exchange rates of around four years, which is in the usual range, and half-lives for the diaggregate data of between four months and two years. They also demonstrate that the degree of heterogeneity is much more marked for the relative price of traded goods than the relative price of non-traded to traded goods and indeed homogeneity restrictions on the persistence properties of real exchange rates cannot be rejected. They also demonstrate that the apparent dominant role of traded goods at long horizons can be traced back to the same aggregation bias that solves the PPP puzzle.

However, Chen and Engel (2005), using new empirical evidence and theoretical reasoning argue that 'aggregation bias does not explain the PPP puzzle'. They demonstrate using a simulation analysis that if q_t^T is constrained to be non-explosive – $1 \leq \hat{\rho}_i$ – then the size of the aggregation bias is much smaller than Imbs et al. claim. Furthermore, in the presence of measurement error in q_t^T which is additive, and not very persistent, then they show that this can make relative prices appear less persistent than they actually are. Using the same data set as Imbs et al but with corrections for data entry errors Chen and Engel show that half-life estimates are in fact in line with Rogoff's consensus estimates. Additionally, using two different bias correction methods they find that the half-life deviations from PPP for this data set turn out to be even higher than Rogoff's consensus estimates. Taylor (2000) argues that the use of low frequency data, such as the annual data used in nearly all of the panel data sets referred to above, does not, by definition, permit the identification of high frequency adjustment. The kind of time aggregation Taylor refers to is time averaging, rather than observational aggregation (i.e. having a daily price process which is only observed on a weekly basis), which is well known from Working (1960) can introduce severe biases into statistical tests and Taylor demonstrates how this imparts an important bias into half-life estimates of the real exchange rate. In particular, Taylor demonstrates, both theoretically and via a simulation exercise, that when the degree of temporal aggregation is greater than the half-life this bias is likely to be very great.

In order to study the dynamic behaviour of the real exchange rate in a setting that is free of the time aggregation bias issue raised by

Taylor (2001), the product aggregation bias of Imbs et al. (2002), and also to reassess the Engel proposition that deviations from the LOOP are the key explanation for systematic real exchange rate movements, the Parsely and Wei (2003) use The Economist's data set on the price of a Big Mac in a number of capital cities. In particular, Parsely and Wei match Big Mac prices with the prices of the underlying ingredients of a Big Mac across countries, which then allows them to decompose Big Mac real exchange rates into tradable, q^T, and non-tradable, q^{NT}, components.

Parsely and Wei (2003) demonstrate that adjustment speeds for real exchange rates calculated using the tradable components of the Big Mac are much lower than that for non-tradables (average half-lives of 1.4 years and 3.4 years, respectively) and the half-life of Big Mac deviations is 1.8 years which is, as we have seen, much smaller than the kind of half-lives reported in the literature using CPI based real exchange rates. In terms of Engel's explanation for real exchange rate behaviour – that it is the relative price of traded goods, rather than the relative price of non-traded to traded goods which dominates – they show that his finding does not hold in general and that factors such as reduced exchange rate volatility, lower transport cost, higher tariffs, and exchange rate pegs generally weaken this explanation.

1.2.2 Econometric explanations for the PPP puzzle

A number of researchers (see, *inter alia*, Heckscher (1916), Beninga and Protopapadakis (1988), Dumas (1992) and Sercu, Uppal and Van Hulle (1995)) have argued that the existence of transaction costs, due largely to the costs of transportation, are a key explanation for the relatively slow adjustment speeds evident in PPP calculations and, in particular, as an explanation for the failure of the law of one price to hold. In the presence of transaction costs, the price of good *i* in location j, p_j^i may not be equalised with its price in location k, p_k^i Instead if there are transportation costs, π^i, the relative price could fluctuate in a range:

$$-\pi_i \leq p_j^i / sp_k^i \leq \pi_i. \tag{1.11}$$

Further, if the transportation costs depend positively on distance, the range of variation in the relative price will also depend on that distance. Dumas (1992) has demonstrated that for markets which are spatially separated, and feature proportional transactions costs, deviations from PPP should follow a non-linear mean-reverting process, with the speed of mean reversion depending on the magnitude of the deviation from PPP. The upshot of this is that within the transaction band, as defined in (1.11), say, deviations are long-lived and take a considerable time to mean revert: the real exchange rate is observationally equivalent to a random walk. However, large deviations – those that occur outside the band – will be rapidly extinguished and for them the observed mean reversion should be very rapid. The existence of other factors, such as the uncertainty of the permanence of the shock and the so-called sunk costs of the activity of arbitrage may widen the bands over-and-above that associated with simple trade restrictions (see, for example, Dixit (1989) and Krugman (1989)). Essentially the kind of non-linear estimators that researchers have applied to exchange rate data may be thought of as separating observations which represent large deviations from PPP from smaller observations and estimating separately the extent of mean reversion for the two classes of observation.

Obstfeld and Taylor's (1997) attempt to capture the kind of non-linear behaviour imparted by transaction costs involves using the so-called Band Threshold Autoregressive (B-TAR) model. If we reparametrise the standard AR1 model, $q_t = \beta q_{t-1} + \varepsilon_t$ as:

$$\Delta q_t = \lambda q_{t-1} + \varepsilon_t \tag{1.12}$$

where the series is now assumed to be demeaned and $\lambda = (\beta - 1)$ (and also detrended in the work of Obstfeld and Taylor, because they do not explicitly model the long-run systematic trend in real exchange rates). Then the B-TAR is:

$$\begin{aligned} &\lambda^{out}(q_{t-1} - \pi) + \varepsilon_t^{out} \text{ if } q_{t-1} > \pi; \\ \Delta q_t = {}&\lambda^{in} q_{t-1} + \varepsilon_t^{in} \text{ if } \pi \geq q_{t-1} \geq -\pi; \\ &\lambda^{out}(q_{t-1} + \pi) + \varepsilon_t^{out} \text{ if } -\pi > q_{t-1}; \end{aligned} \tag{1.13}$$

where ε_t^{out} is $N(o,\sigma_t^{out})^2$, ε_t^{in} is $N(o,\sigma_t^{out})^2$, $\lambda^{in} = 0$, and λ^{out} is the convergence speed outside the transaction points. So with a B-TAR, the equilibrium value for a real exchange rate can be anywhere in the band $[-\pi,+\pi]$ and does not necessarily need to revert to zero (the real rate is demeaned). The methods of Tsay (1989) are used to identify the best-fit TAR model and, in particular, one which properly partitions the data into observations inside and outside the thresholds. This involves a grid search on π to maximise the log likelihood ratio, LLR = $2(L_a - L_n)$, where L is the likelihood, the subscript *n* denotes the null model and *a* is the alternative TAR model. This is computationally simple, since for a given value of π, TAR estimation in this context amounts to an OLS estimation on partitioned samples – sets of observations with q_{t-1} wholly inside or wholly outside the thresholds.

Using the data set of Engel and Rogers (1995), discussed above, Obstfeld and Taylor find that for inter-country CPI-based real exchange rates, the adjustment speed is between 20 and 40 months, when a simple AR1 model is used, but only 12 months for the TAR model. When dissagregate price series are used to test the law of one price the B-TAR model produces evidence of mean reversion which is well below 12 months, and indeed as low as two months in some cases. Obstfeld and Taylor also show that measures of economic distance – distance itself, exchange rate volatility and trade restrictions – are all positively related to the threshold value and these variables also have a consistent inverse relationship with convergence speed. Many other studies have followed Obstfeld and Taylor's pioneering study (see inter alia Michael, Nobay and Peel (1997), O'Connell (1996), O'Connell and Wei (1997), Bec, Ben-Salem and MacDonald (2000), Taylor, Peel and Sarno (2001)) and provide support of the non linear adjustment of real exchange rates and its role in explaining the PPP puzzle. However, as we shall see below other (linear) explanations can explain the slow mean reversion of real exchange rates and so we sound a cautionary note about non-linear estimators since they must be regarded as something of a black box. Furthermore, these kinds of models are based on the premise that the LOOP should hold once the non-linearities implied by the existence of transactions costs are allowed for. However, as we have argued, the stylised facts suggest that the kind of goods entering international trade are imperfect substitutes and not perfect substitutes as suggested in the LOOP. Additionally, the LOOP relies crucially on the activity of arbitrage. But who carries out such arbitrage? Clearly, although individuals can take advantage of price differences when they travel internationally, this will only have a very limited, if any, effect on the equalisation of goods prices across countries. Wholesalers seem a more natural unit to take advantage of price differences across countries. However, this is only likely to be feasible for goods which are regarded as generic (cereals, for example, and perhaps also certain electronic components may be regarded in this way), but for the vast majority of goods there will likely be institutional or legal constraints which limit the ability of even wholesalers to engage in the goods arbitrage process. The absence of an effective arbitrage process in modern international trade makes it difficult to interpret non-linear results which rely on such a process.

Perhaps the best-known explanation for systematic movements of the real exchange rate, which relies on the $q^{NT,T}$ component of the real exchange rate, is the so-called Balassa-Samuleson (BS) productivity hypothesis. The BS effect is usually derived from a two sector – traded and non-traded – small open economy model. Capital is assumed to be perfectly mobile between the two sectors and across countries. Labour is also assumed to be mobile across the two sectors, but crucially it is not mobile internationally. The law of one price is assumed to hold for the prices of traded goods and nominal wages are determined in the tradable sector.[4]

Tests of the BS hypothesis have proceeded in one of two ways. The first set of tests are indirect and rely on testing which of the two relative price effects embedded in expression (7) dominates the behaviour of the overall real exchange rate: is it movements in the relative price of traded goods (i.e. violations of the LOOP) or the relative price of traded to non-traded goods? These tests (see for example Engel (1993) (2000) and Engel and Rogers (1995)) are not supportive of the BS proposition since they indicate that it is movements in the relative price of traded goods which in large measure explain the time series behaviour of real exchange rates. However, these indirect tests do not preclude a significant direct relationship between productivity and exchange rate movements. Other tests of BS rely on building measures of productivity in the traded and non-traded sectors and regressing the CPI-based real exchange rate and/ or the internal price ratio onto these productivity measures.

For example, Hsieh (1982), Marston (1990) and DeGregorio and Wolf (1994) examine the relationship between the CPI-based real exchange rate and productivity in growth terms. Results favourable to the Balassa–Samuelson hypothesis are reported, in the sense that the coefficients on productivity in the two sectors are statistically significant and correctly signed.[5] As Chinn and Johnston (1999) point out, however, the use of growth rates in these papers allows for permanent shocks to the relationship in levels, which is perhaps undesirable. Canzoneri, Cumby and Diba (1999) use panel co-integration methods to test the relationship between the relative price of non-traded to traded goods and relative productivity in the traded to non-traded sectors, where productivity is measured using labour productivity differentials. Canzoneri et al. report results supportive of the Balassa–Samuelson proposition, in the sense that the relative price of non-traded to traded goods is co-integrated with productivity differentials.

Ito, Isard and Symansky (1997) report a statistically significant relationship between the real exchange rate change and the change in per capita GDP, their proxy for the Balassa–Samuelson effect, for a group of Asian currencies. However, they do not find an association between the per capita differential and the relative price of non-traded to traded goods. As they recognize, one explanation for this latter result could be that per capita GDP is not a good proxy for productivity differences. Chinn and Johnston (1999) use OECD sectoral total factor productivity to analyse the relationship between CPI-based real exchange rates and the relative price of traded to non-traded goods and productivity differences. They report significant co-integrating relationships, suggesting long-run relationships, and point estimates, which are supportive of the Balassa–Samuelson proposition. MacDonald and Ricci (2000) also use the OECD sectoral database to build productivity measures which are then used in panel regressions of the CPI-based real exchange rate. They find that when the difference between productivity in the traded and non-traded sector is entered as a differential it is correctly signed, strongly significant and has a plausible magnitude (in particular, they find a point estimate on relative productivity of around 0.8, which is consistent with its interpretation as the share of expenditure on non-traded goods). However, MacDonald and Ricci demonstrate that the Balassa–Samuelson prediction that the coefficients on productivity in the traded and non-traded sectors are equal and opposite is strongly rejected. Furthermore, when the wage enters the panel regression, productivity on the traded sector becomes significantly negative. If the Balassa–Samuelson hypothesis is correct the introduction of the wage, which is the conduit through which productivity in the traded sector influences the CPI-based real exchange rate, should render the coefficient on tradable productivity to be zero. MacDonald and Ricci interpret this effect as indicating that the LOOP does not hold. One other interesting aspect of MacDonald and Ricci's work is that by conditioning the real exchange rate on productivity differentials, and other 'real' determinants of the real exchange rate, nearly all of the PPP puzzle may be explained.[6]

Dornbusch (1987) and Krugman (1987) were the first to argue that market structure may be important in explaining deviations from PPP. The market structure story is an attempt to explain systematic movements in the real exchange rate in terms of the relative price of traded goods, q_t^T. Perhaps the best known aspect of market structure is pricing to market and recently the role of a country's distribution sector – its wholesale and retail sectors – has been cited as important in explaining the PPP puzzle. Why should the price of a good produced in a foreign country, but sold in the domestic country not reflect the full change in any exchange rate change? That is to say, what explains price stabilisation in the local currency (or relatedly the degree of pass-through)? A number of hypotheses have been given in the literature to explain this phenomenon. Among them are imperfect competition, costs of adjustment in supply, menu costs, concern for market share and the role of particular currencies in the international financial system. In terms of the latter, if the price which is used to invoice an export is the home currency then exchange rate fluctuations will not affect the home currency price and there will be zero pass-through from the exchange rate to domestic prices. Since so many traded goods are invoiced in terms of US dollars, perhaps the US is the best example of a country where LCP is likely to be effective. However, for countries whose currencies are not widely used for invoicing purposes, pricing to market (PTM) (a term introduced by Krugman (1980)) the existence of differentiated products and imperfectly competitive firms, who price discriminate across export markets, can also generate a stabilisation of local currency prices and zero pass-through. For example, such firms may alter the mark-up of price over marginal cost as the exchange rate changes in order to protect their market share in a particular location. However, it is worth noting that the alternative paradigm of a perfectly competitive firm structure can also generate this result. For example, say there is an appreciation of a country's currency and this appreciation is correlated with a rise in world demand, which pulls up marginal costs. In this case pass-through would also be less than complete (i.e. the tendency for the local currency price to fall as the exchange rate appreciated would be offset by the rising marginal cost).

Knetter (1989) provides a classic partial equilibrium example of pricing to market for an exporting firm assumed to sell to N foreign destinations. His model captures the basic result of price discrimination: the price in the exporter's currency is a mark-up over marginal cost, where the mark-up is determined by the elasticity of demand in the various destination markets. In this context if the exporter faces a constant elasticity of demand schedule then the price charged over marginal cost will be a constant mark-up and in this case there will be complete pass-through; that is, the price in terms of the exporter's currency will stay unchanged as the exchange rate depreciates and so the price in terms of the destination market will fully reflect the exchange rate change. However, in this example although marginal cost is common across destinations, it may nonetheless vary over time and the mark-up can therefore vary across destinations. For a monopolist who discriminates across export markets, demand schedules that are less convex (i.e. more elastic) than a constant-elasticity schedule will produce a stabilisation of local currency price and therefore pricing to market: as the exchange rate depreciates the mark-up will fall. However, if the monopolist's demand schedule is more convex (inelastic) then a constant-elasticity schedule will produce the opposite effect – mark-ups increase as the buyer's currency depreciates. Feenstra and Kendall (1997) provide a variant of the partial equilibrium model in which the exporter hedges some of his exposure to foreign exchange risk in the forward exchange market. More recent work on pricing to market has sought to embed the concept in the general equilibrium framework exploited by the new open economy macro model of Obstfeld and Rogoff (1996) (see, for example, Betts and Devereux (2000), discussed below).

A number of papers have sought to test the empirical implications of pricing to market. For example, Mann (1986) analysed a data set consisting of the movement of four-digit industry US import prices relative to a trade weighted average of foreign production costs and found that profit margins are adjusted to mitigate the impact of exchange rate changes on dollar prices of US imports. Interestingly, she found that US exporters did not adjust mark-ups in response to exchange rate changes. Knetter (1989, 1993) uses panel methods and finds considerable evidence of pricing to market The percentage of point estimates that imply LCPS are as follows: Germany 89 per cent; Japan 79 per cent, the UK 67 per cent and the US 45 per cent. One of the paper's most striking results is that, in contrast to Knetter (1989), there is very little evidence that the destination market is important in determining the extent of LCPS. In particular, there is little evidence to suggest that foreign exporters treat the US differently to any other market. This suggests that the large swings observed in the dollar are not responsible for the existence of PTM. Also, and in contrast to other research in this area, there is little evidence of differences in behaviour within common industries. However, there is clear evidence of different behaviour across US and UK industries and Knetter argues that future research should look at industry characteristics rather than, for example, focusing on trying to understand exchange rate behaviour using atheoretical methods, such as the permanent and transitory decompositions of exchange rates.

Giovannini (1988) presents evidence that the relative export price (the export price, in foreign currency relative to the domestic price) of a narrow sectoral set of Japanese manufacturers' prices – things like ball bearings, nuts and bolts, – fluctuate widely over the period 1973–1983 (+/− 20 per cent), and on many occasions these appear to be systematically related to the exchange rate (the yen-dollar rate). These kinds of movements are suggestive of some form of price discrimination. The novelty of Giovannini's work is that it provides a neat way of unravelling whether these effects arise from *ex ante* discrimination or they could not have been predicted and are simply the outcome of exchange rate surprises. In the first stage of his analysis, Giovannini uses a set of forecasting equations to determine if deviations from the LOOP (that is the relative export price scaled by the nominal exchange rate) are predictable. These equations involve projecting the deviation from the LOOP onto information publicly available in period-t. The regressions clearly demonstrate that there is predictability in these deviations and this implies that firms either discriminate ex ante or prices are preset for more than one month in advance, or both. In a second stage these two effects are unravelled by estimating relative price equations which incorporate price staggering. The results show that, even allowing for price staggering, there is clear evidence that firms engage in *ex ante* price discrimination.

Ghosh and Wolf (2001) have criticised the standard pass-through equation noted above. In particular, they argue that in the context of standard pass-through equations it is difficult to distinguish between pricing to market and menu cost pricing. For example, with menu costs the expectation is that there would be a long sequence of non-zero pass-through followed by a single price change with complete pass-through of the cumulative change in the exchange rate since the last price change. If menu costs differ across products and price changes are staggered then a regression of aggregate price on the exchange rate will, since it averages the two sets of observations across many products, likely yield a non-unitary and non-zero estimate of price pass through, which is similar to pricing to market. The two alternative explanations for a lack of complete pass have very different implications for PPP. The LOOP remains valid, in the long term, with menu costs, while deviations from the LOOP are permanent in most models of strategic pricing.

In order to address the relative importance of menu costs and pricing to market in explaining imperfect pass-through, Ghosh and Wolf (2001) examine the properties of the prices of the Economist and Business Week using a panel of 11 countries for the period January 1973 to December 1995 (The Economist) and January 1980 to December 1995 (for Business Week). Their analysis of this data set reveals the following. First, they find a small pass-through from contemporaneous exchange rates to prices (3 and 11 per cent for The Economist and Business Week, respectively). Second, they find a much larger pass-through of cumulative exchange rate changes since the last price adjustment to the current price change. Third, the pass-through elasticity increases sharply if the sample is restricted to those months in which prices are changed, although the elasticity is well below unity. The conclusions Gosh and Wolf draw from this evidence is that menu costs play an important role in addition to strategic pricing decisions.

Cheung, Chinn and Fujii (1999) seek to explore the consequences of market structure for the persistence of deviations from PPP. The capture persistence using the mean reversion coefficient for industry i of country j as $MRC_i^j = 1 + \delta$. This is then regressed onto two measures of market structure and a number of macroeconomic variables. The first measure of market structure is the price cost margin (PCM) which approximates profits of an industry and is intended to give a measure of how competitive an industry is:

$$PCM_{i,t}^{j} = \frac{V_{i,t}^{j} - M_{i,t}^{j} - W_{i,t}^{j}}{V_{i,t}^{j}} \tag{1.11}$$

where V is the value of total prod, M is cost of materials and W is the wage. The second measure is the intra-industry trade index (IIT) defined as:

$$ITT_{i,t}^{j} \equiv 1 - \frac{|EX_{i,t}^{j} - IM_{i,t}^{j}|}{(EX_{i,t}^{j} + IM_{i,t}^{j})} \tag{1.12}$$

where EX and IM represent sectoral exports and imports. A large value of ITT represents a high level of market power due to product differentiation.

Using sectoral real exchange rate data (for nine manufacturing sectors) from 15 OECD countries over the period 1970–1993 Cheung et al show that both market structure effects are significantly positively related to the mean reversion speed and robust to different specifications; the macro variables are, however, not robust to different specifications. They also show that industries with high PCMs have slowest mean reversion.

It is clear, therefore, that there are a number of potential economic and econometric explanations of the PPP puzzle. We favour explanations which rely on real factors, such as productivity differentials and net foreign assets. Such explanations imply that PPP is not a good measure of a country's equilibrium exchange rate.

1.3 The volatility puzzle

There is a widespread perception that when exchange rates are floating they tend to be very volatile. There are two aspects to this volatility: inter-regime volatility and intra-regime volatility. The former measure of volatility may be illustrated by comparing the behaviour of exchange rates in the Bretton and post-Bretton Woods periods. Hallwood and MacDonald (2001) note that the volatility of nominal exchange rates increases approximately six-fold in the move from Bretton Woods to post- Bretton Woods. A number of researchers have tried to ascertain if this kind of increase in exchange rate volatility is matched by the volatility in the macroeconomic fundamentals. For example, Baxter and Stockman (1989) examine the variability of output, trade variables and private and government consumption and the real exchange rate between Bretton Woods and post-Bretton Woods and they are: 'unable to find evidence that the cyclic behaviour of real macroeconomic aggregates depends systematically on the exchange rate regime. The only exception is the well-known case of the real exchange rate'. In sum in moving from fixed to floating rate regimes the volatility of the fundamentals remains unchanged but the volatility of the nominal and real exchange rates changes dramatically. The issue of intra regime volatility has been made by Frankel and Meese (1987) and MacDonald (1999) who note that it has become something of a stylised fact in the post-Bretton Woods regime that nominal exchange rates s are clearly more volatile than a standard set of macroeconomic fundamentals – they are excessively volatile. How may such volatility be explained? We argue that there are a number of forward-looking monetary models which can be used to explain intra- regime volatility.

1.3.1 The forward-looking monetary relationship and the magnification effect

The base line forward-looking model is based on the standard monetary reduced form:

$$s_t = m_t - m_t^* - \beta_0(y_t - y_t^*) + \beta_1 E_t(s_{t+1} - s_t), \tag{1.13}$$

which, in turn, may be rearranged for the current exchange rate as:

$$s_t = z_t + \theta E_t(s_{t+1}), \tag{1.13'}$$

where:

$$z_t = (1 + \beta)^{-1}[m_t - m_t^* - \beta_0(y_t - y_t^*)],$$

and

$$\theta = \beta_1(1 + \beta_1)^{-1}.$$

With rational expectations the expected exchange rate in period t + 1 may be obtained by leading (1.13′) one period and taking conditional expectations: $E_t s_t = E_t z_{t+1} + \theta E_t s_{t+2}$.

By recursively substituting out the expected exchange rate for all future periods the forward extension of the monetary model may be obtained as:

$$s_t = \sum_{i=0}^{\infty} \theta^i E_t[z_{t+i}] \tag{1.14}$$

where the transversality or terminal condition – $\lim_{i=\infty} \theta^i E_t s_{t+i+1} = 0$ – is assumed to hold. A key implication of (1.14) is that changes in current fundamentals can have a more than proportionate or magnified, effect on s to the extent they influence future profile of expectations. This may be seen more clearly by posing the following example: what does a current change in the money supply signal to agents? To answer this question we assume the time series properties of the composite fundamental term have an AR1 representation:

$$z_t = \phi z_{t-1} + u_t \quad |\phi|<1. \tag{1.15}$$

Using this expression in (1.14) a closed form solution for the exchange rate may be derived as:

$$s_t = (1 - \phi\theta)^{-1} z_t, \tag{1.16}$$

since the term $(1 - \phi\theta)^{-1}$ is greater than unity a current change in m will have a magnified effect on s. So in answer to the above question a current change in the money supply, by signalling to agents through (16) further changes in the future, produces a more than proportionate movement in the current exchange rate relative to current fundamentals.

On the basis of the above, one potential explanation for the apparent excess volatility of the exchange rate with respect to current fundamentals is that such a comparison misses the dramatic effect that expectations can have on exchange rate volatility. In discussing exchange rate volatility it is useful to introduce so–called variance inequality of variance bounds relationship, popular from the stock market literature. If we denote the solution (1.15) as market fundamentals or 'no-bubbles' and label it $\hat{s}_t$, where:

$$\hat{s}_t = \sum_{i=0}^{\infty}\theta^i E_t[z_{t+i}] \tag{1.14'}$$

Expression (1.14′) may be rewritten as:

$$\hat{s}_t = E_t s_t^*, \tag{1.17}$$

Where s_t^* has the interpretation of the perfect foresight exchange rate (the rate that would prevail if there is no uncertainty):

$$s_t^* = \sum_{i=0}^{\infty}\theta^i z_{t+i}.$$

With rational expectations it follows that:

$$s_t^* = \hat{s}_t + u_t, \tag{1.18}$$

or

$$s_t^* = s_t + u_t \tag{1.18'}$$

where u_t is a purely random forecast error. Taking the variance of the left and right hand sides of (18′) we obtain:

$$Var(s_t^*) = Var(s_t) + Var(u_t)$$

Since the error term is a purely random term it must follow that $Cov(\hat{s}_t, u_t) = 0$ and therefore:

$$Var(s_t^*) \geq Var(s_t) \tag{1.19}$$

If the magnification story is correct then the variance of the perfect foresight exchange rate should be at least as large as the variance of the actual exchange rate. As we shall see below, a number of tests suggests the opposite is the case in practice.

Another explanation for exchange rate volatility can be derived from the forward monetary model by relaxing the terminal condition assumption. In particular, if $\lim_{i \to \infty} \theta^i E_t s_{t+i+1} = 0$, does not hold, then there are potentially multiple solutions to (1.13′) each one of which may be written in the form:

$$s_t = \hat{s}_t + b_t. \tag{1.20}$$

For (20) to be a rational bubble, and therefore a solution to (13) it must evolve in the following way:

$$b_t = \theta E_t b_{t+1}. \tag{1.21}$$

This is regarded as a rational bubble because it provides a solution to the model which is equivalent to (13′). The existence of an explosive bubble violates the transversality condition which may be seen by substituting (1.21) into the limit condition for the final period expected exchange rate condition:

$$\theta^{t+k} E\hat{s}_{t+k} = \theta^{t+k} E_t s_{t+k} + \theta^{t+k} E_t b_{t+k} = b_t.$$

The bubble term will eventually dominate the exchange rate process and push it away from the fundamental path. The implications of a rational speculative bubble for excess volatility of the exchange rates can be demonstrated by constructing a 'variance inequality' which is comparable to (1.19). In presence of speculative bubble we know from (1.20) that $\hat{s}_t = s_t - b_t$ and so we have to replace (1.18) with:

$$s_t^* = s_t - b_t + u_t \tag{1.22}$$

Since, *a priori*, a correlation between b_t and s_t cannot be ruled out, the variance decomposition now has the following form:

$$Var(s_t^*) = Var(s_t) + Var(b_t) + Var(u_t) - 2Cov(s_t, b_t) \tag{1.23}$$

which indicates that in the presence of speculative bubbles, exchange rates may be excessively volatile relative to fundamentals-based values. In other words, if a researcher were to test the inequality (1.19) and find it were reversed, then such violation would represent *prima facie* evidence of a speculative bubble.

A recent example of this kind of approach has been made by Engel and West (2004) who consider the following variant of the monetary model:

$$s_t = z_t^f + u_t \tag{1.24}$$

where $z_t^f = \sum_{i=0}^{\infty} \theta^i E_t z_{t+i}^f$ and is the discounted sum of current and expected future fundamentals that the econometrician observes and u_t is that part of the exchange rate not determined by z_t^f and could represent other fundamentals not observable to econometrician, noise, non-rational bubbles etc. Expression (24) may then be used to produce the following decomposition:

$$Var(\Delta s_t) = Var(\Delta z_t^f) + Var(\Delta u_t) + 2Cov(\Delta z_t^f, \Delta u_t). \tag{1.25}$$

Engel and West (2004) show that the variability of observable fundamentals accounts for around 40 per cent of exchange rate volatility. One of the novel features of this approach is that estimates of $Var(\Delta z_t^f)$ based on the true information set and that of the econometrician are equivalent when the discount factor approaches 1 and z is I(1).

Obstfeld and Rogoff (2000c) use a stochastic version of the NOEM model to generate a variant of the forward-looking monetary model. The basic difference here is that the introduction of uncertainty means that the forward-looking reduced form features a risk premium term:

$$s_t = \frac{\bar{i}\varepsilon}{1 + \bar{i}\varepsilon} \sum_{s=t}^{\infty} \left(\frac{1}{1 + \bar{i}\varepsilon} \right)^{s-t} E_t \left[m_s - m_s^* + \frac{v_s - v_s^*}{\bar{i}\varepsilon} \right] \tag{1.26}$$

where the risk premium, $v_t - v_t^*$, is given by:

$$v_t - v_t^* = \frac{1}{2}(\sigma_{p^*,t}^2 - \sigma_{p,t}^2) + \rho(\sigma_{cp^*,t} - \sigma_{cp,t}) \tag{1.27}$$

where the subscript p denotes the log of the price level and the overbar above the interest rate term reflects a nonstochastic steady state value (which arises because the nonlinearity of money equilibrium condition makes it necessary to approximate it in the neighbourhood of a nonstochastic steady state), and ε is the consumption elasticity of the demand for money. The term involving $[v_s - v_s^*]_{s=t}^{\infty}$ is referred to as the 'level' risk premium, and is not exactly equal to the standard forward market risk premium because of the existence of $1/\bar{i}\varepsilon$. There are two key insights here. First, the risk premium can affect the level of the exchange rate, and not just the predictable excess return, which has been studied extensively in the literature. This is important because it means that higher moments of economic variables can affect the volatility of the exchange rate and not just the first moments – if the forward risk premium is quite volatile, this could have important implications for exchange rate volatility. Second, the effect of the risk premium on the exchange rate may potentially be very large because of the scaling factor, $1/\bar{i}\varepsilon$. A rise in the covariance of c and p would lead to a fall in v which, in turn, would produce a fall in the interest rate and exchange rate appreciation. Obstfeld and Rogoff view this as capturing the idea of a portfolio shift toward the home currency or, equivalently, of a 'safe haven' effect on the home currency.

Duarte (2003) uses a variant of the two country NOEM model in which asset markets are incomplete and prices are set one period in advance in the buyer's currency (i.e. local currency pricing) to address the intra-regime volatility issue, that the conditional variance of the real exchange rate changes sharply across exchange rate regimes. In the model, the home agent holds home currency and trades a riskless bond, *B*, which pays one unit of home currency with certainty one period after issuance, with the foreign agent (i.e. there is a single bond and so asset markets are incomplete). Duarte's equation for the nominal exchange rate can be obtained as:

$$s_t = \frac{P_t\, u^*_{c,t} \;\; E_t[u_{c,t+1}/P_{t+1}]}{u_{c,t}\, P^*_t\, E_t[u^*_{c,t+1}/s_{t+1}P^*_{t+1}]} \tag{1.28}$$

where $u_{c,t}$ represents the marginal utility function of home consumption in period *t* and other terms have the same interpretation as before. This equation differs from the standard Lucas (1985) model, in which asset markets are complete, in that the nominal exchange rate is an explicit function of expectations of future variables. This follows on from the assumption of incomplete asset (bond) markets and product market segmentation.[7] It then follows that changes in expectations about future variables can translate into changes in the exchange rate without directly affecting other macroeconomic variables, thereby offering an explanation for the excess volatility result. This result would not occur, of course, in a model with complete risk-sharing.

Duarte studies the properties of this model in the context of a simulation exercise in which the utility function is fully specified, along with technology and monetary shocks. This exercise clearly generates a sharp increase in the volatility of the real exchange rate following a switch from fixed to flexible rates, with no similar change in the volatilities of output, consumption, or trade flows. The intuition for this result is quite simple: because prices are set one period ahead in the buyer's currency, allocation decisions are disconnected, at the time of impact, from unexpected changes in the nominal exchange rate and so the volatilities of output, consumption and trade flows are unaffected.

Duarte and Stockman (2005) exploit the same two country model used in Duarte (2003) and by writing the equivalent expression to (1.28) for the forward exchange rate, *f*, are able to rewrite (1.28) as:

$$s_t = \frac{Q_t}{Q^*_t}(rp_t + E_t[s_{t+1}]), \tag{1.29}$$

where rp_t is the risk premium defined in the conventional way as $f_t - E(s_{t+1})$ and the *Q* terms contain the marginal utility ratios. This equation is a first-order stochastic difference equation for the exchange rate and, in words, shows that the expected growth of the exchange rate depends on the household's perception of the relative risk of holding the two nominal assets rp_t, normalised by the level of the exchange rate. The risk premium is given by:

$$rp_t = \frac{cov_t(s_{t+1}, u_{c,t+1})}{E_t[u_{c,t+1}]}. \tag{1.30}$$

where $u_{c,t+1}$ denotes the marginal utility of the home household in period t+1. Equation (1.30) shows that the risk premium arises from the covariance between the nominal exchange rate and the marginal utility of consumption. When the next period's covariance between s and $u_{c,t+1}$ is high, the foreign bond tends to pay a high (low) real return when the marginal utility of consumption is also high (low). The foreign bond is therefore more risky to the home agent the lower is $cov(s_{t+1}, u_{c,t+1})$.

The key prediction of the model is that new information which results in agents revising their perceptions of the risk premium can produce exchange rate volatility without there being any changes in the current macroeconomic variables. Exogenous shocks to money growth and productivity growth, with time-varying second moments, cause endogenous changes in the risk premium. Such shocks result from regime shifts which affect the co-variances of shocks, and these generate 'rational speculation', in the sense of altering equilibrium risk premia. The model of Duarte and Stockman generates a strong correlation between changes in exchange rates and changes in risk premia. However, it turns out that the magnitude of the risk premium is too small to match the data and, as a result, the exchange rate changes they produce are also too small. Duarte and Stockman suggest that further modifications to the model, such as modelling the equity-premium and the introduction of irrational speculation may help to generate sufficient exchange rate variability.

Montacelli (2004) takes a stochastic small open economy version of the NOEM model, in which there is an explicit role for capital accumulation (where capital is assumed to be a function of Tobin's q) and pricing to market, in order to examine the issue of intra-regime volatility. The main novelty of this work is to introduce into this class of model an open economy variant of a Taylor style interest rate monetary rule which allows an analysis of the short run dynamic effects of a change in the nominal exchange rate regime. Specifically, the equation for the target for the nominal interest rate is:

$$(1 + \bar{i}_t) = \left(\frac{P_{H,t}}{P_{H,t-1}}\right)^{\omega_\pi} Y_t^{\omega_y} S_t^{\frac{\omega_s}{1-\omega_s}}. \tag{1.31}$$

From this expression the monetary authority reacts to the contemporaneous level of the nominal exchange rate (a forward-looking jump variable) and to contemporaneous inflation and output. The use of this rule allows Montacelli to consider fixed and floating exchange rate regimes in the context of the NOEM. If $\omega_s = 0$ this implies a flexible rate regime whereas if $\omega_s \in [0,1]$ this allows for a range of managed to fixed exchange rates. It is then assumed that the monetary authority smooths interest rates using the following rule:

$$(1 + i_t) = (1 + \bar{i}_t)^{1-\chi}(1 + i_{t-1})^{\chi}, \tag{1.32}$$

and by taking a log-linear approximation of these two equations it is possible to obtain:

$$i_t = \tilde{\omega}_\pi \pi_{H,t} + \tilde{\omega}_y y_t + \tilde{\omega}_s s_t + \chi^i_{t-1}, \tag{1.33}$$

where

$$\tilde{\omega}_\pi = (1 - \chi)\omega_\pi,\ \tilde{\omega}_y = (1 - \chi)\omega_y,\ \tilde{\omega}_s = (1 - \chi)(\omega_s/1 - \omega_s),$$

$$i_t \approx log(1 + i_t/1 + i).$$

The model is then calibrated and solved numerically for the instances of complete and incomplete pass-through. In the complete pass-through case, Monacelli (2004) shows that in moving from fixed to flexible exchange rates there is a proportional rise in the volatility of the nominal exchange rate which is coupled with a rise in the real exchange rate which roughly mimics what we observe in the data and the interest rate smoothing objective is crucial in generating this result. Furthermore, the close correlation between real and nominal exchange rates in a flexible rate regime is mimicked in this model and these results are robust with respect to the sources of the underlying shocks. However, this version of the model produces a correlation between nominal depreciation and inflation which is too high relative to the actual correlation in the data. Nonetheless, it is demonstrated that this correlation can be made consistent with the data when there is incomplete pass-through of exchange rate changes.

A further attempt to explain the excess volatility of exchange rates using a variant of the NOEM is made by Devereux and Engel (2001). They attempt to shed light on a conjecture of Krugman (1989) that exchange rate volatility is so great because fluctuations in the exchange rate matter so little for the economy. They use a variant of the NOEM in which there is a combination of local currency pricing, heterogeneity in international price setting and in the distribution of goods (for example, some firms market their products directly in the foreign market and charge a foreign price while some exporters use foreign distributors, charging a price set in the exporter's currency) and, crucially, the existence of noise traders who impart expectational biases into international financial markets. They derive an expression for the unanticipated change in the exchange rate of the following form:

$$\hat{s}_t = \frac{(1 + \frac{\sigma}{r})(\hat{m}_t - \hat{m}_t^*) + \frac{\sigma}{r}v_t}{\left[\frac{\sigma}{r} + \rho(\theta - (1 - \theta^*))\right]} \tag{1.34}$$

Where θ is the fraction of home firms that sell directly to households in the foreign country at a foreign price (with $1-\theta$ selling their product to home-based distributors at a home price), θ^* is the fraction of foreign firms that sell directly to households in the home country at a home currency price (with $1-\theta^*$selling their product to home-based distributors at a foreign currency price), v is the bias in foreign exchange dealers' prediction of the exchange rate due to the existence of noise traders, ρ is the elasticity of intertemporal substitution, σ is a function of the elasticity of intertemporal substitution, the intratemporal elasticity of substitution and a leisure – work parameter. How volatile the exchange rate is with respect to the fundamentals can be gauged by calculating the conditional variance of the exchange rate:

$$Var_{t-1}(\hat{s}_t) = \frac{(1 + \frac{\sigma}{r})Var_{t-1}(\hat{m}_t - \hat{m}_t^*)}{\Phi^2\left[1 - \left[\frac{\lambda\sigma}{r\Phi}\right]^2\right]}, \Phi = \left[\frac{\sigma}{r} + \rho(\theta - (1 - \theta^*))\right]. \quad (1.35)$$

Where, of terms not previously defined, $\lambda > 0$ and $Var_{t-1}(v_t) = \lambda Var_{t-1}(s_t)$; that is the volatility of the bias in noise traders' expectations is determined by exchange rate volatility. Given this expression (1.35) says that the conditional volatility in the exchange rate depends only on fundamentals which in this case are the volatility in relative moneys. Given (1.35) it turns out that as $\theta + \theta^* \rightarrow 1$ and with $\lambda = 1$, the conditional volatility of the exchange rate rises without bound. This is because in this model the combination of local currency pricing, along with asymmetric distribution of goods and noise trading implies a degree of exchange rate volatility which is far in excess of the underlying shocks.

The basic intuition for this result is that the presence of local currency pricing and domestic distributors tends to remove both the substitution and wealth effects of exchange rate movements at any point in time. In the absence of noise traders an unanticipated shock to the exchange rate will drive a wedge between the real interest rate in the home and foreign country and this in turn will limit the degree of exchange rate movement in so that the current account adjusts to maintain expected future levels of consumption. However, with noise traders, of the type assumed in this model, the response of the exchange rate is no longer governed by the intertemporal current account parameters.

Bacchetta and Wincoop (2003) produce another variant of the forward-looking monetary model: introduce heterogeneous expectations which has two sources – heterogeneous expectations about future macro fundamentals and heterogeneity due to non-fundamental traders – noise traders and rational traders trading for non-speculative reasons – liquidity trades. Their forward-looking equation has the following representation:

$$s_t = \frac{1}{1+\alpha}\sum_{k=0}^{\infty}\left(\frac{\alpha}{1+\alpha}\right)^k \bar{E}_t^k(f_{t+k} - \alpha\gamma\sigma_{t+k}^2 b_{t+k})$$

where f_t is the fundamental, $\gamma\sigma_{t+k}^2 b_{t+k}$ is a risk premium $\bar{E}_t$ is the average rational expectation across all investors, $\bar{E}_t^0(x_t) = x_t, \bar{E}_t^1(x_{t+1}) = \bar{E}_t(x_{t+1})$ and higher order expectations are defined as: $\bar{E}_t^k(x_{t+k}) = \bar{E}_t\bar{E}_{t+1} \ldots\ldots \bar{E}_{t+k-1}(x_{t+k})$. The basic feature of this kind of heterogeneous model is that the law of iterated expectations does not hold; i.e. $\bar{E}_t\bar{E}_{t+1}(s_{t+2}) \neq \bar{E}_t(s_{t+2})$. In dynamic systems this leads to an infinite regress problem and as the discounting horizon goes to infinity the dimensionality of the expectation term also goes to infinity. Bacchetta and Wincoop demonstrate in a calibrated version of the model that there is a substantial magnification effect due to the role of these higher order expectations.

Betts and Devereux (1996) take the NOEM of Obstfeld and Rogoff, combined with pricing to market of the local currency pricing variety to obtain the following expression for the log change in the exchange rate:

$$\hat{s} = \frac{\varepsilon(\hat{M} - \hat{M}^*)}{(1-\nu)(\varepsilon + \theta - 1) + \nu}$$

where of variables which do not have an obvious interpretation, ε is the consumption elasticity of the demand for money, θ is the elasticity of substitution and ν is the pricing to market term. A rise in ν represents an increase in pricing to market and this will increase the response of the exchange rate to monetary changes so long as $\varepsilon > 2 - \theta$. Betts and Devereux (1996) show that with reasonable parameter values, the variance of S is three times greater than in absence of PTM.

In this section we have given a number of different explanations for exchange rate volatility all of which are consistent with forward-looking behaviour. This would seem to provide a positive message for the usefulness of macroeconomic fundamentals in explaining exchange rate behaviour. Does the empirical evidence offer support for these kinds of explanations?

1.3.2 Empirical evidence on inter- and intra-regime volatility

A number of researchers have sought to test the base line monetary model captured in equation (1.14) (see, inter alia, Huang (1981), Hoffman and Schlagenhauf (1983), Kearney and MacDonald (1987), Ghosh (1993), MacDonald-Taylor (1993)). Although these studies offer some limited support for this model often the so-called cross equation restrictions, which are seen as the hallmark of these models, are rejected, especially when appropriate recognition is made of non-stationarity issues. We return to different types of tests of intra-regime volatility below.

Flood and Rose (1995,1999) empirically test inter-regime volatility by constructing so-called Virtual Fundamentals (VF) and Total Fundamentals (TF). Consider again the monetary reduced form:

$$s_t = m_t - m_t^* - \beta_0(y_t - y_t^*) + \beta_1(i_t - i_t^*), \tag{1.38}$$

which can be rearranged as:

$$s_t - \beta_1(i_t - i_t^*) = m_t - m_t^* - \beta_0(y_t - y_t^*), \tag{1.39}$$

where the LHS becomes the 'Virtual Fundamental' $VF_t = s_t - \beta_1(i_t - i_t^*)$ and the RHS is the 'Traditional Fundamental', $TF_t = m_t - m_t^* - \beta_0(y_t - y_t^*)$, Frankel and Rose estimate the conditional volatility of VF and TF (and also for variants in which they allow money demand disturbances) for a sample period spanning both the Bretton Woods and post-Bretton Woods periods. The countries studied: UK, Canada, France, Germany, Holland, Italy, Japan, Sweden and the numeraire country/currency is the US. In sum, their results indicate that the volatility of VF increases dramatically as countries move from fixed to floating, but the volatility of TF does not. Frankel and Rose demonstrate that this finding is robust to different values of the coefficients specifications. Flood and Rose's key conclusion is that exchange rate models cannot explain the volatility of the exchange rate in the recent floating period. They draw the implication that what changes in the move from fixed to flexible exchange rates is the market microstructure and so this should be the focus in trying to understand high frequency exchange rate movements.

Arnold, de Vries and MacDonald (2005) (AVM) revisit the Flood and Rose finding and argue that it is important to turn the question from why do exchange rates appear excessively volatile in flexible rate regimes to why are fundamentals not more volatile in fixed rate regimes? In this regard they argue it is important to recognise the role played by distortions in fixed rate regimes and modify the monetary exchange rate equation to:

$$s = \mathrm{E}[m_j - m_j^*] - \mathrm{E}[x_j - x_j^*] + \ln\frac{R}{I} - \ln\frac{\tau^*\omega^*}{\tau\omega} + \mathrm{E}[\ln \tau_j + \ln \omega_j^* - \ln \omega_j] + \Omega \tag{1.40}$$

where τ capital control distortion and ω trade distortion and Ω is the risk premium comprising the sum of variances and co-variances of the individual variables

$$\Omega = \frac{1}{2}\{[\sigma^2_{m^*_j} - \sigma^2_{m_j}] + [\sigma^2_{x_j} + \sigma^2_{\ln \tau_j/\omega_j} + 2\sigma_{p^*_j, x_j} - 2\sigma_{p^*_j, \ln \tau_j/\omega_j} - 2\sigma_{x_j, \ln \tau_j/\omega_j}]$$
$$- [\sigma^2_{x^*_j} + \sigma^2_{\ln \omega^*_j} + 2\sigma_{p^*_j, x^*_j} + 2\sigma_{p^*_j, \ln \omega^*_j} + 2\sigma_{x^*_j, \ln \omega^*_j}]\}$$

Arnold, de Vries and MacDonald (2005) tackle Flood and Rose (1995) in terms of two key distortions: IMF support and capital controls. In a monetary framework volatility should show up in reserves under fixed exchange rates, but Flood and Rose have argued there is no volatility of reserves trade-off. AVM show, with a specific case study for the UK through Bretton Woods and post-Bretton Woods, that IMF credit facilities can dramatically distort the relationship and they show that IMF support is quantitatively important enough to include in an analysis of the volatility tradeoff and when it is there indeed appears to be a volatility trade-off.

Using the off-shore/on-shore interest rate differential as a measure of capital controls we show for the UK during Bretton Woods and post-Bretton Woods that it is striking how marked the volatility of the onshore – offshore differential is for this period and it turns out to be almost the reverse of the stylised exchange rate volatility – i.e. highly volatile in Bretton Woods and hardly any volatility in the floating rate period. Also we demonstrate this is an important source of for France and Italy during subperiod when capital controls in force in ERM (i.e. 79.01–83.03).

AVM also assess the post-Bretton Woods intra-regime volatility by constructing standard deviations of Δs and Δf i.e $\Delta((m - m^*) - (y - y^*))$, with both US and Germany as alternate numeraire. They report the striking result: the order of magnitude of volatility in total fundamentals is not very different from Δs.

A further finding of AVM is that they demonstrate for the ERM period that the magnitude of exchange rate volatility is clearly dependent on whether realignments are excluded or not. With realignments included, exchange rate volatility is much greater compared to the non-realignment position. Flood and Rose (1995) and others do not include *s* realignments in their work and this therefore could be another explanation for their failure to find much exchange rate volatility in the Bretton Woods period. AVM conclude that the intra- and inter-regime volatility disconnection is overplayed – in their view there is a clear connection between macroeconomic fundamentals in both the intra- and inter-regime contexts, especially if the appropriate fundamentals are utilised.

1.4 The levels puzzle and out-of-sample forecasting

Perhaps the most devastating indictment against fundamentals-based exchange rate modelling was made by Meese and Rogoff (1983), who examined the out-of-sample forecasting performance of the model. Ever since the publication of the Meese and Rogoff paper the ability of an exchange rate model to beat a random walk has become something of an acid test, indeed, *the* acid test of how successful an exchange rate model is. It has become the equivalent of the R squared metric in the economics of exchange rate literature.

Meese and Rogoff (1983) consider variants of the monetary model and estimate these models for the dollar-mark, dollar-pound, dollar-yen and the trade-weighted dollar. The sample period studied was March 1973 to November 1980, with the out-of-sample forecasts conducted over the sub-period December 1976 to November 1980. In particular, the models were estimated from March 1973 to

November 1976 and one- to 12-step-ahead forecasts were constructed. The observation for December 1976 was then added in and the process repeated up to November 1980. Rather than forecast all of the right-hand-side variables from a particular exchange rate relationship simultaneously with the exchange rate, to produce real time forecasts (that is, forecasts which could potentially have been used at the time), Meese and Rogoff gave the monetary class of models an unfair advantage by including actual data outcomes of the right-hand-side variables. Data on the latter variables were available to them due to the historical nature of their study, but of course they would not have been available at the time of forecasting to a forecaster producing 'real time' forecasts. To produce the latter all of the right-hand-side variables would have had to be forecast simultaneously with the exchange rate. Out-of-sample forecasting accuracy was determined using the mean bias, mean absolute bias and the root mean square error criteria. The benchmark comparison was a simple random walk with drift:

$$s_t = s_{t-1} + \kappa + \varepsilon_t, \tag{1.41}$$

where κ is a constant (drift) term and ε_t is a random disturbance. Since the *RMSE* criterion has become the measure that most subsequent researchers have focussed on we note it here as:

$$RMSE = \sqrt{\frac{\sum(F_t - A_t)^2}{n}},$$

where F is the forecast and A is an actual outcome. By taking the ratio of the *RMSE* obtained from the model under scrutiny, to the *RMSE* of the random walk process, a summary measure of the forecasting performance can be obtained as:

$$RMSE^r = \frac{RMSE^m}{RMSE^{rw}}, \tag{1.42}$$

where $RMSE^r$ is the root mean square error ratio (this is equivalent to the Theil statistic).

In sum, Meese and Rogoff were unable to outperform a random walk at horizons of between one and 12 months ahead, although in four instances (out of a possible 224) the VAR model produced a ranking which was above the random walk at longer horizons (one outperformance at six months and three out-performances at 12 months), although this is still a number which is less than that expected by chance. The reason why the Meese and Rogoff finding has been interpreted as a particularly telling indictment against fundamentals-based models is because they deliberately gave their models an unfair advantage by using actual data outcomes of the fundamentals, rather than forecasting them simultaneously with the exchange rate. The Meese and Rogoff result has been confirmed more recently by Mark (1995) and Chinn and Meese (1995), although these researchers do find that predictability kicks in at 'longer horizons', that is horizons of 36 months and above. We return to the forecast performance of the monetary model in the next Section.

The Meese and Rogoff (1993) finding has had an enduring impression on the economics profession. For example, surveying the post-Meese and Rogoff literature Frankel and Rose (1995) argue (emphasis added): ' … the Meese and Rogoff analysis of short horizons [less than 36 months] has never been convincingly overturned or explained. It continues to exert a pessimistic effect on the field of empirical exchange rate modelling in particular and international finance in general'.

One potential reason why Meese and Rogoff may have been unable to beat a random walk is because all but one of their empirical relationships were either static or had very limited dynamics. However, we know from our discussions of the PPP proposition which underpins the monetary model, that exchange rate dynamics tend to be quite complex and adjustment to PPP takes a considerable number of periods. A similar story is true for the money market relationships which are so central to the monetary model – all of the available evidence from money demand studies indicates that adjustment to equilibrium is often quite complex. Clearly for an empirical exchange rate model to be successful it should incorporate these kinds of dynamics. As we shall now demonstrate, when these dynamics are accounted for in the estimation process the random walk model is convincingly beaten.

One potential reason for the dynamics in the relationships underpinning the monetary model is structural instability. One way of allowing for such instability would be to let the coefficients in the reduced form equation evolve over time and this has been done in a number of studies, such as Wolff (1987) and Schinasi and Swamy

(1987). These studies report a consistent outperformance of the random walk model at horizons as short as one or two months.

Another way of addressing the dynamic adjustments underlying the monetary equation is to use a modelling method, such as the so-called general-to-specific dynamic modelling approach proposed by Hendry (1995) and others. Although in one of their estimated models, Meese and Rogoff did allow for rich dynamic interactions using a VAR, it is likely that such a system is over-parameterised in terms of its use of information and such systems generally do not forecast well. Interestingly, Meese and Rogoff in a footnote cite this as a potential reason for the poor performance of the VAR-based implementation of the model. The general-to-specific approach can be used to produce parsimonious VARs or parsimonious VECM models.

The general-to-specific approach to exchange rate modelling, and its implications for exchange rate forecastability, can be illustrated using the approach of MacDonald and Taylor (1991). In particular, they estimate a dynamic error correction equation of the following form:

$$\begin{aligned}\Delta s_t = \underset{(0.073)}{0.244}\Delta s_{t-2} - \underset{(0.235)}{0.417}\Delta_2\Delta m_t - \underset{(0.343)}{0.796}\Delta y_t - \underset{(0.003)}{0.008}\Delta^2 i_t^* \\ - \underset{(0.013)}{0.025} z_{t-1} + \underset{(0.003)}{0.005} \qquad (1.43)\end{aligned}$$

This equation was shown to pass a standard set of in-sample diagnostic tests (not reported here). Of perhaps more significance, however, is the ability of this model to outperform a random walk in an out-of-sample forecasting exercise. In order to produce truly dynamic out-of-sample forecasts, MacDonald and Taylor implemented a dynamic forecasting exercise over the last 24 observations using the procedure of Meese and Rogoff (1983); that is they sequentially re-estimated the model for every data point from 1989:1 onwards, computing dynamic forecasts for forecast horizons of one to twelve months ahead. In each case the root mean square error (*RMSE*) statistic for each horizon was less than the comparable *RMSE*s from a random walk model.

These results are in marked contrast to those of Meese and Rogoff, in the sense that the random walk model is beaten at all of the estimated horizons, even at one month ahead (it is worth noting that the consensus view, according Frankel and Rose (1995) is that the benchmark random walk model cannot be beaten at horizons of less than 36 months). However, despite the apparent success in beating a random walk, MacDonald and Taylor continue to use the actual right-hand-side variables in their forecasting exercise and therefore, although this is consistent with the original Meese and Rogoff article, these forecasts could not have been used by practitioners to make 'real time' exchange rate forecasts. Furthermore, although the *RMSE* ratios are less than unity, it is not clear that they are significantly less than one. In order to address these kind of issues MacDonald and Marsh (1996) propose a modelling technique which produces fully simultaneous forecasts of all of the model variables and they also provide significance levels for the *RMSE* ratios. MacDonald and Marsh take the so-called UIP-PPP approach, which involves combining relative interest rates with the nominal exchange rate and relative prices to produce a stationary (co-integrating) relationship. That is, they focus on the following vector: $x' = [s, p, p^*, i^l, i^{l*}]$.

The modelling approach involves the Structural Econometric Modelling of Hendry and Mizon (1993) and Johansen and Juselius (1994). Essentially this involves moving from a VECM representation to a constrained VAR (CVAR), a parsimonious VAR (PVAR) and finally to a simultaneous equation model (SEM). In the final SEM, each equation is fully specified in that it may have contemporaneous as well as lagged dynamic terms, and may contain long-run equilibria. A key advantage of this SEM modelling approach is that it results in a full system of equations, rather than a single reduced form, and can therefore be used to provide forecasts for all of the variables in the model. The essential point made by MacDonald and Marsh is that an exchange rate model which incorporates a sensible long-run equilibrium and dynamic properties, which are rich enough to capture the underlying data generating process, should do better than a static model or one with very simple dynamics (which is essentially the kind of model used by other researchers).

MacDonald and Marsh focus on the yen, mark and pound against the US dollar, over the period January 1974 to December 1992, with the last 24 observations held back for forecasting purposes. The forecasts constructed are fully simultaneous and dynamic and could therefore have been used by a potential forecaster. The success of the forecasts is gauged in three ways. First, using the $RMSE^r$ criterion, discussed above. Second in terms of the directional ability calculated as:

$$D = \frac{(1 \text{ if forecast direction} = \text{actual,else } 0)}{n} \tag{1.44}$$

On the basis of chance D is expected to be 0.5, and therefore any number above 0.5 means that the model does better in terms of its predictive ability than simply tossing a coin. Finally, *RMSE* ratios were constructed for the model projections relative to a panel of 150 professional forecasts, located in the G7 financial centres, and as collected by Consensus Economics of London (gauged using the $RMSE^r$ criterion).

MacDonald and Marsh's forecasting results demonstrate that the random walk model can be convincingly beaten at horizons as short as two months ahead and many of the $RMSE^r$ statistics are significantly less than unity. Additionally, all of the models seem to have very good directional forecasting powers and across the three currencies and forecast horizons, the models of MacDonald and Marsh outperform the professional forecasters. It is also worth noting that the *RMSE* ratio of the estimated SEM models relative to a VAR in first differences is always less than unity. This would seem to underscore the point that such models are likely to underperform, both because they are over-parameterised and also because of their failure to incorporate the 'long-run' information contained in the co-integrating vector.

In a follow-up paper, MacDonald and Marsh (1999) extend their earlier analysis by using a tripolar model of the yen, dollar and German mark and their results again demonstrate the ease with which the random walk model can be beaten in an out-of-sample forecasting context once appropriate dynamics and long-run relationships have been incorporated into an exchange rate model.

La Cour and MacDonald (1998) show that the random walk model can be beaten in a dynamic error correction monetary model in which the long-run co-integrating relationships are fully specified (that is multiple co-integrating vectors are identified both economically and statistically), for horizons as short as four months ahead.

Mark and Sul (2001) use their panel estimates of the monetary model to construct one and 16 quarter ahead out-of-sample forecasts and compares these to forecasts produced using a random walk model, in terms of the *RMSE*^{r}. Using the US dollar as the numeraire, the root mean squared error ratio has a model value of unity at the one-quarter horizon. However, at 16 quarters the monetary model dominates a random walk for 17 out of the 18 exchange rates and this difference is statistically significant. For the other two numeraire currencies (the yen and Swiss franc) the monetary model also significantly outperforms a random walk for the vast majority of countries. In contrast to the US results, however, the majority of *RMSE* ratios for the one-quarter forecasts, using the Swiss franc as numeriare, are significantly below unity, while the number of ratios below unity for the yen is slightly below half of the total number of countries. Mark and Sul conclude by noting: 'There is a preponderance of statistically superior predictive performance by the monetary model exchange rate regression'.

Cheung, Chinn and Pascual (2002), estimate a monetary approach reduced forms and variants, which incorporate 'real' factors such as a Balassa Samuelson effect. Their sample period is 1973 quarter two to 2000 quarter four and they consider five currencies against the US dollar and Japanese yen. They report that 'no model consistently outperforms a random walk, by a mean squared error criterion; however, along a direction-of change dimension, certain structural models do outperform a random walk with statistical significance'. In the light of our discussion above this result seems surprising especially since Cheung et al use an error correction specification, in addition to a first difference specification. However, crucially the error correction models estimated are not rendered parsimonious by the deletion of insignificant dynamics and MacDonald and Marsh have shown this aspect of exchange rate modelling is crucial in the process of obtaining accurate exchange rate forecasts.

We believe that the research presented in this section demonstrates clearly that the random walk paradigm no longer rules the roost in terms of exchange rate forecasting. There is now a sufficient body of evidence to suggest that the random walk can be beaten in a large variety of samples and for a number of different currencies. This of course is not to say that the random walk model can always be beaten, but it does, at least, indicate that the pessimism that many have levelled against fundamentals-based exchange rate models is unwarranted: the levels puzzle is not really a puzzle at all.

1.5 Summary and conclusions

In this paper we have overviewed three key exchange rate puzzles – the PPP puzzle, and what we have referred to as the levels and volatility puzzles, and we have sought to provide an explanation for these puzzles. We have argued that the PPP Puzzle – the combination of a high volatility of real and nominal exchange rates with the slow mean reversion of real exchange rates – can be explained in a number of ways, from product and time aggregation biases to pricing to market, non-linear adjustment, real factors and imperfectly substitutable goods. Our own preferred explanation for the PPP puzzle is a combination of pricing to market and real factors, such as the effects of productivity differentials on exchange rates. This conclusion has clear implications for the measurement of equilibrium values of currencies.

The levels puzzle concerns the supposed poor out-of-sample forecasting properties of exchange rate models and, in particular, the findings of Meese and Rogoff (1983) that fundamentals-based models cannot outperform a random walk. We have argued in this paper that the random walk paradigm can be convincingly overturned at horizons as short as two months, and this seems a robust result. The key to overturning this result is the use of econometric methods which capture the underlying data dynamics and the long-run relationships.

The volatility puzzle concerns the apparent excessive volatility of exchange rates in flexible rate regimes – intra- regime volatility – and the sharp rise in both real and nominal exchange rate volatility in the move from fixed to floating exchange rates – inter-regime volatility. In this paper we have argued that excessive exchange rate volatility is entirely consistent with a number of forward-looking exchange rate models and in fact the empirical evidence suggests that intra- regime volatility may be something of a chimera. On the basis of recent work by Arnold, de Vries and MacDonald (2005), we have also argued that the issue of inter-regime volatility may also be overplayed since once the role of distortions are recognised in fixed rate regimes fundamentals become more volatile.

In sum, we would argue that although there are still a number of puzzles in the exchange rate literature the three key puzzles considered in this paper have been resolved.

Notes

1. It is important to note that β and therefore $\bar{q}$ will not equal zero if price indices are used instead of price levels.
2. They distinguish between these terms by the inclusion or exclusion of product/country fixed effects in their panel tests: relative LOOP includes fixed effects while the tests of absolute PPP excludes these terms and therefore tests if price differences are converging towards zero in the long-run.
3. See Jorion and Sweeney (1996) and Pappell (1997) for a further discussion.
4. Our derivation of the Balassa–Samuelson model is based on Asea and Cordon (1994) which, in turn, is based on Balassa (1964).
5. Hsieh (1982) defines productivity in the traded sector as the ratio of the index of manufacturing to employed man-hours in manufacturing, Marston uses labour productivity while DeGregorio and Wolf (1994) employ the OECD sectoral database to build measures of total factor productivity in the traded and non-traded sectors.
6. MacDonald and Ricci (2000) argue that a country's distribution sector is an important determinant of the real exchange rate. MacDonald and Ricci (2001) provide a model based on New Trade Theory to re-examine the links between productivity and the real exchange rate.
7. For example, in a model with a complete set of state-contingent nominal assets, complete risk sharing across markets implies that $s_t = (P_t/u_{c,t})(u^*_{c,t}/P_t)$.

References

Abuaf, Niso, and Philippe Jorion, (1990) 'Purchasing Power Parity in the Long Run', *Journal of Finance*, Vol. 45, pp. 157–74.

Arnold, I., R. MacDonald and C. de Vries (2005) 'Fundamental volatility is regime specific' mimeo, University of Glasgow.

Baillie, Richard T., and David D. Selover, 'Cointegration and Models of Exchange Rate Determination', *International Journal of Forecasting*, Vol. 3, No. 1 (1987), pp. 43–51.

Balassa, B. (1964), 'The Purchasing Power Parity Doctrine: A Reappraisal', *Journal of Political Economy*, 72, 584–596.

Banerjee, Anindya, and others, 'Exploring Equilibrium Relationships in Econometrics Through Static Models: Some Monte Carlo Evidence', *Oxford Bulletin of Economics and Statistics*, Vol. 48 (August 1986), pp. 253–77.

Baxter, M. and A. Stockman (1989), 'Business Cycles and the Exchange-Rate System', *Journal of Monetary Economics*, 23, 377–400.

Bayoumi, T. and R. MacDonald (1998), 'Deviations of Exchange Rates from Purchasing Power Parity: A Story Featuring Two Monetary Unions', IMF Working Paper 98/ (Washington: International Monetary Fund, March 1998), IMF Staff Papers, 1999.

Betts, C. and M. Devereux (1996), 'The exchange rate in a model of pricing to market', *European Economic Review*, 40, 1007–1021.

Campbell, John Y., and Pierre Perron, 'Pitfalls and Opportunities: What Macroeconomists Should Know About Unit Roots', in *NBER Economics Annual 1991*, ed. by Olivier Jean Blanchard and Stanley Fisher (Cambridge: MIT Press, 1991).

Canzoneri, M.B., R.E. Cumby and Behzad Diba (1996), 'Relative Labour Productivity and the Real Exchange Rate in the Long Run: Evidence for a Panel of OECD Countries', Journal of International Economics, 47, 245–266.

Cheung, Yin-Wong, and Lai, Kon. S., 'Long-Run Purchasing Power Parity During the Recent Float', *Journal of International Economics*, Vol. 34 (February 1993), pp. 181–92.

Cheung, Yin-Wong, and Lai, Kon. S., (2000) 'On the Purchasing Power Parity Puzzle', *Journal of International Economics*, Vol. 52, pp. 321–330.

Cheung, Y-W, M. Chinn and E. Fujii (1999), 'Market Structure and the Persistence of Sectoral Real Exchange Rates', mimeo, University of California at Santa Cruz.

Chinn, M. and L. Johnston (1996+1999), 'Real Exchange Rate Level, Productivity and demand Shocks: Evidence from a Panel of 14 Countries', *NBER* Discussion paper No 5709.

Chinn, M. and R. Meese (1995), 'Banking on Currency Forecasts: How Predictable is the change in Money?', *Journal of International Economics*, 38, 161–78.

Darby, Michael R., 'Does Purchasing Power Parity Work?' NBER Working Paper No. 607 (Cambridge, Massachusetts: National Bureau of Economic Research, December 1980).

DeGregorio, J. and H. Wolf (1994), 'Terms of Trade, Productivity and the Real Exchange Rate', NBER Working Paper No. 4807.

Devereux, M. and C. Engel (2001), 'Endogenous Currency price setting in a dynamic open economy model', *mimeo*.

Diebold, Francis X., Steven Husted, and Mark Rush, 'Real Exchange Rates Under the Gold Standard', *Journal of Political Economy*, Vol. 99 (December 1991), pp. 1252–71.

Dixit, A.K. (1989), 'Hysteresis, Import Penetration, and Exchange Rate Pass Through', *Quarterly Journal of Economics*, 104, 205–228.

Duarte, M. (2003), 'Why don't macroeconomic quantities respond to exchange rate variability?', *Journal of Monetary Economics*, 50, 889–913.

Duarte, M. and A.C. Stockman (2003), 'Rational speculation and exchange rates', *Journal of Monetary Economics*, 52, 3–29.

Dumas, B. (1992), 'Dynamic Equilibrium and the Real Exchange Rate in a Spatially Separated World', *Review of Financial Studies*, 5, 153–180.

Edison, H.J., 'Purchasing Power Parity in the Long Run: A Test of the Dollar/Pound Exchange Rate (1890–1978)', *Journal of Money, Credit and Banking*, Vol. 19 (August 1987), pp. 376–87.

Enders, Walter, 'ARIMA and Cointegration Tests of PPP Under Fixed and Flexible Exchange Rate Regimes', *Review of Economics and Statistics* (August 1988), pp. 504–08.

Engel, C. (1993), 'Real Exchange Rates and Relative Prices: An Empirical Investigation', *Journal of Monetary Economics*, 32, 35–50.

Engel, C. (2000a), 'Long-run PPP may not hold after all', *Journal of International Economics*, 57, 243–273.

Feenstra, R.C. and J.D. Kendall (1997), 'Pass-through of exchange rates and purchasing power parity', *Journal of International Economics*, 43, 237–261.

Flood, R.P. and A.K. Rose (1995), 'Fixing Exchange Rates: A Virtual Quest for Fundamentals', *Journal of Monetary Economics*, 36, 3–37.

Flood, R.P. and A.K. Rose (1999), 'Understanding Exchange Rate Volatility without the Contrivance of Macroeconomics', *Economic Journal*, F660-F672.

Frankel, J.A. and R. Meese (1987), Are exchange rates excessively variable?, S. Fischer ed. NBER Macroeconomics Annual, Cambridge: MIT Press, pp. 117–153.

Frankel, Jeffrey A. and Andrew Rose (1995), 'A Survey of Empirical Research on Nominal Exchange Rates', *The Handbook of International Economics*, Vol. 3 (eds) S. Grossman and K. Rogoff, Amsterdam: North Holland.

Frankel, J. and A. Rose (1995), 'A Panel Project on Purchasing Power Parity: Mean Reversion Within and Between Countries', NBER Working Paper No. 5006 (Cambridge, Massachusetts: National Bureau of Economic Research, February 1995).

Frenkel, J., 'Flexible Exchange Rates, Prices and the Role of 'News': Lessons from the 1970s', *Journal of Political Economy*, Vol. 89, (August 1981), pp. 665–705.

Froot, K.M. Kim and K. Rogoff (1995), The law of one price over 700 years', NBER working Paper No 5132.

Ghosh, A. and H Wolf (2001), 'Imperfect Exchange Rate Passthrough: Strategic Pricing and Menu Costs' CESifo Working paper No 436.

Giovannini, A. (1988), 'Exchange rates and traded goods prices', *Journal of International Economics*, Vol. 24, 45–68.

Grilli, Vittorio, and Graciela Kaminsky, 'Nominal Exchange Rate Regimes and the Real Exchange Rate: Evidence from the United States and Great Britain, 1885–1986', *Journal of Monetary Economics*, Vol. 27 (April 1991), pp. 191–212.

Hansen, Bruce E., 'Tests for Parameter Instability in Regression with I(1) Processes', *Journal of Business and Economic Statistics*, Vol. 10 (July 1992), pp. 321–35.

Heckscher, E.F. (1916), Vaxelkursens Grundval vid Pappersmyntfot, *Ekonomisk Tidskrift*, 18, 309–312.

Hendry, D.F. and G. Mizon (1993), 'Evaluating Dynamic Econometric Models by Encompassing the VAR', in P.C.B Phillips (ed.), *Models, Methods and Applications of Econometrics*, pp. 272–300, Oxford: Blackwell.

Hoffman, D.L and D.E. Schlagenhauf (1983), 'Rational Expectations and Monetary Models of Exchange Rate Determination: An Empirical Examination', *Journal of Monetary Economics*, 11, 247–60.

Hsieh D. (1982), 'The Determination of the Real Exchange Rate: The Productivity Approach', *Journal of International Economics*, 12, 355–362.

Huang, R.D. (1981), 'The Monetary Approach to the Exchange Rate in an Efficient Foreign Exchange Market: Tests Based on Volatility', *Journal of Finance*, 36, 31–41.

Imbs, J.H. Mumtaz, M. Ravn, H. Rey (2002), 'PPP strikes back: Aggregation and the real exchange rate', NBER No 9372.

Johansen, Søren, 'Statistical Analysis of Cointegrating Vectors', *Journal of Economic Dynamics and Control*, Vol. 12 (June–September 1988), pp. 231–54.

Jorion, P. and R. Sweeney (1996), Mean Reversion in Real Exchange Rates: Evidence and Implications for Forecasting, *Journal of International Economics*, 40, 112–30.

Kearney, C. and R. MacDonald (1987), 'Intervention and Sterilisation under Floating Exchange Rates: the UK 1973–1983', *European Economic Review*, 30, 345–64.

Knetter, M. (1989), 'Price Discrimination by US and German Exporters', *American Economic Review*, 79, 198–209.

Knetter, M. (1993), 'International Comparisons of Pricing-to-market Behaviour', *American Economic Review*, 83, 473–486.

Krugman, P.R. (1979), 'A Model of Balance of Payments Crisis', *Journal of Money Credit and Banking*, 11, 311–25.

Krugman, P. (1989), *Exchange Rate Instability*, MIT Press: Cambridge MA.

Kugler, Peter, and Carlos Lenz (1993), 'Multivariate Cointegration Analysis and the Long-Run Validity of PPP', *Review of Economics and Statistics*, Vol. 75, pp. 180–4.

La Cour, L. and R. MacDonald (2000), 'Modelling the ECU Against the US Dollar: A Structural Monetary Interpretation', *Journal of Business Economics and Statistics*, September.

Levin, Andrew, and Chien-Fu Lin, 'Unit Root Tests in Panel Data: Asymptotic and Finite Sample Properties' (Unpublished; Washington: Federal Reserve Board of Governors, 1992,1994).

Lothian, J. (1997), 'Multi-Country Evidence on the Behaviour of Purchasing Power Parity Under the Current Float', *Journal of International Money and Finance*.

Lothian, J. and M. Taylor (1995), 'Real Exchange Rate Behaviour: The Recent Float From the Behaviour of the Past Two Centuries', *Journal of Political Economy*.

MacDonald, R. (1985), 'The Norman Conquest of $4.86 and the Asset Approach to the Exchange Rate', *Journal of International Money and Finance*, 4, 373–387.

MacDonald, R., 'Long-Run Purchasing Power Parity: Is It for Real?' *Review of Economics and Statistics*, Vol. 75 (November 1993), pp. 690–5.

MacDonald, R. (1995a), 'Long-Run Exchange Rate Modeling: A Survey of the Recent Evidence', *Staff Papers, International Monetary Fund*, Vol. 42, 3, 437–489.

MacDonald, R. (1995b), 'Asset Market and Balance of Payments Characteristics: An Eclectic Exchange Rate Model for the Dollar, Mark, and Yen', *Open Economies Review* 10, 1, 5–30.

MacDonald, R.(1999), 'Exchange Rates: Do Fundamentals Matter?', *Economic Journal*.
MacDonald, R. and I.W. Marsh (1997), 'On Casselian PPP, Cointegration and Exchange Rate Forecasting', *Review of Economics and Statistics*, November.
MacDonald, R. and I.W. Marsh (1999), *Exchange Rate Modelling*, Kluwer: Boston.
MacDonald, R. and I.W. Marsh (2004), 'A Tripolar forecasting model of bilateral exchange rates', *Journal of International Money and Finance*, forthcoming.
MacDonald, R., and M. Moore, (1996) 'Long-Run Purchasing Power Parity and Structural Change', *Economie Appliquee*, XLIX, 11–48.
MacDonald, R. and M.P. Taylor (1991), 'The Monetary Model of the Exchange Rate: Long-Run Relationships and Coefficient Restrictions', *Economics Letters*, 37, 179–85.
MacDonald, R. and M.P. Taylor (1993), 'The Monetary Approach to the Exchange Rate: Rational Expectations, Long-run Equilibrium and Forecasting', *IMF Staff Papers*, 40, 89–107.
MacDonald, R. and M.P. Taylor (1994), 'The Monetary Model of the exchange rate: long-run relationships, short-run dynamics and how to beat a random walk', *Journal of International Money and Finance*, 13, 276–290.
Mark, N.C. (1990), 'Real and Nominal Exchange Rates in the Long-Run: An Empirical Investigation', *Journal of International Economics*, Vol. 28, pp. 115–36.
Mark, N.C. (1995), 'Exchange Rates and Fundamentals: Evidence on Long-Horizon Predictability', *American Economic Review*, 85, 201–218.
Marston, R. (1990), 'Pricing to Market in Japanese Manufacturing', *Journal of International Economics*, 29, 217–236.
Meese, R, and K. Rogoff (1983), 'Empirical Exchange Rate Models of the Seventies: Do They Fit Out of Sample?', *Journal of International Economics*, 14, 3–24.
Michael, P,. A.R. Nobay and D.A. Peel (1997), 'Transaction Costs and Nonlinear Adjustment in Real Exchange Rates: An Empirical Investigation', *Journal of Political Economy*, 105, 4.
Monacelli, T. (2004), 'Into the Mussa puzzle: monetary policy regimes and the real exchange rate in a small open economy', *Journal of International Economics*, 62, 191–217.
Obstfeld, M. and A.M. Taylor (1997), 'Nonlinear Aspects of Goods-Market Arbitrage and Adjustment: Hecksher's Commodity Points Revisited', *Journal of Japanese and International Economies*, 11, 441–479.
Obstfeld, M. and K. Rogoff (1995), 'Exchange Rate Dynamics Redux', *Journal of Political Economy*, 103, 624–660.
Obstfeld, M. and K. Rogoff (1996), *Foundations of International Macroeconomics*, MIT Press.
Obstfeld, M. and K Rogoff (2000c), 'Risk and Exchange Rates', NBER Working Paper No 6694.
O'Connell, P. (1996), 'Market Frictions and Relative Traded Goods Prices', *Journal of International Money and Finance*, forthcoming.

O'Connell, P. (1997), 'The Overvaluation of Purchasing Power Parity', *Journal of International Economics*, 44, 1–19.

O'Connell, P. and S-J. Wei (1997), 'The Bigger They Are the Harder They Fall: How Price Differences Across US Cities are Arbitraged', *mimeo*.

Oh, K-Y. (1996), 'Purchasing Power Parity and Unit Root Test Using Panel Data', *Journal of International Money and Finance*, 15, 405–418.

Papell, D.H. (1997), 'Searching for Stationarity: Purchasing Power Parity Under the Current Float', *Journal of International Economics*, 41, 313–32.

Papell, D.H. and H. Theodoris. (1997), 'The choice of Numeraire Currency in Panel Tests of Purchasing Power Parity', *mimeo*, University of Houston.

Patel, Jayendu, 'Purchasing Power Parity as a Long-Run Relation', *Journal of Applied Econometrics*, Vol. 5 (October–December 1990), pp. 367–79.

Pedroni, P. (1997), 'Panel Cointegration: Asymptotic and Finite Sample Properties of Pooled Time Series Tests with an Application to the PPP Hypothesis', *mimeo*, Indiana University.

Pedroni, P. (2001), 'PPP in Cointegrated Panels', *Review of Economics and Statistics*, 4, 727–731.

Rogoff, K. (1996), 'The Purchasing Power Parity Puzzle', *Journal of Economic Literature*, XXXIV, 647–668.

Roll, Richard, (1979), 'Violations of Purchasing Power Parity and their Implications for Efficient International Commodity Markets', in *International Finance and Trade*, Vol. 1, ed. by Marshall Sarnat and Giorgio P. Szegö (Cambridge, Massachusetts: Ballinger), pp. 133–76.

Sercu, P. Uppal and Van Hulle (1995), 'The Exchange Rate in the Presence of Transaction Costs: Implications for Tests of Purchasing Power Parity', *Journal of Finance*, 50, 1309–1319.

Tsay, R.S. (1989), 'Testing and Modeling Threshold Autoregressive Processes', *Journal of the American Statistical Association*, 84, 231–240.

Wei, S-J. and D. Parsley (1995), 'Purchasing Power Disparity during the Recent Floating Rate Period: Exchange Rate Volatility, Trade Barriers and Other Culprits', *Quarterly Journal of Economics*.

Wolff, C. (1987), 'Time-Varying Parameters and the Out-of Sample Forecasting Performance of Structural Exchange Rate Models', *Journal of Business and Economics Statistics*, 5: 87–97.

2

The Real Exchange Rate Misalignment in the Five Central European Countries – Single Equation Approach

Jan Frait, Luboš Komárek and Martin Melecký

2.1 Introduction

Both policy makers and market participants have a strong interest in appropriate estimates of equilibrium real exchange rates and their prospective movements. They have also a keen interest in understanding determinants of the equilibrium real exchange rate and the factors behind implied misalignments of the actual rate from its equilibrium level. The real exchange rate is viewed as a key indicator of external competitiveness. Hence, a real appreciation of the exchange rate is often interpreted as a loss of price competitiveness. Nevertheless, this applies only if the real exchange rate becomes overvalued in relation to the equilibrium one. At the same time, real exchange rate appreciation can simply reflect improved competitiveness thanks to an increase in productivity. In this sense, the study of the determinants of the real exchange rates may shed some light on whether a real appreciation causes a loss in competitiveness or reflects the improvements in it (see also Frait and Komárek (1999, 2001)). The real exchange rate misalignments may be rather costly. Both overvalued and undervalued currencies have their negative implications. From policymakers' perspective, the risks implied by the overvaluation are more important. There is an empirical support for the view that an overvalued currency leads to lower economic growth, especially via the impact on the manufacturing (see e.g. Razin and Collins, 1997). Additionally, an overvalued currency may lead to an unsustainable current account deficit, increasing external debt and the risk of possible speculative attacks (see e.g. Kaminski, Lizondo and Reinhart, 1997). An undervalued currency seems to have an equivocal effect, though the risk should not be underestimated too. The potential misalignment is one of the most important policy issues faced by the new EU Member States that are supposed to adopt the euro in the future. The challenges constitute the participation in the exchange rate mechanism, ERM II, which is part of the criterion related to exchange rate stability, with a chosen central parity, and the future announcement of their euro-locking rate. ECB (2003) recommends in its position documents related to ERM II participation that '*... the central rate should reflect the best possible assessment of the equilibrium exchange rate at the time of entry into the mechanism. This assessment should be based on a broad range of economic indicators and developments while also taking account for the market rate.*' In broad terms, the 'equilibrium' exchange rate refers to the rate, which is consistent with medium-term macroeconomic fundamentals. The medium term, usually defined as two to six years, is often chosen as a benchmark in order to assess the level towards which the actual exchange rate is meant to gravitate. The overall objective of this paper is the evaluation of the real exchange rate misalignments by purely statistical as well as behavioural approaches applied to the five new EU Member States (EU5), namely in the Czech Republic, Hungary, Poland, Slovakia and Slovenia. In Section 2, we focus on the development of real exchange rates and their determinants in EU5. The long-term trends leading to real exchange rate appreciation are described while pointing to the differences in the individual countries. We also provide a survey of existing empirical literature on the real exchange rates in transitional countries. In Section 3, we briefly mention various approaches that can be used for the estimation of the equilibrium real exchange rates. From the available options we decided to build on the main determinants of the real exchange rate movements considered by the BEER approach (Behavioral Equilibrium Exchange Rate). The advantage is a simple structure suitable for looking at a number of countries with a problematic data sources. Nevertheless, the drawback of the approach is the ad hoc specification. Section 4 then presents the results of the estimations of the misalignments of the real exchange rates in the individual countries. The estimations were made by means of the purely statistical (Hodrick-Prescott and Band-Pass filter) as well as the BEER-like approaches, which were estimated by two single equation techniques (Engle-Granger and ARDL). In the concluding part we report that the real exchange rates have generally evolved in line with the determinants that are believed to be fundamental. The differences among the individual countries can sometimes be explained by different development of their fundamentals.

2.2 Development and determinants of the real exchange rates

2.2.1 The real exchange rate developments in the new EU Member States

The real convergence of all post-socialistic new EU Member States (NMS) was accompanied by sustained appreciation of the real exchange rate.[1] The left hand side of Figure 2.1 shows that all EU5 countries experienced significant real exchange rate appreciation between 1993 and 2004. At the same time, on average, the real exchange rate appreciation was slower during 2000–04 compared to 1993–99, but surprisingly not so much.

There is also a trend regarding the relative importance of the exchange rate and inflation channels in the process of real exchange rate appreciation. The right-hand-side of Figure 2.1 brings evidence that during 1993–99 the economies relied on nominal exchange rate depreciation and real exchange rate appreciation was achieved via much higher inflation. The outlier is the Czech Republic which experienced nominal exchange rate appreciation and low inflation over the whole period. However, at the end of the decade nominal exchange rate appreciation ceased to be the preferred solution, and nominal exchange rates became rather stable or even appreciating also in the other economies. This reflects their ambitions to bring the inflation close to the inflation criterion required for the euro adoption as well as the worldwide preference for a very low inflation.

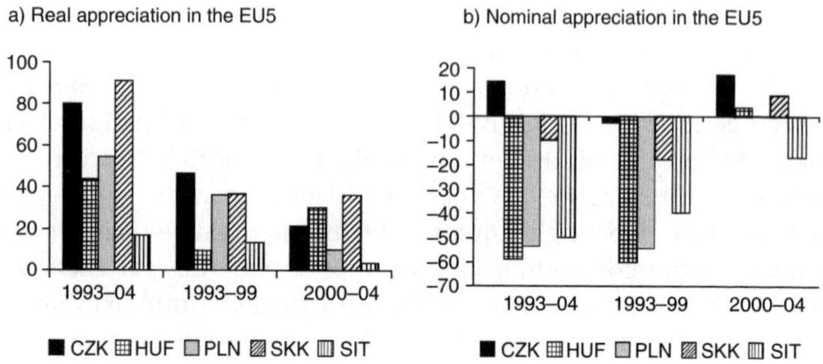

Figure 2.1 Real exchange rate and ERDI of the EU5 countries

Note: (+) appreciation, (−) depreciation, in (%).

Sources: Eurostat, IMF-IFS CD-ROM and authors' calculations.

Table 2.1[2] shows the results of the decomposition of the real exchange rates on nominal exchange rates[3] and inflation differentials for all NMS and the group of 'old' Member States comprised of the catching-up countries (Spain, Portugal, Ireland and Greece). The appreciation of real exchange rates can be generally found during the two or five years preceding the end of sample evaluation period (group A and B) or factual acceptance to the euro area (group C). The variability of the real exchange rate, which we monitor by normalised standard deviations, was lower during the shorter (two years) than longer (five years) period, as might be expected.

Despite a slowdown in real appreciation in recent years, there still must be scope for further real appreciation in some countries as evidenced by calculations of the Exchange Rate Deviation Index (ERDI) – the ratios of the nominal exchange rate over the PPP-implied exchange rate (see Figure 2.2). In principle, equally developed countries have similar price levels expressed in the same currency unit (E.P* = P).[4] Consequently, in the steady state, the ERDI of countries with the same GDP per capita should equal to 1 (E.P*/P = 1).[5] Regarding transition countries with much lower GDP per capita, their exchange rates are normally undervalued relative to those of more developed countries implying that the ERDI is higher than one.[6] However, if the price level of a transition country is in line with its productivity level, this undervaluation can be viewed as an

Table 2.1 The average changes in exchange rates and inflation differentials

		Real exchange rate				Nominal exchange				Inflation differential			
		2y backwards		5y backwards		2y backwards		5y backwards		2y backwards		5y backwards	
Country/variable		Mean	SD	Mean	SD	Mean	SD	Mean	SD	Mean	SD	Mean	SD
Group A	Estonia (EEK)	−0.633	0.967	−1.963	1.397	0.000	0.000	0.000	0.000	0.646	0.980	1.985	1.436
	Lithuania (LTL)	1.126	1.728	−3.778	6.284	−0.917	1.744	−4.855	5.870	−2.019	0.589	−1.090	1.039
	Latvia (LVL)	6.018	4.151	−1.005	7.948	7.940	3.483	0.678	4.756	1.848	1.417	1.360	1.195
	Cyprus (CYP)	−1.154	1.375	−1.298	1.599	0.843	0.933	0.192	0.914	2.037	1.524	1.529	1.448
	Malta (MTL)	3.032	2.720	−0.963	4.329	3.010	1.916	−0.258	3.678	0.002	1.156	0.746	1.220
Group B	Czech Rep (CZK)	0.497	5.878	−3.152	5.891	0.162	5.898	−2.122	5.304	−0.332	0.933	1.109	1.469
	Hungary (HUF)	−1.673	4.582	−5.072	4.643	2.201	5.039	0.336	8.076	3.933	1.140	6.089	2.351
	Poland (PLN)	12.040	4.873	−0.141	11.849	12.903	4.490	2.848	9.756	0.064	0.794	3.308	3.603
	Slovakia (SKK)	−7.693	3.869	−7.150	5.140	−2.343	2.325	−0.700	4.558	5.886	2.643	7.075	3.946
	Slovenia (SIT)	−0.864	0.910	−1.010	0.951	3.389	0.673	4.632	1.483	4.302	1.441	5.706	1.573
Group C	Spain (ESP)	−0.034	0.569	−0.856	5.630	0.455	0.491	2.156	4.881	0.491	0.554	1.578	1.034
	Portugal (PTE)	−1.048	1.814	−0.533	3.663	−0.041	1.793	1.163	4.170	1.023	1.048	1.694	0.972
	Ireland (IEP)	−2.372	6.448	0.564	4.558	−1.737	7.298	−0.478	6.073	0.598	1.073	0.360	0.832
	Greece (GRD)	4.886	3.989	0.088	6.081	1.199	2.867	1.314	4.049	−3.355	5.146	1.469	5.244

Notes:
a) calculations based on average monthly market exchange rate against DEM/EUR and monthly CPI indexes.
b) (−) national currency appreciation/decrease, (+) national currency depreciation/increase; the numbers thus express the appreciation or depreciation of the euro against national currencies, not vice versa. Shadow parts alert to appreciation periods.
c) calculation for 2 and 5 years before the hypothetical (group A, B) and real (group C) euro area entry, i.e. for group A and B: end of June 2004 and 2 (5) years backwards, for Spain, Portugal and Ireland: January1997–December1998, (January1994–December 1999) and for Greece: January 1999–December 2000 (January 1996–December 2000).

Sources: Eurostat, IMF-IFS CD-ROM and authors' calculations.

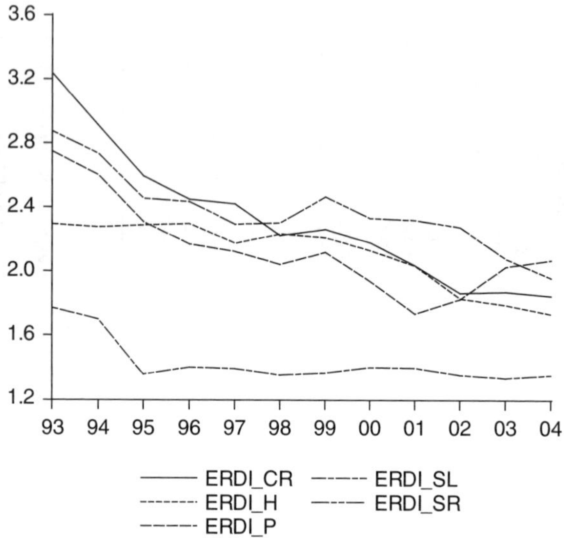

Figure 2.2 Exchange rate deviation index of the EU5 countries

Note: ERDI = Exchange rate deviation index, CR = Czech Republic, H = Hungary, P = Poland, SL = Slovenia, SR = Slovakia.

Sources: Eurostat, IMF-IFS CD-ROM and authors' calculations.

equilibrium undervaluation in PPP terms. In addition, there may be a gap between the actual ERDI and the one implied by GDP per capita. This particular gap should close during the initial phase transition to a large extent thanks to the elimination of the inefficiencies and structural distortions. A successful catch-up process should thus cause the real exchange rate to appreciate first towards the ERDI values implied by GDP per capita and then, in the very long run, towards the ERDI value of 1, representing the PPP 'target' value.

The calculations of the ERDI show that their values for the EU5 countries have been relatively far from the steady state value of 1, but also from the average 'entrance' value of countries of group C defined above. This value was for all these countries on average 1.3 – from the lowest value 1.23 (Spain) to the highest value 1.45 (Portugal). The only exception is the ERDI for Slovenia which is not so far from the average for the Group C countries. However, the other four countries have still significantly higher values of ERDI, but with a clear long-run trend towards the lower number. Real exchange rate appreciation thus should continue in the years prior to the euro adoption. Admittedly, there is a major uncertainty as to the speed of the real appreciation in the more advanced phases of transition.

2.2.2 The fundamental factors affecting the real exchange rate

According to the abundant empirical literature on the determinants of real exchange rate,[7] the key variables which drive real exchange rate development are productivity or productivity differentials, net foreign assets, terms of trade, real interest rates differentials, foreign debts and foreign direct investment to GDP ratios. Higher growth of *average productivity* at home compared to the foreign country is believed to lead unambiguously to real exchange rate appreciation. Next, an increase in the *net foreign asset position*, by augmenting the amount of foreign assets owned by the residents, is expected to increase the value of domestic currency and contribute to real exchange rate appreciation. The *terms of trade*, the ratio of export to import prices, are implicitly linked with the price component of the real exchange rate. If the terms of trade improve, then relative domestic prices rise, which leads to real exchange rate appreciation. The *real interest rate differential*, as an indicator of attractiveness of domestic currency on international markets, may also have at least positive short-term impact on the real exchange rate. Conversely, high ratio of *foreign debt to GDP* undermines the confidence in the currency and contributes to nominal or subsequently a real depreciation. Other possible explanatory variables are the degree of openness or the shares of investment, government or private consumption on GDP. We note that the individual theories and models may view the impact of the fundamentals differently. Especially time horizon is what matters. Some determinants are believed to cause the real exchange rate appreciation in the short run and depreciation in the medium- or long-run, and vice versa. This is a crucial challenge for the estimates of equilibrium real exchange rates.[8]

Regarding the transition countries, Frait and Komárek (2001) split the factors affecting the real exchange rate into two broad groups: those that affect the tradables sector and those that affect the non-tradables sector. They sort the main factors affecting the real exchange rate, and which cause real appreciation of the exchange rate in transition economies, into two groups – the supply and demand factors. The supply factors include the Balassa–Samuelson effect, the relative factor endowment hypothesis, the costs of developing the network and regulated sectors, and the 'Dutch disease'. The demand factors include the income elasticity of demand for non-tradables and capital inflows following liberalisation of the financial (capital) account.

Égert (2003) provides an extensive survey of empirical studies that lists a vast number of variables that are believed to have a lasting impact on real exchange rate. Productivity or a proxy of it appears to enter almost always the real exchange rate equation. There is strong evidence that an increase in productivity leads to an appreciation of the real exchange rate. However, the findings of the literature regarding the signs of the other variables are mixed. Approximately a third of the papers find that government expenditures in GDP, the openness ratio, net foreign assets, the foreign real interest rate or the real interest differential and the terms of trade have had a significant impact on the real exchange of the NMS. Besides, a couple of other variables such as foreign debt, private expenditures and investment relative to GDP have also been detected in a handful of papers to exert an influence on the real exchange rate. Mixed results with respect to other variables except for the productivity are sometimes due to the difference in time horizon (e.g. use of 3-month versus 10-year real interest rates), methodological differences and also because the theoretical explanation itself is unambiguous (see Appendix 2).

2.3 The equilibrium real exchange rate concepts

As far as the future steps towards adopting the euro are concerned, the central parity chosen by a particular country should reflect the best possible assessment of the equilibrium real exchange rate at the time of the entry into the ERM II. From the literature presented, see for example Égert (2003), MacDonald (2000), it is clear that a wide variety of approaches for estimating the equilibrium exchange rates could be applied.

2.3.1 Methods based on an economic theory[9]

The analysis of the real equilibrium exchange rate could be divided into two main categories; the fundamental (normative) and behavioural (positive) ones.[10] Nevertheless, a common starting point to infer about the equilibrium exchange rate is to use the purchasing power parity approach. However, there is a strong consensus in the literature that PPP (Purchasing Power Parity) is not an appropriate measure for the developing and transition economies. Countries in a catch-up process may experience a trend appreciation of the real exchange rate, for which simple version of PPP theory cannot account.[11]

A more medium-term concept, and thus more useful for policy purposes is the fundamental equilibrium exchange rate (*FEER*) developed by Williamson (1994), which defines the equilibrium exchange rate as the real exchange rate that satisfies simultaneously internal and external balances. The cornerstone of this approach is current account sustainability, i.e. the level of current account deficits/surpluses that matches long-term capital inflows/outflows. The FEER approach needs a normative judgment regarding the size of long-term capital flows. This is a very important and also sometimes tricky aspect, especially for small, open and transition economies, such as NMS. Also, FEER estimates are usually derived from large-scale macroeconometric models or partial trade blocks of a given economy. To circumvent normativity and the use of macro models, the macroeconomic balance (*MB*) approach, which has been sharpened and widely used by the IMF,[12] estimates directly the sustainable level of current account deficits (surpluses) based on the saving and investment balance.

Similar in spirit to these approaches is the *NATREX* (Natural Rate of Exchange) model advocated by Stein[13] in that it is also based on the notions of internal and external balances. However, contrary to FEER, it does not only consider the medium term, but also the long run, when capital stock and foreign debt are assumed to converge to their long-run steady state.

The behavioral equilibrium exchange rate (*BEER*) put forth by MacDonald (1997) and Clark and MacDonald (1998) draws on the real interest parity through which the real exchange rate can be connected to the fundamentals. However, this approach is rather a statistical one, linking the real exchange rate to a set of macroeconomic variables through a single equation setting. Thus, the choice of the fundamentals is more ad hoc than based on a theory. The fitted value of the estimated equation, which may be derived either on the basis of observed series or using long-term values of the fundamentals, represents the estimated equilibrium exchange rate.

The permanent equilibrium exchange rate (*PEER*), a variant of BEER refers to the approach that aims to decompose the long-term co-integration vector (fitted value) into a permanent and transitory component[14] with the permanent component being interpreted as the equilibrium exchange rate. This means that the PEER method filters out the disturbance of the fundamentals. Wadhwani (1999) presents a relatively similar BEER type model, which was named the intermediate term model-based equilibrium exchange rate (*ITMEER*).

Another approach explains the persistence in real exchange rates, and also derives well-defined measures of the equilibrium exchange rate. The capital enhanced equilibrium exchange rate (*CHEER*), as it is called, involves exploiting the vector which consists of the nominal exchange rate, price level and interest rates in domestic and foreign country. The main idea of the approach is that the exchange rate may be away from its PPP determined rate because of non-zero interest rate differential – this is in accordance with the basic Casselian view of the PPP. CHEER approach has been popularised for example by Johansen and Juselius (1992). According to MacDonald (2000), the CHEER is a medium-run concept in a sense that it does not impose stock-flow consistency.

2.3.2 Outline of the behavioural model for EU5 countries

The popularity of the behavioural models is brought about by the observation that they can explain well the real exchange rate movements even when estimated in a reduced form. The behavioural models do not approach the equilibrium real exchange rate from the point of view of internal and external equilibria, but rather from the point of view of consistency with relevant fundamentals. We start building the BEER model for the NMS using the equation for the actual real exchange rate based on real uncovered interest parity (UIP):

$$q_t = E_t(q_{t+k}) - (r_t - r_t^*) + \omega_t \tag{1}$$

where q_t is the actual real exchange rate (RER), r_t and r_t^* are the domestic and foreign real interest rates with a maturity $t + k$, E_t (q_{t+k}) is the conditional expectation of the $t + k$ period real exchange rate and ω_t is the time-varying risk premium. Further, $r_t = i_t - E_t\ (\pi_{t+k})$, is the *ex ante* real interest rate, where i_t is the nominal interest rate with a maturity $t + k$ and E_t (π_{t+k}) is the conditional expectation of inflation, π_t in period $t + k$. An increase in the risk premium ω_t is deemed to induce a depreciation of the RER which, given the model structure, generates an expected appreciation. The risk premium can be written out in full as:

$$\omega_t = \mu + \lambda_t + e_t \tag{2}$$

where μ is a constant, λ_t is some proxy for the unobserved risk premium and e_t is a white noise process. Following Clark and McDonald (1998) the proxy is assumed to be a positive function of the relative fiscal stance fs_t / fs_t^*:

$$\lambda_t = f^{+}\left(fs_t / fs_t^*\right) \tag{3}$$

hereafter the function $f(\cdot)$ is restricted to be linear. For instance, an increase in the relative supply of the outstanding domestic debt increases the risk premium on the domestic currency and induces a depreciation of the current real exchange rate.

Now, consider again equation (1). The conditional expectation is also restricted to be a linear function of the information set we will condition upon. It is convenient at this point to elaborate on the conditional expectation of the $t + k$ period RER given that we deal with some specifics related to an economy in transition. For this reason, let us decompose the expectation into two parts:

$$E\left(q_{t+k} \mid I_t\right) = E\left(q_{t+k} \mid I_t^*\right) + E\left(q_{t+k} \mid I_t^T\right) \tag{4}$$

where I_t^* involves the traditional determinants of RER of developed economies (see e.g. McDonald, 1997), and I_t^T is a set of determinants that are effective only during transition periods and their effect on the RER ceases to be significant as the countries accomplish their transitions (convergence to developed economies). Applying the assumption of linearity and using equations (2)–(4), (1) can be expressed as:

$$q_t = \mu + \theta_1 X_{1,t} + \theta_2 X_{2,t} + \theta_3(r_t - r_t^*) + \theta_4(fs_t - fs_t^*) + e_t \quad (5)$$

where $X_{1,t}$ is a subset of I_t^* and similarly $X_{2,t}$ is a subset of I_t^T, θ_1 is expected to be non-zero, $\theta_2 \to 0$ as t approaches the end of the transition period, θ_3 is expected to be equal to negative one if the real UIP holds, and θ_4 is expected to be positive.

2.4 Empirical evaluation and evidence for the EU5 countries

2.4.1 Empirical techniques

By using a combination of statistical and reduced form methods to estimate the equilibrium RER we aim to address difficulties concerning regarding the data availability for CEE countries, i.e. 1) a lack of time series for some variables recommended by the theory and 2) short time span. Quarterly time series were used covering the period from 1995Q1 to 2004Q1 (37 observations). The time series were transformed into logarithms, except for the real interest rate differential. The relevant series were seasonally adjusted by means of Tramo/Seats method, where it was not possible by X12 procedure. All the data used are described in the Appendix 1. The simplest, purely statistical method of estimation of exchange rate misalignments is to detrend the RER series. We employ two types of filters for this purpose – Hodrick-Prescott filter (HP) and Band-Pass filter (BP). Subsequently, we apply two co-integration methods of Engle-Granger (EG) and the ARDL method to the reduced-form BEER model. Both types of techniques are then compared.

Hodrick–Prescott filter

The assumption of this approach, used for example in Csajbók (2003), is that in the sample period as a whole, the real exchange rate has been on average in equilibrium. The shorter the sample period, the less plausible this assumption is, as there are examples of long-lasting misalignments. Fitted values are obtained by applying the HP-filter with the generally recommended smoothing parameter $\lambda = 1600$ for the quarterly time series (see part b in Figures 2.3–2.7).

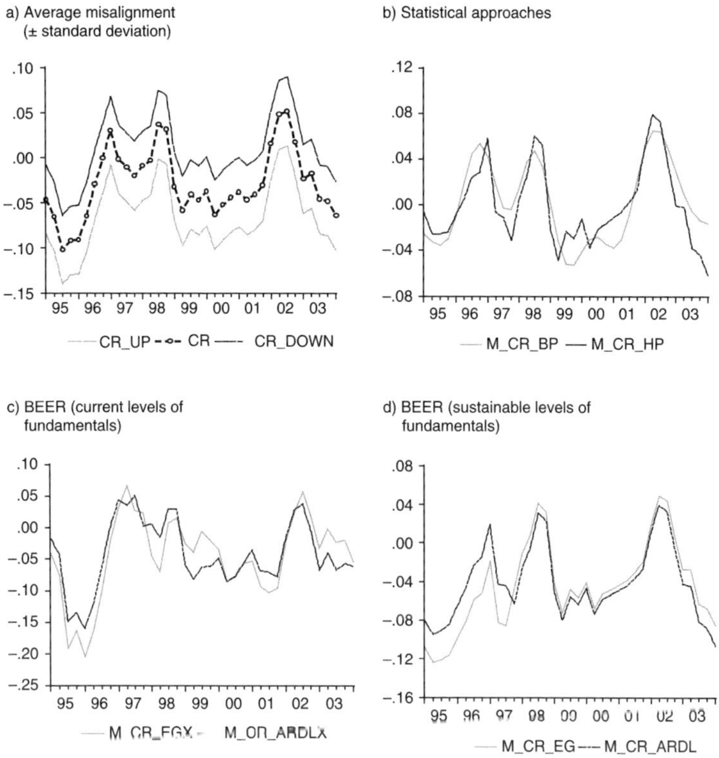

Figure 2.3 Real exchange rate misalignments of the Czech koruna

Note: Misalignment = fitted – actual values. Positive values correspond to overvaluation. Current levels of fundamentals measure short run misalignment, sustainable levels of fundamentals medium-run misalignment. CR = the Czech Republic. Part (a): CR_UP = average misalignment + standard deviation, CR_DOWN = average misalignment – standard deviation, CR = average misalignment; part (b) M_CR_BP = misalignment based on Band–Pass filter, M_CR_HP = misalignment based on Hodrick–Prescott filter; part (c) M_CR_EGX = short-run misalignment based on Engle–Granger method, M_CR_ARDLX = short-run misalignment based on ARDL method; part (d): M_CR_EG: middle-run misalignment based on Engle–Granger method, M_CR_ARDL: middle-run misalignment based on ARDL method.

Sources: Authors' calculations based on Eurostat and IMF-IFS data.

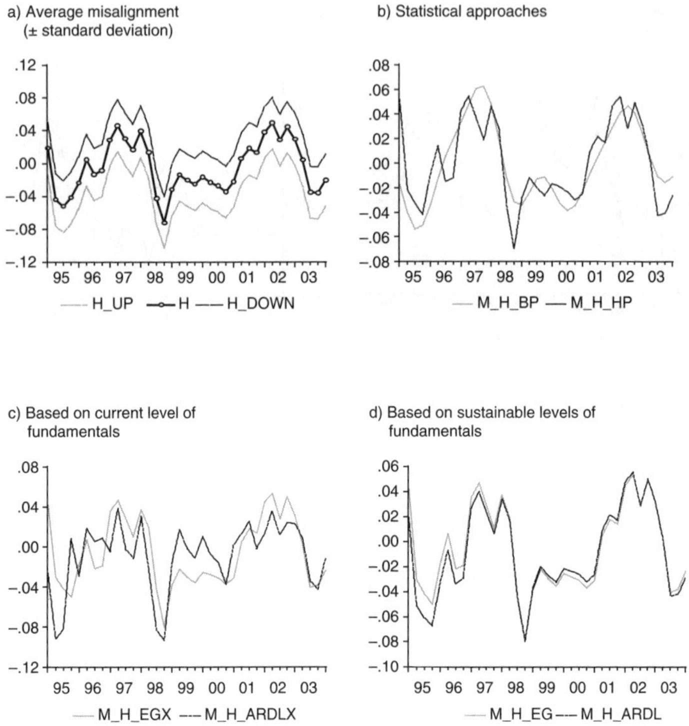

Figure 2.4 Real exchange rate misalignments of the Hungarian forint

Note: H = Hungary. Further description is similar to Figure 2.3.

Sources: Authors' calculations based on Eurostat and IMF-IFS data.

Band–Pass filter

Another method, which can be used in this context, is to compute several forms of Band–Pass (frequency) filters. This method identifies the cyclical component of the time series given a pre-specified range for its duration. The band–pass filter is a linear filter that passes a limited range of frequencies between the specified lower and upper bounds. The band–pass filter is then computed by weighting the resulting two-sided moving average filters. We use the full-length asymmetric filter introduced by Christiano and

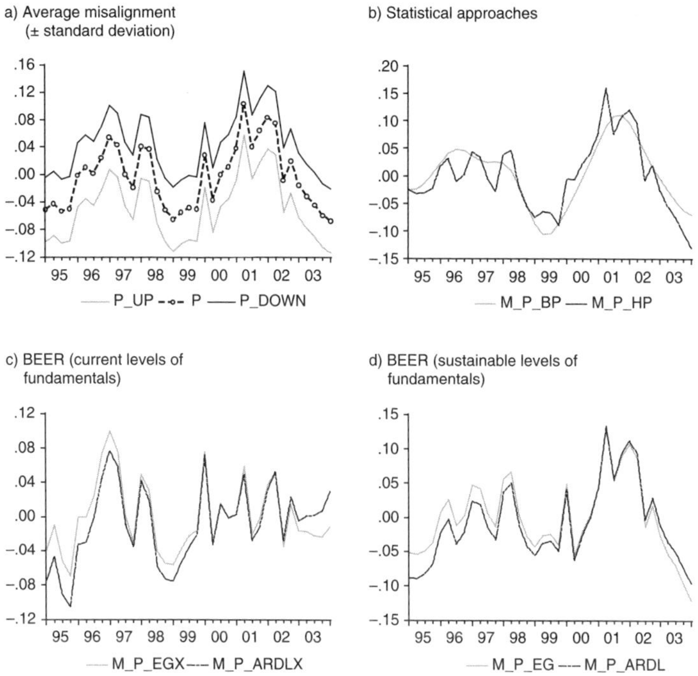

Figure 2.5 Real exchange rate misalignments of the Polish zloty

Note: P = Poland. Further description is similar to Figure 2.3.

Sources: Authors' calculations based on Eurostat and IMF-IFS data.

Fitzgerald (1999, 2003) to construct the misalignments presented in Figures 2.3–2.7 (part b).

Engle–Granger method

As a starting point, we use the Engle–Granger methodology exposited in e.g. Enders (2004, pp. 335–339). According to this approach, a dependent variable Y_t and exogenous variables $X_{i,t}$ form a long-term relationship (6) if all variables are integrated of the same order and the residuals e_t are stationary.

$$Y_t = \beta_0 + \sum_{i=1}^{n} \beta_i X_{i,t} + e_t \qquad (6)$$

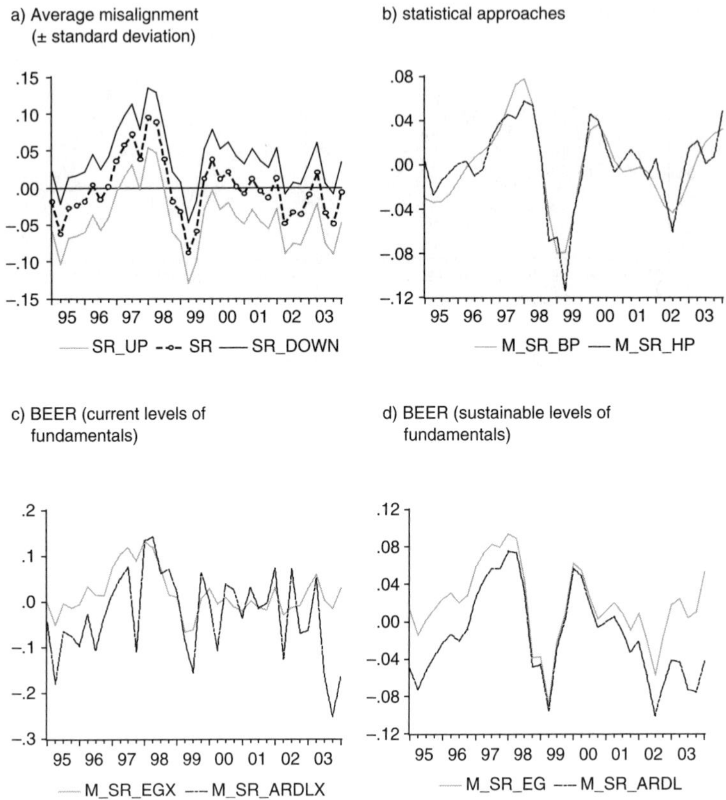

Figure 2.6 Real exchange rate misalignments of the Slovak koruna

Note: SR = Slovakia. Further description is similar to Figure 2.3.

Sources: Authors' calculations based on Eurostat and IMF-IFS data.

Stationarity of the regression residuals e_t is tested by applying the augmented Dickey-Fuller (ADF) unit root test:

$$\Delta\hat{e}_t = a_1\hat{e}_{t-1} + \sum_{i=1}^{n} a_{i+1}\Delta\hat{e}_{t-i} + \varepsilon_t \qquad (7)$$

Since the actual distribution of regression residuals $\hat{e}_t$ is not known, special critical values of the ADF statistics should be used to assess

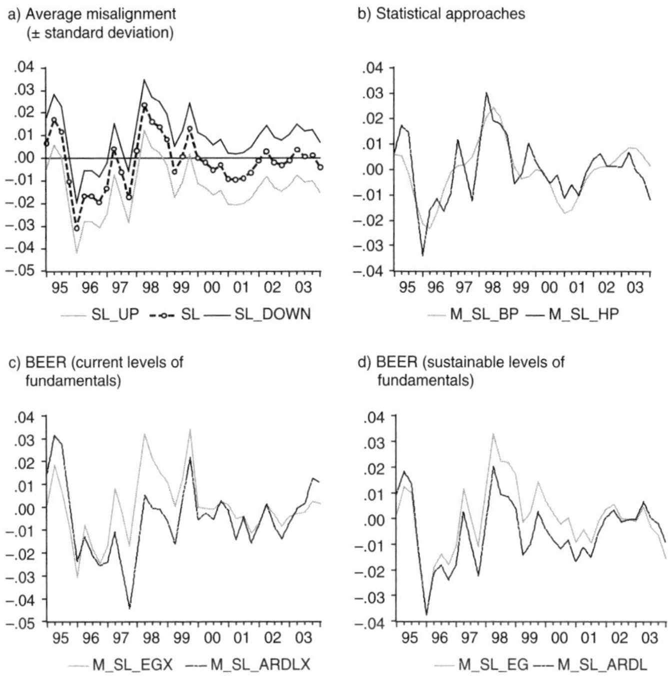

Figure 2.7 Real exchange rate misalignment of the Slovenian tolar

Note: SL = Slovenia. Further description is similar to Figure 2.3.

Sources: Authors' calculations based on Eurostat and IMF-IFS data.

stationarity. Critical values are obtained using the following formula: $C_k(p,T) = \beta_\infty + \beta_1 T^{-1} + \beta_2 T^{-2}$ where p and T are the significance level and the sample size respectively, and the betas are parameters of response surface estimates provided in MacKinnon (1991). The results are presented in Figures 2.3–2.7, parts c and d.

ARDL method

The error correction form of the ARDL model is given by equation (8) where the dependent variable in first differences is regressed on the lagged values of the dependent and independent variables in levels and first differences.

$$\Delta Y_t = \beta_0 + \rho(Y_{t-1} + \beta_1 X_{t-1}) + \sum_{j=1}^{l_1} \eta_j \Delta Y_{t-j} + \sum_{j=0}^{l_2} \gamma_{i,j} \Delta X_{i,t-j} + e_t \qquad (8)$$

Pesaran (2001) employ a bound testing approach. Using conventional F-tests, the null of H_0: $\rho = \beta_1 = \ldots = \beta_n = 0$ is tested against the alternative hypothesis of $H_1 : \rho \neq 0, \beta_1 \neq 0, \cdots, \beta_n \neq 0$. Pesaran et al. (2001) tabulate two sets of critical values, one for the case when all variables are I(1), i.e. the upper-bound critical values and another one when all variables are I(0), i.e. the lower-bound critical values. Critical values are provided for five different models, of which model (8) with restricted intercept and no trend is used in this paper. If the test statistic is higher than the upper bound critical value the null of no co-integration is rejected in favour of the presence of cointegration. The results are presented in Figures 2.3–2.7, parts c and d.

2.4.2 Misalignments of the EU5 countries' currencies

When employing the behavioural approach, it is possible to distinguish between two types of misalignments, i.e. deviations of the actual exchange rate from an estimate of its equilibrium values. The first deviation of interest is the *current (speculative) misalignment*, which is defined as the deviation of the actual real exchange rate from the estimated equilibrium real exchange rate given by the conditioning set of actual fundamentals. This kind of misalignment measures the actual deviations from the equilibrium exchange rate of the EU5 countries in the short-run (see part c in Figures 2.3–2.7).

The second deviation is the *total (cyclical plus speculative) misalignment* defined as the deviation of the actual real exchange rate from the estimated equilibrium real exchange rate based on the sustainable values of the fundamentals. The sustainable values of the estimated equilibrium exchange rate are obtained by applying some cyclical filter to the latter estimates; one example being the Hodrick–Prescott (HP) filter to the original time series (see part d in Figures 2.3–2.7). This misalignment measures the equilibrium exchange rate in the medium-run perspective. Below we comment on the estimations for each of EU5 countries with the emphasis on the result at the end of the period (first quarter of 2004). Finally, we average over statistical and econometrical approaches to take a broad view upon the estimated misalignments.

These average misalignments are presented in Figures 2.3–2.7 (part a) together with ± standard deviation.

Czech Republic

Both the EG and ARDL methods find the productivity differential, net foreign direct investment and terms of trade as significant determinants of the real exchange rate (see Appendix 5). All variables were significant at the 1 per cent level and had the expected sign. Both sets of results were tested for serial correlation in residuals, appropriate functional form, non-normality and heteroscedasticity and all these tests produced satisfactory results. The error correction equation also works out well. The error correction term has a negative sign at the 1 per cent significance level. This coefficient indicates that the Czech koruna in real terms returns to its equilibrium level approximately in two quarters. The average misalignment (the average of all six estimations) of the Czech koruna was roughly 6 per cent; i.e. the real exchange rate was 6 per cent undervalued compare to the equilibrium exchange rate at the end of the first quarter of 2004. The results of both statistical methods support the outcomes from co-integration analysis.

Hungary

The EG method finds the productivity differential, net foreign assets, openness and foreign direct investment as significant determinants of the real exchange rate of the Hungarian forint (see Appendix 5). All these explanatory variables bear the expected sign. The ARDL method identifies similar determinants of the forint's exchange rate except for the net foreign direct investment which appear to be insignificant at the 10 per cent level. All diagnostic tests are satisfied. The error correction term was significant but relatively high, which indicates relatively quick movement of the real exchange rate to its equilibrium level. The forint was – in real terms – approximately 2.5 per cent undervalued at the end of the first quarter of 2004. The results for both statistical methods are similar to the co-integration outcomes.

Poland

The results of the EG and ARDL methods (Appendix 5) show that the degree of openness, the productivity differential, and real interest rates are significant in explaining the real exchange behavior of the Polish zloty. All these explanatory variables have the expected sign.

The change of the exchange rate regime in Poland was also tested – the dummy variable was significant. Other explanatory variables, i.e. approximation of the B-S effect, net foreign assets, government spending and terms of trades were not significant at the 10per cent level. The results of diagnostic tests rule out the presence of serial correlation, non-normality, inappropriate functional form and heteroscedasticity. Also the error correction term has the expected negative sign and its level indicates that the real exchange rate regresses to its equilibrium level within two quarters. The zloty was – in real terms – approximately 7.5 per cent undervalued at the end of the first quarter of 2004. The results for both statistical methods are in line with the co-integration outcomes.

Slovakia

The results of the EG and ARDL methods (Appendix 5) show that the productivity differential, the productivity differential and foreign direct investment are significant determinants of Slovak koruna's real exchange rate. The EG method also finds openness as relatively significant variable (at the 12 per cent level). Nevertheless, the FDI variable has the opposite sign than was expected. The other explanatory variables, i.e. the real interest rates differential, net foreign assets, terms of trades and government spending cannot explain the movements in the Slovak koruna. In addition, the Russian and Asian crises had an important effect on the koruna. Overall, the estimated outcomes and their diagnostic tests work quite well and also the error correction term is significantly negative. The overall conclusion about the over/under valuation of the Slovak koruna is ambiguous. Purely statistical results indicate a 3per cent overvaluation of the Slovak koruna at the end of the period. However, there are striking differences between both methods and between the current and total misalignments. The volatility of FDI seems to be the main reason for these differences. Due to the developments of other fundamental factors in the Slovak economy, we emphasise the results obtained using the sustainable levels of the fundamentals. The Slovak koruna was appreciating really fast in line with recent economic reforms.

Slovenia

Both EG and ARDL methods are in line with purely statistical approaches and show that Slovenia has a stable currency in real terms. Tolar was approximately 0.5 per cent undervalued at the end of the first quarter of 2004. Both methods find that the productivity differential, net foreign assets and government spending are the significant determinants of the tolar real exchange rate (see Appendix 5). The results for the ARDL method show better diagnostic properties as the tests reject the hypothesis of serial correlation, inappropriate functional form, non-normality and heteroscedasticity. In addition, the error correction term was relatively high (0.665) and significant.

2.5 Conclusion

The real convergence of the new EU Member States has been accompanied by sustained appreciation of the real exchange rate. This was closing the gap between the PPP exchange rates and the actual exchange rates in such a way that the ERDI (Exchange Rate Deviation Index) was approaching more reasonable levels. This trend is supposed to continue in the years prior to the euro adoption. However, there is a major uncertainty as to the speed of the real appreciation in the more advanced phases of transition. Understanding determinants of the equilibrium real exchange appreciation is therefore very important from the policymakers' perspective, not only because misalignments of the actual rate from its equilibrium level may turn rather costly. In particular, an overvalued currency may lead to an unsustainable current account deficit, and in the long run, to lower economic growth. Besides that, potential misalignment is an important policy issue faced by the new EU Member States that are supposed to participate in the exchange rate mechanism, ERM II, and then adopt the euro in the future. That will require first setting a central parity in ERM II and later the euro-locking rate for the final conversion.

The primary objective of this paper was to analyse the misalignment of the real exchange rate in five New EU Member States (Czech Republic, Hungary, Poland Slovakia, Slovenia) with the use of purely statistical as well as behavioural approaches. The behavioural model of the equilibrium exchange rate in the tradition of MacDonald (1997, 2000) was employed in this paper and the actual and sustainable misalignments were calculated accordingly. Besides the behavioural model, the statistical techniques like the Hodrick–Prescott and Band–Pass filter were utilised to answer similar questions.

The results of the paper indicate that the tendency towards real exchange rates' appreciation in the economies under consideration have been driven primarily by fundamental determinants. They also signal that at the beginning of 2004, which was the ultimate date of our sample, the currencies of the EU5 countries were generally undervalued in real terms. The subsequent appreciation of some of these countries' currencies may thus be viewed as natural phenomenon. Besides that the dynamics of misalignments suggest that all currencies behave similarly, probably because they are being affected by similar factors. In addition, the under/over valuation periods had roughly similar timing, expect for the existence of periods of bubbles (which resulted in the strong appreciation followed by the correcting depreciation) or turbulences. These results will have to be confirmed by the future research since the problems with the availability and shortness of time series call for their cautious interpretation.

Appendix 1: Construction and stationarity of data[15]

The real exchange rate (*rer*) – the index of the nominal exchange rate against DEM (EUR) deflated by the consumer price index (CPI) in the given economy and in Germany. The decrease in this index denotes any real exchange rate appreciation. The quarterly indices were obtained by averaging the monthly indices. Data source: IMF IFS database. All time series were integrated in order one.

Productivity differential (*dprod*) – the differential between productivity in the EU5 countries and Germany calculated as the ratio of the real GDP over employment in both countries. Data source: IMF IFS and Eurostat, New Cronos databases (seasonal adjustment by authors). All time series were integrated in order one.

Approximation of the Balassa–Samuelson effect (*bs*) – this is a ratio calculated as the relative price of non-tradable goods to tradable goods. An increase in this ratio should induce an appreciation of the real exchange rate. Clark and MacDonald (1998) approximate the Balassa–Samuelson effect as the ratio of CPI to WPI (PPI) in the home country relative to the foreign country.[16] In this paper, the modification of this ratio is used in a form of the service component of the consumer price index to the producer price index (PPI) in the home country over the same ratio in foreign country (Germany). Data source: IMF IFS database (seasonal adjustment by authors). All time series were integrated in order one.

Foreign direct investment (*fdi*) – the ratio of net foreign direct investments over nominal GDP calculated from the four quarters' moving averages, both denominated in national currency. The increase in this ratio leads to the appreciation of the real exchange rate. Data source: IMF IFS database (seasonal adjustment by authors). All time series were integrated in order one. All time series were integrated in order one.

Terms of trade (*tot*) – the standard ratio of the export and import indices in each economy. The increase in this ratio leads to the appreciation of the real exchange rate. Data source: Eurostat, New Cronos database (seasonal adjustment by authors). All time series were integrated in order one.

Openness (*open*) – the ratio of the sum of exports and imports relative to nominal GDP, all denominated in national currency. The effect of openness to the real exchange rate is ambiguous. Data source: Eurostat, New Cronos databases (seasonal adjustment by authors). All time series were integrated in order one, expect for Slovenia, for which is openness type I(0).

Net foreign assets (*nfa*) – The percentage ratio of the net foreign assets relative to nominal GDP, both denominated in national currency. The increase of this ratio leads to the appreciation of the real exchange rate. Data source: IMF IFS database (seasonal adjustment by authors).

Government spending (*gs*) – due to lack of data the total government consumption over nominal GDP was used as a proxy for non-tradable government consumption, both denominated in national currency. The decrease of this ratio leads to the appreciation of the real exchange rate (though the theme may be rather specific dynamics originally leading to depreciation). Data source: IMF IFS and Eurostat, New Cronos databases (seasonal adjustment by authors). All time series were integrated in order one, except for Hungary, for which is openness type I(0).

Real interest rate differential (*dlrr*) – The differential of the home and foreign (German) lending rates deflated by both home and foreign (German) inflation rates. The decrease of this ratio leads to the appreciation of the real exchange rate. Generally, one intends to use long-term interest rates but time series like this are not available for the whole period and for all EU5 countries. Data source: IMF IFS database. All time series were integrated in order one.

Appendix 2: Overview of the real exchange rate determinants from the empirical studies

STUDY	A	B	C	D	E	F	G	H	I	J	K	Σ
Alberola (2003)	–			?								2
Alonso-Gamo et al. (2002)	–			+								2
Avallone & ahrèche-Révil (1999)	–	–	+			–			–			5
Begg et al. (1999)	–	–	–									3
Beguna (2002)		–	–			–					–	4
Bitans (2002)	–	+	+									3
Bitans & Tillers (2003)	–			–		+						3
Burgess et al. (2003)	–			+								3
Coricelli and Jazbec (2001)	–	–							–			3
Coudert (1999)	–							+				2
Csajbók (2003)	–	–	–	–	–	–						6
Darvas (2001)	–			–	?							3
De Broeck and Sløk (2001)	–		+									2
Dobrinsky (2003)	–	–										2
Égert &Lahrèche-Révil (2003)	–											1
Égert & Lommatzsch (2003)	–		+		–			?		–		5
Filipozzi (2000)	–						–					2
Fischer (2002)	–	–			?	+						4
Frait & Komárek (1999, 2001)	–				+	–			–		–	4
Halpern & Wyplosz (1997)	–	–										2
Hinnosar et al. (2003)	–			–		–						3
IMF (1998)	–	+	–				+					4
Kazaks (2000)	–		+									2
Kim & Korhonen (2002)	–	–	+				–					4
Krajnyák & Zettelmeyer (1998)	–											1
Lommatzsch & Tober (2002b)	–			+	–							3
MacDonald & Wójcik (2002)	–			?	–					–		4
Maurin (2001)	–	–			–			+				4
Rahn (2003)	–			–								3
Randveer & Rell (2002)	–					–						2
Rawdanowicz (2003)	–				–	–						3
Rubaszek (2003)				–	–							2
Vetlov (2002)	–		+		+							3
Number of '–'	31	10	4	8	9	7	2	1	2	2	2	X
Number of '+'	0	2	7	5	3	2	1	3	0	0	0	X
Total number of studies	31	12	11	11	10	9	3	3	2	2	2	X

Appendix 3: The development of the different real exchange rates in the EU5 countries

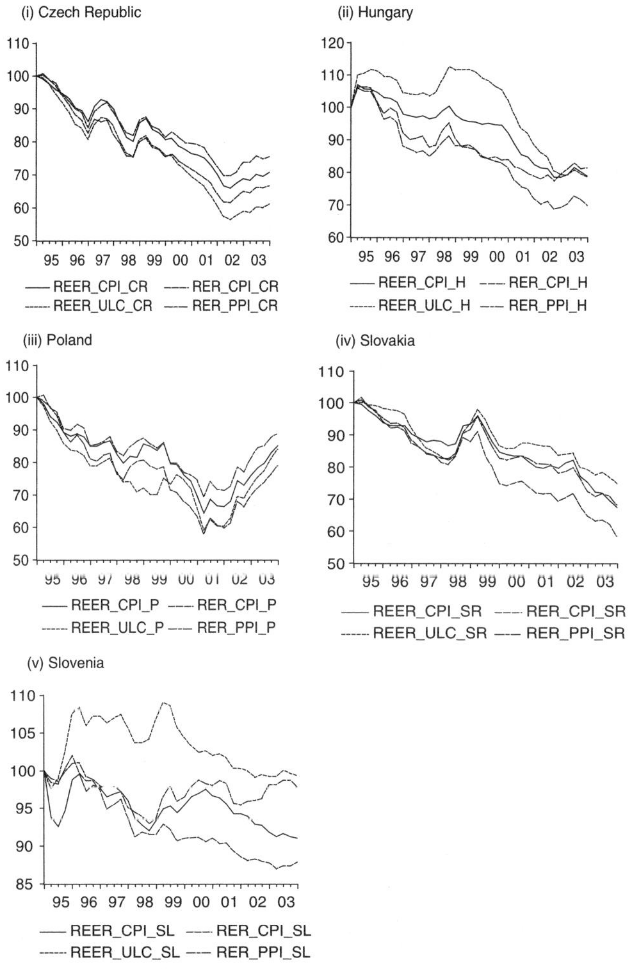

Notes: a) The decrease in the index of the real and nominal exchange indicate the real and nominal appreciation. b) 1995:Q1 = 100. c) REER_CPI = real effective exchange rate deflated by CPI indices, REER_ULC = real effective exchange rate deflated by the unit labour costs.

Source: Authors calculations based on IMF International Monetary Statistic and Eurostat New Cronos.

Appendix 4: Exchange rate regimes in EU5 countries from 1993

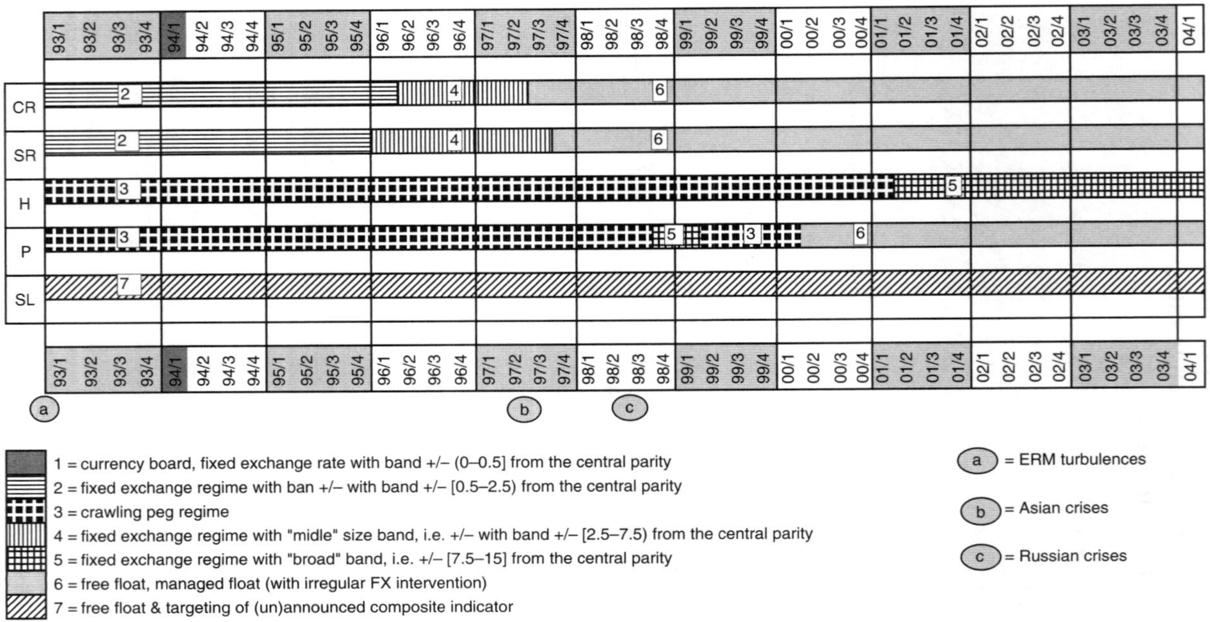

Appendix 5: Co-integration results: Engle–Granger and ARDL method

	Engle–Granger method	ARDL method
CR	$R = 24.59 - 2.88dprod - 0.93fdi - 0.0896dllr - 0.528tot$ (1.50) (0.22) (0.14) (0.19) (0.26)	$R = 22.15 - 3.021dprod - 0.087fdi - 0.849tot$ (1.97) (0.29) (0.16) (0.30)
H	$R = 14.59 - 2.367dprod - 0.01fdi - 0.457open$ (1.43) (0.20) (0.005) (0.19) $+ 0.091nfa + 0.069drc$ (0.038) (0.18)	$R = 14.03 - 2.248dprod - 0.302open - 0.083nfa + 0.782drc$ (1.35) (0.176) (0.193) (0.30) (0.218)
P	$R = 8.6394 - 0.776dprod + 0.461open - 0.021dlrr$ (1.12) (0.23) (0.13) (0.029)	$R = 8.7928 - 0.787dprod + 0.607open - 0.0206dlrr$ (2.08) (0.421) (0.261) (0.005)
SR	$R = 10.946 - 0.749dprod + 0.061fdi - 0.0576bs - 0.093dllr$ (1.02) (0.285) (0.048) (0.12) (0.02) $-0.139open$ (0.088)	$R = 17.383 - 1.175dprod + 0.295fdi - 1.356bs$ (3.13) (0.66) (0.106) (0.12)
SL	$R = 6.6284 - 0.336dprod + 1.12gs - 0.0525nfa$ (1.18) (0.527) (0.048) (0.22)	$R = 6.14 - 0.205dprod + 1.157gs - 0.126nfa$ (0.22) (0.527) (0.539) (0.42)

Appendix 6: List of main abbreviations

	Countries / group of countries		Variables
BG	Bulgaria	**FX**	Foreign exchange market
CEEC	Central and Eastern European countries (CR, H, P, SL, SR)	**CPI**	Consumer price index
CR	the Czech Republic	**PPI**	Producer price index
E	Estonia	**WPI**	Wholesale price index
EU15	The members of the EU before 1st May 2004	**RER, REER**	Real exchange rate, real effective exchange rate
EU5	5 new Member States of the EU	**OPEN**	Openness
FSU	Former Soviet Union countries	**PROD**	Productivity differential
H	Hungary	**RER**	Real exchange rate
HR	Croatia	**NER**	Nominal exchange rate
LA	Latvia	**ID**	Inflation differential
LI	Lithuania	**TOT**	Terms of trade
P	Poland	**NFA**	Net foreign assets
RO	Romania	**FDI**	Foreign direct investment
RU	Russia	**GS**	Government consumption
SL	Slovenia	**CA**	Current account
SR	Slovakia	**RIRD**	Real interest rates differential

Notes

1. We sort the NMS into two groups: *Group A* – countries with relatively fixed exchange rate regimes and *Group B* – countries following a more flexible regime (see also Appendix 4). The countries in these groups will be compared with the development of the former EU catching-up countries – *Group C*.
2. Table 2.1 presents average means and standard deviations of year-over-year percentage changes for the nominal and the CPI-based real exchange rates and also for inflation differential. We take the two periods for the NMS, i.e. two-year (July 2002–June 2004) and five-year (July 1999–June 2004) intervals from the end of the evaluation period. We compare these results with the similar periods, i.e. two and five years backwards from the entry date of selected current euro area members (Ireland, Spain, Portugal and Greece).

3. The countries' nominal exchange rate paths against the euro can be broken down, according to the common features of their nominal exchange rate indices, into those which, between the start of 1993 and the present, have predominantly appreciated, depreciated or have been (by definition of their exchange rate regime) stable against the DEM/EUR or ECU/EUR rates.
4. E = nominal exchange rate, P = domestic price level, P* = foreign price level.
5. Of course, there are factors which may cause the price level to deviate from one another, such as different taxation, direct and indirect trade barriers and in particular transportation costs.
6. The exchange rate must be defined as units of domestic currency per one unit of foreign currency.
7. See, for example, the classic studies by Faruqee (1995), MacDonald (1997), Clark and MacDonald (1998), and a more recent overview by Frait and Komárek (1999, 2001) and Égert (2003).
8. The determinants of real exchange rates can be distributed also over time in the following way. In the short run, movements in the real exchange rate are determined by changes in the nominal exchange rate. This means that the correlation between the nominal and real exchange rate is very high in the short run. In the medium run the real exchange rate is determined chiefly by factors associated with the balance of payments (real interest rates, which determine developments on the financial account; the current account position, which determines net foreign assets; and aggregate labour productivity) and by 'real shocks' to the economy (significant technological changes, significant changes in the terms of trade, and significant changes in state finances, for example rises or falls in expenditure on arms or infrastructure investment). In the very long run, the real exchange rates of advanced nations that are near to a steady state can be more or less constant, unless they exhibit different trends in the overall productivity or thrift.
9. This is only a brief sketch of the methods. For a more-in-depth analysis, see MacDonald (2000) and Égert (2003).
10. For more details see Frait and Komárek (1999, 2001).
11. A well-known phenomenon explaining trend appreciation is the Balassa–Samuelson effect, which is based on market-based non-tradable price inflation driven by fast productivity gains. However, there are two other factors that can contribute to the trend appreciation of the real exchange rate: (1) the trend appreciation of the tradable price-based real exchange rate for example due to the improvements in terms of trade (2) administered/regulated prices changes. For more detail, see Égert and Lommatzsch (2003) and Égert (2003).
12. See Isard and Faruqee (1998) for an overview.
13. See Stein (1994, 1995, 2002).
14. See Gonzalo and Granger (1995).
15. We used data in logarithmic form except the time series for the real interest differential.

16. There might be a problem that the dependent variable (real exchange rate) is also defined by means of CPI indices, which might produce problems in the estimations.

References

ALBEROLA, E. (2003): Real Convergence, External Disequilibria and Equilibrium Exchange Rates in EU Acceding Countries. Bank of Spain.

AVALLONE, N. – LAHRECHE-RVIL, A. (1999): Le taux de change réel d'équilibre dans les pays en transition: le cas de la Hongrie, TEAM, Université Paris 1, Cahiers blancs 1999/91.

BABETSKI, J. – ÉGERT, B. – KOMÁREK, L. – MELECKÝ, M. (2004): An Appropriate level of the exchange rate for ERM II and Euro Conversion of the Czech Koruna. Internal Policy Notes, the Czech National Bank, mimeo.

BAFFES, J. – ELBADAWI, I. A. – O'CONNELL, S. A. (1997): Single-equation Estimation of the Equilibrium Real Exchange Rate. The World Bank Development Research Group, *Policy Research Working Paper*, no. 1800 (August).

BALASSA, B. (1964): The Purchasing Power Parity Doctrine: A Reappraisal. *Journal of Political Economy*, vol. 72, pp. 584–596.

BAXTER, M. – KING, R. (1995): 'Measuring Business Cycles Approximate Band-Pass Filters for Economic Times Series.' NBER Working Paper, No. 5022, February.

BEGG, D. – HALPERN, L. – WYPLOSZ, CH. (1999): Monetary and Exchange Rate Policies, EMU and Central and Eastern Europe. *Forum Report on the Economic Policy Initiative* No. 5. London: CEPR and New York, Prague: EastWest Institute.

BEGUNA, A. (2002): Competitiveness and the Equilibrium Exchange Rate in Latvia. University of Latvia and EuroFaculty. EuroFaculty working Paper in Economic, no. 16 (August).

BURDA, M. C. – GERLACH, S.: (1990) Exchange Rate Dynamics and Currency Unification: The Ostmark-DM Rate/*CEPR Discussion Paper*, no. 485.

CHRISTIANO, L. – FITZGERALD, T. (1999): The Band Pass Filter. NBER Working Paper, No. 7257, July.

CHRISTIANO, L. J. – FITZGERALD, T. J. (2003): The Band Pass Filter. *International Economic Review*, 44(2), 435–465.

CLARK, P. – MACDONALD, R. (1998): Exchange Rates and Economic Fundamentals: A Methodological Comparison of BEERs and FEERs. *IMF Working Paper*, no. WP/98/67, May 1998.

COUDERT, V. (1999): Comment Définir un Taux de Change D¥équilibre Pour Les Pays Émergents? *Economie internationale*. 77. 1er trimestre. 45–65.

CSAJBÓK, A. (2003): The Equilibrium Real Exchange Rate in Hungary: Results from Alternative Approaches. Paper presented at the 2nd workshop on Macroeconomic Policy Research. Magyar Nemzeti Bank, October.

DE BROECK, M. – SLØK, T. (2001): Interpreting Real Exchange Rate Movements in Transition Countries. *IMF Working Paper*, no. 56/01.

DETKEN C. – DIEPPE, A. – HENRY, J. – MARIN, C. – SMETS, F. (2002): Model Uncertainty and the Equilibrium Value of the Real Effective Euro Exchange Rate. *European Central Bank Working Paper*, no. 160 (July).

ECB (2003): Policy position of the Governing Council of the ECB on Exchange Rate Issues Relating to the Acceding Countries. *European Central Bank*, Frankfurt am Main (18 December 2003).

ÉGERT, B. – LAHRÉCHE-RÉVIL, A. (2003): Estimating the Equilibrium Exchange Rate of Central and Eastern European Countries: The Challenge of euro adoption. Weltwirtschaftliches Archiv. 139(4). 683–708.

ÉGERT, B. – LOMMATZSCH, K. (2003): Equilibrium Real Exchange Rates in CEE Acceding countries: How Large Is Our Confidence (Interval)? *Focus on Transition,* No. 2, pp. 107–137.

ÉGERT, B. (2003): Assessing Equilibrium Exchange Rates in CEE Acceding Countries: Can We Have DEER with BEER without FEER? A Critical Survey of the Literature, Oesterreichische Nationalbank, *Focus on Transition*, No. 2., pp. 38–106.

ENDERS, W. (2004): Applied Econometric Time Series. 2nd edition. Wiley publisher.

FARUQEE, H. (1995): Long Run Determinants of the Real Exchange Rate: A Stock-flow Perspective. *IMF Staff Papers*, March.

FISCHER, C. (2002): Real Currency Appreciation in Accession Countries: Balassa-Samuelson and Investment Demand. *BOFIT Discussion Paper no. 8*. Institute for Economies in Transition (BOFIT). Suomen Pankki.

FRAIT, J. – KOMÁREK, L. (1999): Long–term determinants of the Equilibrium Real Exchange Rate of Czech Koruna. Czech National Bank Working Paper, No. 9. [in Czech].

FRAIT, J. – KOMÁREK, L. (2001): Real Exchange Rate Trends in Transitional Countries, *Warwick Economics Research Papers*, Department of Economics, The University of Warwick, July 2001, No 596.

GONZALO, J. – GRANGER, C. W. (1995): Estimation of Common Long-Memory Components in Cointegrated Systems. *Journal of Business Economics and Statistics*, Vol. 13, pp. 27.35.

HALPERN, L. – WYPLOSZ, CH. (1997): Equilibrium Real Exchange Rates in Transition Economies. *IMF Staff Papers*, No. 4 (December).

HINNOSAR, M., – R. JUKS, H. – KAADU – L. UUSKÜLA. (2003): Estimating the Equilibrium Exchange Rate of the Estonian Kroon. Bank of Estonia, mimeo.

ISARD, P. – FARUQEE, H. (eds) (1998): *Exchange rate assessment: extensions of the macroeconomic balance approach*. IMF Occasional Paper, No. 167, Washington DC.

JOHANSEN, S. – JUSELIUS, K. (1998): Testing Structural Hypothesis in a Multivariate Cointegration Analysis of the PPP and the UIP for the UK. *Journal of Econometris*, Vol. 53, pp. 211–244.

KAMINSKI, G. – LIZONDO, S. – REINHART, C. (1997): Leading Indicators of Currency Crises. *IMF Working Paper*, no. 97/79 (July).

KIM, B.Y. – Korhonen, I. (2002): Equilibrium Exchange Rates in Transition Countries: Evidence from Dynamic Heterogeneous Panel Models. *BOFIT Discussion Papers*, no. 15.

KRAJNYÁK, K. – ZETTELMEYER, J. (1998): Competitiveness in Transition Economies: What Scope for Real Appreciation? *IMF Staff Papers*, no. 45/98.

LOMMATZSCH, K. – TOBER, S. (2002): 'What is Behind the Real Appreciation of the Accession Countries' Currencies? An investigation of the PPI-based Real Exchange Rate.' Presented at 'Exchange rate strategies during the EU Enlargement'. Budapest. 27–30 November.

MacDONALD, R. (2000): Concept to Calculate Equilibrium Exchange Rate: An Overview. *Deutsche Bundesbank Discussion Paper* 3/00. Economic Research Group of the Deutsche Bundesbank.

MacDONALD, R. – STEIN, J. L. (eds) (1999): *Equilibrium exchange rates*. London: Kluwer Academic Press.

MacDONALD, R. – WÓJCIK, C. (2002): Catching Up: The Role of Demand and Supply Side Effects on the Real Exchange Rate of Accession Countries. Oesterreichische Nationalbank. Focus on Transition, no. 2/2002.

MacDONALD, R. (1997): What Determines Real Exchange Rate? The long and short of it. *IMF Working Paper*, no. WP/97/21, January 1997.

MacKINNON, J. G. (1991): Critical values for co-integration tests. In: R. F. Engle and C. WJ. Granger (eds). *Long-run economic relationships*. New York, Oxford University Press. 267–276.

MAESO-FERNANDEZ, F. – OSBAT, CH. – SCHNATZ, B. (2004): Towards the Estimation of Equilibrium Exchange Rates for CEE Acceding Countries: Methodological Issues and a Panel Cointegration Perspective. *European Central Bank Working Paper Series*, no. 353 (April).

MAURIN, L. (2001): Fundamental Determinants of RER for Transition Countries. In: M. H. Stierle and T. Birringer (eds). *Economics of Transition: Theory, Experiences and EU-Enlargement*. Berlin: Verlag für Wissenschaft ufn Forschung.

MELTZER, A. (1993): Real Exchange Rates: Some Evidence for the Post-war Years. In: Dimensions of Monetary Policy. Proceedings of the Seventeenth Annual Economic Policy Conference of the Federal Reserve Bank of St. Louis, Federal Reserve Bank of St. Louis Review (March/April).

PESARAN, M. H. – SHIN, Y. – SMITH, R. J. (2001): Bounds testing approaches to the analysis of level relationships. *Journal of Applied Econometrics*, 16(3), pp. 289–326.

PESARARAN, M. H. – SHIN, Y. (1995): An Autoregresive Distributed Lag Modelling Approach to Cointegration Analysis, DAE Working Paper, No 9514, Department of Applied Economics, University of Cambridge.

RAHN, J. (2003): Bilateral Equilibrium Exchange Rates of the EU Accession Countries Against the Euro. BOFIT Discussion Papers No. 11.

RAZIN, O. – COLLINS, S. (1997): Real Exchange Rate Misalignments and Growth. In: A. Razin – E. Sadka (eds). *International Economic Integration: Public Economics Perspectives*. Cambridge, Cambridge University Press, 1997.

SAMUELSON, P. A. (1964): Theoretical Notes on Trade Problems. *Review of Economics and Statistics*, vol. 46, pp. 145–154.

STEIN, J. – ALLEN, P. (eds), (1995): *Fundamental Determinants of Exchange Rates*. Oxford: Clarendon Press.

STEIN, J. (1994): The Natural Real Exchange Rate of the US-dollar and Determinants of Capital Flows. In: J. Williamson. *Estimating Equilibrium Exchange Rates*. Washington, D. C.: Institute for International Economics, pp. 133–176.

WADHWANI, S. (1999) 'Sterling's Puzzling Behaviour'. Bank of England Quarterly Bulletin November.

WILLIAMSON, J. (1994): *Estimating equilibrium exchange rates*. Washington, D.C.: Institute for International Economics.

3
Real Equilibrium Exchange Rate in China. Is the Renminbi Undervalued?

Virginie Coudert and Cécile Couharde

3.1 Introduction

China's exchange rate regime was a *de facto* peg to the dollar, from 1995 to July 2005 causing automatically an effective depreciation of renminbi (RMN) when the dollar depreciated significantly in 2003 and 2004. As China runs a current account surplus, this depreciation of the exchange rate has raised the question of a possible undervaluation of the renminbi. The shift to a managed float with a reference to a currency basket and the 2 per cent revaluation of the RMB, announced on the 21st of July 2005, has not greatly changed the terms of the debate, as the 2 per cent revaluation is not sufficient to have any impact on external imbalances.

According to Bergsten (2004), China's de facto peg to the dollar explains the reluctance of Asian countries to let their currencies rise against the dollar and the limited fall of the dollar's effective exchange rate, despite its substantial decline from 2002 to 2004 against several currencies. As a result, this has impeded the necessary adjustment of the US current deficit. World growth may have dampened as the adjustment burden falls only on a few countries, such as those of the euro area, where exchange rates are flexible but the rate of growth is already low. Dooley et al. (2004) think that the issue of undervaluation is linked to the very low productivity of millions of workers in China, who need to join the 'modern' sector in the coming years. In this framework, the so-called undervaluation of the currency may simply be a recipe for absorbing disguised unemployment.

Indeed, some of the 'usual suspects' that characterise an undervaluation can be observed in the Chinese case: the real effective exchange rate depreciation along with the dollar since the beginning of 2002, the surge in foreign exchange reserves and the current account surplus. Several papers studying the issue already found a large undervaluation of the renminbi, although they use different methods of assessment (Goldstein, 2003; Jeong and Mazier, 2003; IMF, 2004a and 2004b; Bergsten, 2004; Bénassy et al., 2004).

This paper tries to revisit the issue by assessing the renminbi's misalignment in using a large sample of emerging countries. We start from a BEER model (*Behavioural Equilibrium Exchange Rate*), as introduced by Clark and MacDonald (1998), that we estimate successively on cross-section and on panel-data. Taking stock of the results for Asia-Pacific real exchange rates obtained by Chinn (2000), we restrict the set of fundamental variables to a 'Balassa effect'. Comparing China with other emerging countries, we evidence the lack of real exchange rate (RER) appreciation in recent years, that would correspond to a 'normal' 'Balassa effect'. The results indicate an undervaluation in both estimations.

The rest of the paper is organised as follows. Section 2 gives some insights about the possible undervaluation of the Chinese currency, by using different economic indicators. Section 3 presents the Balassa effect and gives the results of cross-section estimations and panel data co-integration. Section 4 discusses the results and compares them with those obtained in other studies. Section 5 concludes.

3.2 Is the renminbi undervalued? The 'usual suspects'

There have been some signs of undervaluation of the real exchange rate of China during the recent years. First, the current account has been in surplus, which is atypical for an emerging country. It reached 2.8 per cent of GDP in 2002 and kept on increasing to 3.2 per cent in 2003 and 4 per cent in 2004. In a context of a booming activity, this surplus may seem a little puzzling. It is sometimes interpreted as a sign of competitiveness advantage for Chinese exports, raising the issue of undervaluation.

Second, the accumulation of foreign reserves has accelerated since the beginning of 2002, reaching \$740 billions at the end of July 2005, which is approximately 42 per cent of GDP. This huge amount makes China the second world owner of foreign exchange reserves, just behind Japan. This is the result of repeated interventions by the central bank, in order to impede the renminbi appreciation. This is also the sign of a disequilibrium in the foreign exchange market, where private demand for renminbi exceeds supply. In the absence of interventions of the monetary authorities, the Chinese currency would spontaneously appreciate, which also can be read as a sign of undervaluation.

Theoretically, there should be an automatic adjustment to this process: the accumulation of foreign exchange reserves as a result of intervention without sterilisation should boost monetary creation, generate inflation and appreciation of the real exchange rate, despite the nominal peg. However, in reality, this adjustment takes time and does not seem to work so well in the case of China. On the one hand, interventions are partly sterilised. On the other hand, the consumer price index showed signs of deflation from 1998 on until the beginning of 2003, despite a sharp two-digit increase in monetary aggregates.

Aside from the official interventions, the appreciation pressures in the foreign exchange market can also be read in the forward rates (Figure 3.1). Expectations for a revaluation began to rise in 2003 and

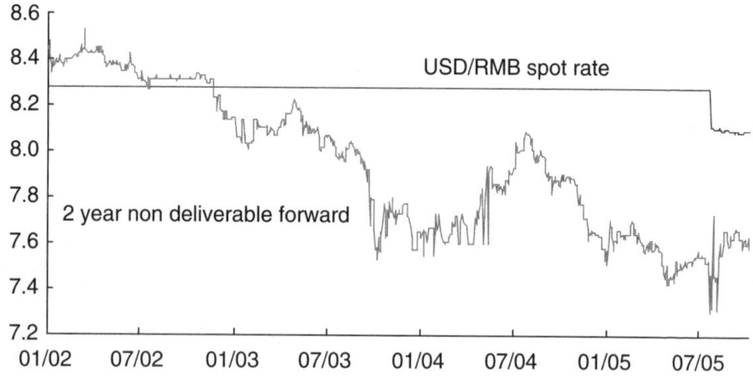

Figure 3.1 Renminbi against dollar, spot and forward exchange rates
Source: Bloomberg.

were especially high just after the Dubai G7 meeting, in September 2003. In October 2003, the two-year non-deliverable forward market indicated an expected appreciation of the renminbi fluctuating between 6 per cent and 9 per cent. The day after the 2 per cent revaluation of the 21st of July, the two-year non- deliverable forward market still indicated an expectation of 8 per cent appreciation.

Third, the real effective exchange rate of the renminbi has been depreciating since the beginning of 2002 (Figure 3.2). From February 2002 to October 2004, it depreciated by 18 per cent. The movement is entirely linked to the dollar evolution against third currencies and also to the low inflation in China. This depreciation raised the issue of the undervaluation of the renminbi and the appropriateness of the dollar peg. However, a depreciation of the real effective exchange rate is not sufficient for detecting an undervaluation.

Even assuming that the purchasing power parity (PPP) holds, a major drawback for drawing any conclusions from the real exchange rate evolution is the lack of a reference period. Indeed, the reference could be the year 1994, when the foreign exchange market was reformed, unifying the black and official markets and triggering a strong devaluation of the official parity. In that case, the present parity does not seem undervalued. However, the 1994 parity may also be considered as undervalued, as Chinese exports surged at that time; this latter view is consistent with the fact that China was not affected

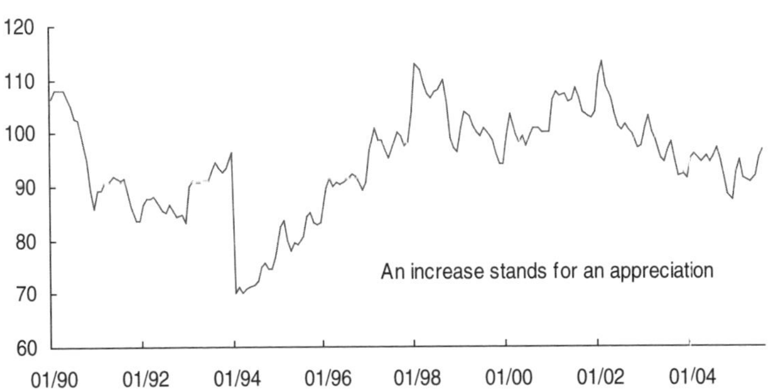

Figure 3.2 Real effective exchange rate in China, year 2000 = 100
Source: Banque de France.

by the wave of devaluations, triggered by the 'Asian' crisis of 1997 (Fernald et al., 1999).

3.3 Estimating the Balassa effect

Long term developments of the Chinese real effective exchange rate do not support any appreciating trend since the beginning of the nineties (Figure 3.2), which contrasts with the principle of real appreciation for catching-up countries, known as the 'Balassa effect'. We use two methods to assess the gap between the evolution of the real exchange rate in China and what would have resulted from the 'normal' Balassa effect: cross-section estimations and panel co-integration.

3.3.1 The Balassa effect

The 'Balassa–Samuelson' effect, first formulated by Balassa (1964) and Samuelson (1964) describes the distortion in purchasing power parity (PPP) resulting from the international differences in relative productivity between the tradable goods sector (constituted more or less by manufacturing and agriculture) and the non-tradable goods sector (roughly speaking, services). Accordingly, during the development process, productivity tends to increase more quickly in the tradable goods sector than in the services sector. Given that the prices of tradable goods are set by international competition, an increase in productivity in this sector leads to an increase in wages, which is not detrimental to competitiveness. Since this increase in wages spreads across the economy as a whole, there is a rise in relative prices in the non-tradable goods sector, where productivity has not grown at the same pace. Given that the price index is an average of these two sectors, there is an increase in the prices of domestic goods relative to those from abroad, which results in an appreciation of the real exchange rate.

Let us take the example of an emerging economy whose exchange rate is calculated against the currency of an advanced foreign country, marked *, for instance the United States. The real exchange rate of the emerging country is defined as:

$$\dot{q} = \dot{e} + \dot{p} - \dot{p}^* \qquad (1)$$

where q and e are the real and nominal exchange rate against dollar respectively; p and p^* are the final demand price index in the emerging country and the United States respectively. The lower-case variables marked with a dot indicate rates of growth (logarithmic derivatives). The nominal exchange rate is expressed as the number of dollars per domestic currency unit; therefore, an increase in the nominal and real exchange rate stands for an appreciation.

The relative price of tradable goods, between the two countries is given by $\dot{q}_T$:

$$\dot{q}_T = \dot{p}_T + \dot{e} - \dot{p}_T^* \tag{2}$$

where $\dot{p}_T$ stands for the tradable price index. By subtracting the two equations (1) and (2), we can express the real exchange rate as the total of the relative price for tradable goods between the two countries and the difference between the two countries of relative prices for goods across the board and the exposed sector T:

$$\dot{q} = \dot{q}_T + [(\dot{p} - \dot{p}_T) - (\dot{p}^* - \dot{p}_T^*)] \tag{3}$$

An equivalent expression can be obtained by expressing the final demand price as a weighted average of prices in the two sectors:

$$\dot{p} = \dot{p}_T + (1 - \gamma)(\dot{p}_N - \dot{p}_T) \tag{4}$$

where $\dot{p}_N$ is the price index in the non-tradable goods sector N and γ is the share of tradable goods in final demand. As this definition is also valid for the United States, the real exchange rate set out in equation (1) can be written:

$$\dot{q} = \dot{q}_T + (1 - \gamma)[(\dot{p}_N - \dot{p}_T) - (\dot{p}_N^* - \dot{p}_T^*)] - (\gamma - \gamma^*)(\dot{p}_N^* - \dot{p}_T^*) \tag{5}$$

The rise in the relative price of non-tradable goods compared with that of tradable goods may stem from a variety of factors, from the supply or the demand side. According to Balassa (1964), it results from larger productivity gains in the manufacturing sector in catching-up countries. To see this, let us start by determining the relative price of non-tradable goods compared with tradable goods in a single economy; this relative price is also called the 'internal exchange rate', given that it compares the price of domestic goods with those exposed to international competition. After setting the usual assumptions (see for example, Coudert, 2004), it may be expressed as follows:

$$\dot{p}_N - \dot{p}_T = \frac{\alpha_N}{\alpha_T}\dot{\theta}_T - \dot{\theta}_N \tag{6}$$

where θ_i designates the total factor productivity in sector $i = N,T$, and α_i the share of labour in the sector i's value added. Thus, the relative price of non-tradable goods, i.e. the 'internal exchange rate', appreciates with productivity gains in the tradable goods sector. Generally, we have: $\theta_T > \theta_N$ and also

$$\frac{\alpha_N}{\alpha_T}\dot{\theta}_T > \dot{\theta}_N$$

i.e. the relative increase in the productivity in tradable goods leads to an appreciation of the 'internal exchange rate', especially in emerging countries.

When considering the external real exchange rate between two countries, this expression is written as

$$\dot{q} = \dot{q}_T + (1-\gamma)\left(\frac{\alpha_N}{\alpha_T}(\dot{\theta}_T - \dot{\theta}_T{}^*) - (\dot{\theta}_N - \dot{\theta}_N{}^*)\right) \tag{7}$$

The second term at the right hand side of the equation $\left(\frac{\alpha_N}{\alpha_T}(\dot{\theta}_T - \dot{\theta}_T^*) - (\dot{\theta}_N - \dot{\theta}_N^*)\right)$ is generally positive, since the productivity gains in the tradable sector are higher than in the reference advanced country, while there is not such great difference for the non tradable sector. Therefore, according to equation (7), the real exchange rate of an emerging country has a tendency to appreciate.

3.3.2 Cross-section estimations

In this framework, one way to assess the misalignment of currencies is to use a PPP criterion corrected by a Balassa effect. A first approximation of this method can be given by a cross-section regression in the spirit of Rogoff (1996), De Broeck and Slok (2001) or others surveyed by Edwards and Savastano (1999). The PPP GDP per capita is generally taken as a proxy for the relative productivity differentials between sectors and used in a regression with the relative price levels of a group of countries.

Here, we regress price levels relative to the United States on GDP per capita also relative to the United States, for a large sample of countries during the year 2003. The relative price levels can be interpreted as deviations of the real exchange rates to PPP. Price levels of different countries are calculated by dividing their GDP in dollars by their GDP in PPP. All variables are taken in logarithms. Data are extracted from the CEPII-CHELEM.

The first regression is carried out on a large sample of 173 countries, including all advanced, emerging and developing countries for which data are available. In order to check that the results do not depend on the sample, we make the same regression on different sub-samples, in order to have more homogeneous data. In sub-sample 1, we leave out the group of very poor countries, with PPP GDP per capita smaller than 5 per cent of the United States' GDP. Sub-sample 2 retains only emerging and developing countries with PPP GDP of less than 70 per cent of the US level. Sub-sample 3 is composed by medium-type countries with PPP GDP per capita comprised between 5 and 70 per cent of USA.

The slope of the regression indicates the average appreciation of the real exchange rate to be expected from a 1 per cent increase in relative GDP per capita across countries. The slope ranges between 0.42 and 0.58, depending on the sample used for the estimates (Table 3.1).

Table 3.1 Estimated misalignment for China's currency for 2003, using several samples (1)

	Whole sample	**Sub-sample 1**	**Sub-sample 2**	**Sub-sample 3**
Number of countries	173	136	152	115
Slope of the regression	0.42	0.58	0.34	0.53
Tstat	*(14.6)*	*(15.6)*	*(9.7)*	*(10.0)*
R^2	0.55	0.64	0.38	0.47
Estimated misalignment for China's currency	−50.5%*	−43.7%*	−47.9%*	−43.4%*

Note: (1) Sub-sample 1 includes countries with PPP GDP per capita above 5% of the US. Sub-sample 2, smaller than 70%, and sub-sample 3 between 5% and 70%.
Significantly different from 0, at 95% threshold.

Source: Authors' calculations using CEPII-CHELEM.

For example in sub-sample 1, we obtain

$$Log(P/P^{US}) = \underset{(15.60)}{0.583}\ Log(Y/Y^{US}) + \underset{(16.69)}{2.01} \quad (8)$$

Where P indicates the price level, calculated as indicated above, Y is the PPP GDP per capita and t-statistics are in brackets below. In this framework, the fitted values could be interpreted as a reference exchange rate for a PPP parity taking into account the Balassa effect. We construct a 95 per cent confidence interval around the regression line. Countries inside the interval are considered to have currencies that are not significantly misaligned. Above the confidence interval, countries have high prices relative to other countries of the same living standards, which implies an overvalued exchange rate. Reversely, countries below the confidence interval have abnormally low prices, which accounts to an undervalued exchange rate. This is the case for China, as shown on Figure 3.3.

Misalignment calculations show that China had a significantly undervalued exchange rate, ranging from 43 to 50 per cent in 2003

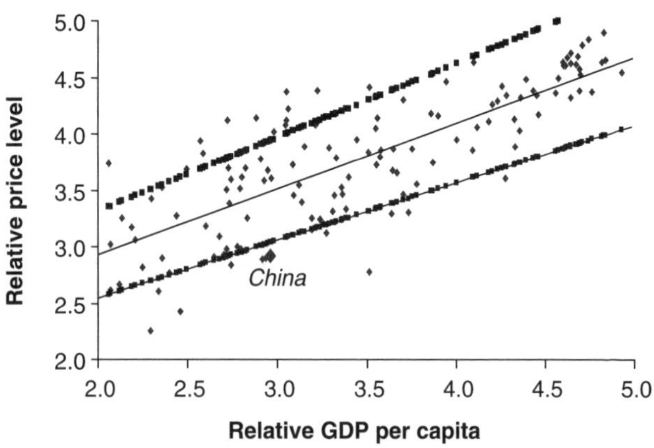

Figure 3.3 Relative price levels and GDP per capita compared to the United States in 2003 (1)

Note: (1) Sub-sample 1 of countries with PPP GDP per capita greater than 5% of the US; data are taken in logarithm, dotted lines around the regression line stand for a confidence interval at 95%.

Source: Authors' calculations using CEPII-CHELEM database.

(see Table 3.1). The misalignment is less pronounced in sub-samples 1 and 3 than in the whole sample, because they exclude some very poor countries, especially those experiencing a war or severe social troubles, which make their prices abnormally high.

In order to check the robustness of results, we performed the same regression again, excluding a group of countries not exceeding one million inhabitants. The rationale is that the presence of these countries may distort the results, by abnormally high prices. Indeed, the initial sample includes very small countries, especially some tiny islands, where the average price levels are high, because of increased transport costs and tourism activity. Although this would have led to a lower calculated undervaluation, the results are only weakly affected by this change (Table 3.2). The estimated undervaluation of the Chinese exchange rate is only slightly smaller, ranging from 41 to 49 per cent.

3.3.3 Panel data estimations

Although this cross-section approach above can give a first insight, it presents two caveats. First, the data sample covers only one year. Second, it is based on price level comparisons, the data of which may lack reliability. In this section, we take over these two drawbacks, by using panel data for a larger period and using real exchange rates in evolution instead of levels. We directly estimate equation (3). This formula is straightforward to use, unlike the usual formulations given by equations (4), (5) and (7), for it requires knowing neither the

Table 3.2 Estimated misalignment for China's currency for 2003, using several samples of countries of more than one million inhabitants (1)

	Whole sample	Sub-sample 1	Sub-sample 2	Sub-sample 3
Number of countries	145	111	127	93
Slope of the regression	0.41	0.59	0.33	0.51
Tstat	(13.4)	(14.3)	(8.6)	(8.6)
R^2	0.56	0.64	0.37	0.45
Estimated misalignment for China's currency	−49.2%*	−41.8%*	−45.6%*	−41.3%*

Note: (1) See note Table 3.1, (*) Significantly different from 0, at 95% threshold.

Source: Authors' calculations using CEPII-CHELEM.

weighting between the sectors γ nor the productivity gains θ. The dependant variable is the real bilateral exchange rate against the US dollar, as defined in equation (1). The explanatory variable is the relative price index, calculated as the ratio of the consumer price index to the producer price index in difference between the home country and the United States. This ratio is usually considered to be a proxy for the relative price between all goods and tradables.

We consider twenty two emerging countries corresponding to Argentina, Brazil, Chile, Colombia, Mexico, Peru, Indonesia, Malaysia, Philippines, Thailand, South Africa, Turkey, Poland, Hungary, Czech Republic, Slovakia, Slovenia, Estonia, Lithuania, Latvia, Estonia and China. The sample covers quarterly data for the period 1980q1 to 2002q4. The panel is unbalanced, because of the unavailability of some countries' data. In particular, for China, the prices data cover only the period from 1998q1 to 2002q4. Data are extracted from the IMF's IFS database and Datastream.

As the size of the sample is large, the test statistics conveniently converge asymptotically to the standard normal distribution. We carried out panel unit root tests on the basis of the Im et al. (2003) test (IPS-t-test).

The structure of the IPS t-test is based on augmented Dickey–Fuller regressions.

$$\Delta y_{it} = \rho_i y_{it-1} + \sum_{j=1}^{p_i} \varphi_{ij} \Delta y_{it-j} + \alpha_i + \gamma_i t + \varepsilon_{it} \tag{9}$$

for $t=1, \ldots T$, *and*; $i=1,\ldots, N$

where T is the time-length of the sample, N is the cross-section dimension. The term $\sum_{j=1}^{p_i} \varphi_{ij} \Delta y_{it-j}$ represents lagged dependent variables with country-specific lag length p_i; ρ_i, φ_{ij}, α_i, γ_i are country-specific coefficients, α_i being an intercept (standing for fixed effects) and γ_i the trend coefficient. The error term ε_{it}, is distributed as a white-noise random variable, with possibly different variance for each member of the panel.

The null hypothesis is that all series have a unit root, that is H_0: $\rho_i = 0$ for all countries i. The test allows for heterogeneity in the value of the autoregressive coefficient under the alternative hypothesis, that is H_1: $\rho_i < 0$ for at least one country i.

The test used here is the group-mean t-bar statistic, based on the t-statistics derived from the N augmented Dickey–Fuller regressions. According to the test, the null hypothesis cannot be rejected. Therefore, we consider that the panel data for real bilateral exchange rate series are I(1). The same result holds for relative prices series (see Table 3.3).

To perform panel co-integration tests, we apply the seven tests proposed by Pedroni (1999). The relationship estimated is the following one:

$$y_{it} = \alpha_i + \gamma_i t + \theta t + \beta_1 x_{1,it} + \ldots + \beta_K x_{K,it} + \varepsilon_{it} \tag{10}$$

where K is the number of regressors and β the elasticities. The deterministic elements are defined as above and $\theta\, t$ are common time effects.

Among the seven Pedroni's tests, four are based on the within dimension (panel co-integration tests) and the three others on the between dimension (group mean panel co-integration tests). All tests are based on the null hypothesis of no co-integration for all countries. Under the alternative hypothesis, for the panel statistics, there is co-integration for all countries. However, the group mean panel co-integration statistics allow for heterogeneity across countries under the alternative hypothesis. Table 3.4 displays the results of Pedroni's tests. All panel and group mean statistics reject the null hypothesis of no co-integration at the 5 per cent threshold, except the panel *adf* statistics. Therefore, it seems reasonable to proceed under the assumption that the variables are co-integrated.

In order to estimate the co-integration vectors for the considered countries, we use the Fully-Modified Ordinary Least Squares (FM-OLS) proposed by Pedroni (1990). According to Pedroni, this method leads to more robust results when working with small size samples than the standard OLS method. We consider two types of

Table 3.3 Panel unit root IPS test

Variable	**Real bilateral exchange rate**	**Relative price ratio**
t-bar [(1)]	−1.05976	−1.30559
p. value	0.28925	0.19169

Note: [(1)] Statistic t-bar with OLS estimations.

Table 3.4 Pedroni panel co-integration test

Panel co-integration tests				Group mean, co-integration tests		
v-stat	rho-stat	Pp-stat	adf-stat	Rho-stat	pp-stat	Adf-stat
5.706	−3.802	−3.187	−1.515	−3.678	−3.714	−1.936
(0,0000)*	(0.0001)*	(0.0014)*	(0.1296)	(0.0002)*	(0.0002)*	(0.0052)**

Notes: p-values are given in parentheses.
* Rejection of the null hypothesis at the 5% significance level (p-values less than 0.05).
** Rejection of the null hypothesis at the 5% significance level (p-values less than 0.10).
Source: Author's calculations.

Table 3.5 Coefficients of the relative prices in the co-integration vectors, country by country estimates

Argentina	−1.45	(−28.17)	Turkey	−0.84	(−6.41)
Brazil	−0.60	(−6.97)	Poland	−1.44	(−13.65)
Chile	−1.94	(−24.83)	Hungary	−0.16	(−29.24)
Colombia	−1.99	(−10.36)	Czech Republic	−1.07	(−4.91)
Mexico	−0.57	(−3.28)	Slovakia	0.79	(−0.64)
Peru	−1.20	(−33.10)	Slovenia	0.73	(−0.47)
Indonesia	−2.31	(−41.08)	Estonia	−2.69	(−7.59)
Malaysia	−1.73	(−11.19)	Lithuania	−3.45	(−12.62)
Philippines	−0.96	(−11.08)	Latvia	−3.50	(−15.13)
Thailand	−1.84	(−7.94)	China	0.64	(−2.43)
South Africa	−3.09	(−7.91)			

Note: t-statistics are given in brackets.
Source: Author's calculations.

estimation: a country by country estimation and a panel estimation with fixed effects. Table 3.5 displays the co-integration vectors estimated country by country.

The coefficients on relative price index generally have the expected sign, supporting a Balassa effect. However, for three countries out of 22, the sign is not the expected one. This is the case for China. This striking feature may be interpreted as a failure of the Balassa effect to explain the Chinese exchange rate behaviour. Another hypothesis is that this is due to the small size of the sample for this country.

Table 3.6 Co-integration vectors, panel estimations with fixed effects

Variables	**Co-integration vectors**
Relative price ratio	−1.37 (−60.89)

Note: t-statistic is given in brackets.
Source: Author's calculations.

The co-integration vector obtained by the panel estimations with fixed effects is shown in Table 3.6. The explanatory variable is significant and correctly signed.

We calculate the real bilateral equilibrium exchange rate of each country as the fitted values obtained with the coefficient of relative price in the panel co-integration vector and with country intercepts. As usual, the misalignments are obtained by comparison with the observed real exchange rate. Table 3.7 reports the results for the year 2002. The renminbi appears undervalued by almost 18 per cent.

3.4 Discussion

3.4.1 Why is there no Balassa effect at work in China?

The empirical results presented above do not confirm the presence of a Balassa effect in China, although they confirm it for the panel of countries, taken as a whole. Moreover, there is a large gap between the fitted value given by the model and the actual behaviour of the exchange rate in China.

In fact, the Balassa effect rests on several restrictive assumptions that may not be valid in the case of China. Although the assumption of the productivity impacts in a two-sector based economy seems to fit the Chinese data, the validity of the perfect mobility of production factors assumptions is questionable. There is no perfect international mobility of capital in China, because of the exchange controls. Internal labour mobility is also restricted, as regulation prevents the labour force to move freely, for example from low-productivity agricultural provinces to the high productivity regions. This policy is aimed at avoiding a massive rural exodus, which would create poverty and social restlessness in urban areas. As a result, wages do not equalise across provinces and also across sectors. Indeed, disparities are important across the 31 regions of China, as regards to prices, wages and productivity.

3.4.2 Comparisons with previous results

Most existing studies find also a large undervaluation of the renminbi, especially against the dollar in the early 2000s (Jeong and Mazier, 2003; Goldstein, 2003; Bénassy-Quéré et al., 2004; Wren-Lewis, 2004) (see Table 3.8). The results of the above mentioned studies can be classified into two groups: those using the FEER approach (*Fundamental Equilibrium Exchange Rate*), and those based on the BEER approach, as this paper.

According to the FEER approach, following Williamson (1994), the equilibrium exchange rate is defined as the real effective exchange rate at which a country could achieve simultaneously 'internal balance' (non-inflationary full employment) and 'external balance'(sustainable current account). Roughly speaking, in this framework, countries having a 'large' structural current account surplus (respectively, deficit) are considered to be undervalued (respectively,

Table 3.7 Real bilateral exchange rate misalignments in 2002, in %

Countries with overvalued currencies		Countries with undervalued currencies	
Brazil	6.1	Argentina	−43.6
Hungary	3.3	Chile	−5.8
Czech Republic	3.8	Colombia	−22.6
Lithuania	32.3	Peru	−10.9
Latvia	5.8	Indonesia	−14.3
		Philippines	−19.7
		Thailand	−16.0
		South Africa	−43.5
		Turkey	−7.3
		Poland	−4.2
		Slovakia	−13.3
		Slovenia	−17.0
		Estonia	−4.3
		China	−17.8

Source: Author's calculations.

overvalued). In most studies, the structural current account in China is found to be greater than 'normal' in the early 2000s. Therefore, estimates using the FEER approach find a large undervaluation of the renminbi (Jeong and Mazier, 2003; Wren-Lewis, 2004; Coudert-Couharde, 2005). The size of the estimated undervaluation depends on the current account target that is fixed and also on the models parameters.

Using the BEER approach, the estimates are generally based on the Balassa effect. This effect is confirmed in all papers using panel-data or cross-section estimations, as it is the case in sections 4 and 5 of this paper. As there was no real appreciation in China despite the rapid GDP growth, it is not surprising that these models result in an undervaluation of the renminbi. In the study of Bénassy-Quéré et al. (2004), another variable is included in the model: net foreign assets, that are supposed to lead to an appreciation of the currency. Here

Table 3.8 Estimates of the renminbi's equilibrium exchange

Author	**Method**	**Exchange rate**	**Period**	**Under-valuation**
Jeong and Mazier (2003)	FEER with a current account target of–1.5%	REER dollar	2000	33% 60%
Wren-Lewis (2004)	FEER, with a current account target of 0	dollar	2002	28%
Couharde-Coudert (2005)	FEER with a current account of −1,5%	REER dollar	2003	23% 44%
Goldstein (2004)	Simplified FEER, with a current account of 1%	REER	2003	15–30%
Bénassy-Quéré et al. (2004)	BEER, panel of G20 countries	dollar	2003	14%–47%
This paper	Regression in level, sample of 93 emerging and developing countries	dollar	2003	41%
This paper	BEER, panel of 21 emerging countries	dollar	2002	18%
Wang (2004)	BEER, 1 country	REER	2003	≈0
Funke and Rahn (2005)	BEER, 1 country	REER dollar	End 2002	3%, ≈ 0 6%

Note: REER: real effective exchange rate.

again, the increase in net foreign assets in China should have resulted in an appreciation of the renminbi.

Wang (2004) and Funke and Rahn (2005) do not find any significant undervaluation. This can be explained by the fact that these two studies estimate a BEER model on a single country: China, instead of a panel of countries. By construction, single-country estimations are likely to understate misalignments. The small size of the sample makes the fitted value of the regression very close to the observed value. Since the misalignment is equal to the residual of the regression, it is not surprising that it is found close to zero.

Other studies also suggest that a large undervaluation, although they do not provide an exact calculation. For example, Williamson (2004) estimates that the Chinese currency is undervalued by around 15 to 25 per cent; Bergsten (2004) gives a similar figure, between 20 and 25 per cent.

3.5 Conclusion

Various approaches were used in this paper to assess the existence and the size of the renminbi's misalignment. First, several economic indicators tend to show some signs of undervaluation of the real exchange rate of the renminbi during recent years : real effective exchange rate depreciation, surging forex reserves, current account surplus. Second, we used cross-section regressions relating the real exchange rate to a 'Balassa effect', on different samples of countries. Third we addressed the issue of the 'Balassa effect' in the framework of a BEER approach using panel-data estimations. These two latter methods resulted in large estimated undervaluation for the Chinese renminbi.

The renminbi misalignment is often considered to have important implications on global imbalances in various parts of the world. However, as the dollar's effective exchange rate is only weakly affected by the renminbi, a revaluation of the renminbi would have only a small effect on the US external deficit. Moreover, we do not think that a hasty shift to a floating exchange rate is a good recipe, especially because of the persistence of capital controls in China. If the Chinese exchange rate was to freely float now, upward pressures in the forex market would likely produce a nominal appreciation of the renminbi; however, a sequenced liberalisation, opening up capital outflows first, could also trigger enormous capital outflows, able to reverse the former market trend. The shift to a managed float with a reference to a basket of currencies that was announced by Chinese authorities in July 2005 seems a more cautious way to gradually adjust the exchange rate.

References

Balassa, B. (1964), «The Purchasing Power Parity : a Reappraisal», *Journal of Political Economy*, vol. 72, no. 6, pp. 584–596.

Bénassy-Quéré, A., «Duran-Vigneron, P., Lahrèche-Révil, A. and V. Mignon (2004), «Distributing Key Currency Adjustment: A G-20 panel cointegration approach», Institute for International Economics workshop on *Dollar Adjustment: How Far ? Against What?*, May 25, Washington DC.

Bergsten, F. (2004), «The Exchange Rate of the Won», Institute for International Economics.

Chinn, M. C. (2000), 'The Usual Suspects? Productivity and Demand Shocks and Asia-Pacific Real Exchange Rates', *Review of International Economics*, vol. 8, no. 1, pp. 20–43.

Clark, Peter B., and R. MacDonald (1998), 'Exchange Rates and Economic Fundamentals: A Methodological Comparison of BEERs and FEERs', IMF WP/98/67.

Coudert, V. (2004), «Measuring the Balassa-Samuelson Effect for the Countries of Central and Eastern Europe?», Bank of France Monthly Bulletin, February.

Coudert, V. and C. Couharde (2005), «Equilibrium Exchange Rate in China», CEPII, Working Paper no 05–01, January.

De Broeck, M. and T. Slok (2001), «Interpreting real exchange rates movements in transition countries», IMF Working Paper 01/56.Dees, S. (1999) The Role of External Variables in the Chinese Economy; Simulations from a macroeconomic model of China, *CEPII Working Paper* no 99–09, June. http:/www.cepii.fr.

Dooley, M.D. Folkerts-Landau and P. Garber (2004), «A Map to the revisited Bretton Woods End Game: Direct Investment, Rising Real Wages and the Disposal of Excess Labor in the Periphery», paper presented at the IMF conference, Madrid, April 2004.

Edwards, S. and M. Savastano (1999), *Exchange rates in emerging countries: What do we know? What do we need to know?*, NBER Working Paper No. 7228.

Fernald J., H. Edison and P. Loungani (1999), «Was China the first domino? Assessing links between China and other Asian economies», *Journal of International Money and Finance*, August, vol. 18, no. 4, pp. 515–535(21).

Frankel, J., S. Schmukler and L. Serven (2002), «Global Transmission of Interest Rates: Monetary Independence and Currency Regime», NBER WP No. 8828.

Funke, Michael and Jörg Rahn, (2005), 'Just how undervalued is the Chinese renminbi?', *The World Economy*, vol. 28, no. 4, pp. 265–289.

Goldfajn, I. and R. Valdés (1996), «The Aftermath of Appreciations,» NBER Working Paper No. 5650.

Goldstein, M (2003), «China's Exchange rate regime», Testimony before subcommittee on domestic and international monetary policy, trade and technology committee on financial services, US House of Representatives, October 1.

Im K. S., Pesaran M. H. Y. and Shin (2003), 'Testing for unit roots in heterogeneous panels', *Journal of Econometrics,* vol. 115, pp. 53–74.

IMF, (2004a), «People's Republic of China», Staff Report for the 2004 Article IV Consultation, 6 July.

IMF, (2004b), «People's Republic of China, Selected Issues», 7 July.

Isard, P., Faruqee, H., Kincaid, G. and M. Fetherston (2001), «Methodology for Current Account and Exchange Rate Assessment», IMF Occasional Paper no. 209.

Jeong, S-E. and J. Mazier (2003), «Exchange Rate Regimes and Equilibrium Exchange Rates in East Asia», *Revue économique,* vol. 54, no. 5, September, pp. 1161–1182.

Pedroni, P. (1999), «Critical Values for Cointegration Tests in Heterogeneous Panels with Multiple Regressors», *Oxford Bulletin of Economics and Statistics,* Special Issue, pp. 653–670.

Pedroni, P. (2000), «Fully Modified OLS for Heterogeneous Cointegrated Panels», *Advances in Econometrics,* vol. 15, pp. 93–130.

Prasad, E. (2004), «China's Growth and Integration into the World Economy: Prospects and Challenges», FMI Occasional Paper No. 232.

Rogoff K. (1996), 'The purchasing parity puzzle', *Journal of Economic Literature,* vol. XXXIV, June.

Williamson, J. (1994), *Estimating Equilibrium Exchange Rates,* (Institute for International Economics).

Williamson, J. (2003), «The Renminbi Exchange Rate and the Global Monetary System», Institute for International Economics.

Wren-Lewis, S. (2004), The Needed Changes in Bilateral Exchange Rates, in Bergsten, C. F. and Williamson, J., *Dollar Adjustment: How Far? Against What?* Institute of International Economics, Washington DC.

Part II

Exchange Rates Dynamics and Pass-Through Effects

4
Exchange Rate Pass-Through Effect and Monetary Policy in Russia

Victoria V. Dobrynskaya and Dmitry V. Levando

4.1 Introduction

The term 'pass-through effect' (PTE) refers to the effect of changes in the exchange rate of a domestic currency for foreign currency (or a trade-weighted portfolio of foreign currencies) on the country's domestic prices for traded and non-traded goods. PTE of exchange rate changes on domestic prices is one of the major factors of transmission of shocks in an open economy. Lafleche (1996) offered a diagram, which described these mechanisms of reaction of domestic prices to depreciation of domestic currency. A variety of mechanisms through which a change in exchange rate affects all domestic prices are thoroughly described in Lafleche (1996). Before the end of the 1970s academic economists did not pay enough attention to this phenomenon. However, in recent years this topic has became increasingly popular in many countries, perhaps in response to globalisation of the international markets and foreign trade growth. Higher PTE implies greater dependence of an open economy on external shocks in the world market and higher volatility of domestic prices due to changes in the exchange rate. Therefore, the government authorities should know the degree of PTE to forecast domestic inflation and conduct adequate inflationary and exchange rate policies.

The existing literature suggests that PTE in all of the studied countries is significant (that is, depreciation of domestic currency leads to inflation), although incomplete (less than 100 per cent) in most cases. The literature also concludes that the degree of PTE depends greatly on the country and types of goods under consideration. One of the conclusions of the authors is that PTE is higher in smaller economies and in developing countries with high import shares.

Since Russia can be described as a developing country with relatively high imports, it can be predicted that PTE in Russia is pretty high. And if this is so, then Russia is highly dependent on world markets and the depreciation of the rouble will result in significant increase in domestic prices. Matters will be even worse if PTE on prices of necessary goods is higher that PTE on prices of luxuries. Then the poor people will suffer more since spending on necessities constitutes most of their income.

To prevent such a situation the government can use its monetary policy to eliminate PTE on prices. In particular, in case of exogenous domestic currency depreciation, the government can conduct contractionary monetary policy in order not to allow prices to rise, thus reducing PTE. Empirical literature on western economies (Parsley and Popper, 1998) concludes that the monetary policy counteracts exchange rate changes and reduces pass-through. Is this the case for Russia? Especially since monetary policy and exchange rates are interdependent due to managed floating exchange rate regime and real exchange rate targeting, as announced by the government.

This paper is devoted to estimation and analysis of PTE in Russia, measured as the percentage change in Russian prices in response to a 1 per cent change in nominal effective exchange rate of the rouble (pass-through elasticity). The purpose of our research is to answer the questions: 'What is the effect of nominal exchange rate changes onto domestic inflation?', 'Does this effect differ across different price categories?' and 'What is the effect of state monetary policy on pass-through?'

This research program is interesting for the following reasons. First, PTE has not been studied properly in Russia: so far there is no single published research paper devoted to this problem. A particular interest arises due to the fact that in August 1998, during the currency and debt crisis, the Russian rouble lost more than 60 per cent of its value against theUS dollar in a week, but this sharp depreciation did not cause a similar and simultaneous burst of the domestic inflation, backed by the expansionary monetary policy, which had an additional effect on domestic prices.

Second, if Russia is indeed an economy with high PTE, the influence of monetary policy on PTE is important. If we conclude that monetary policy does not decrease price volatility due to exchange rates (i.e. does not diminish pass-through), then this will mean that Russia is more dependent on external shocks and has a more unstable economic situation and higher social costs (e.g. menu costs).

So, in this paper we estimate and compare different-term PTE on different price categories (the consumer price index (CPI), the producer price index (PPI)[1] and their components) from the beginning of 1995 until the end of 2002. We explain the differences in PTE on consumer and producer prices, on traded and non-traded goods and in different industries of the Russian economy and we analyse the influence of monetary policy on PTE. To estimate PTE, we apply a two-stage procedure of constructing an Error Correction Model, which takes into account the long-run relationship. Based on economic theory, the existing literature and empirical observations, the following *hypotheses* are tested in this research:

1) PTE is incomplete in the short run and long run;
2) PTE is different for consumer and producer prices;
3) PTE is different for the components of CPI (food, goods and services) and the components of PPI (export- and domestic market-oriented industries);
4) Monetary policy decreases PTE.

So, this in an empirical research which is important from the theoretical point of view and has some practical implications.

The results of the research may be interesting from both microeconomic and macroeconomic points of view. First, the results may be used by enterprises in different industries to forecast future cash flows and profits, for developing pricing strategies and analysis and management of exchange rate risk. For example, if PTE on the price of some product is low, costs of Russian firms expressed in the domestic currency, which arise from purchase of imported intermediate and final goods, will rise more in case of rouble depreciation than the revenues which arise from selling these goods on the domestic market, because it is impossible to pass the whole exchange rate change onto prices of the sold goods. In such a case the Russian importer will not only lose a part of its profits, but also might find itself in a situation when it cannot repay its debt to the foreign creditor, which is expressed in foreign currency terms. Therefore, a high exchange rate risk exists in industries with low PTE, which should be hedged against beforehand.

From a macroeconomic point of view, this research may be useful for the government and the Central bank for forecasting inflation in Russia on an aggregate level and in different industries, for determination of monetary and exchange rate policies and regulation of national industries. For example, if PTE on consumer prices in a country is large, then in order to maintain the targeted inflation rate and to reduce prices volatility (also to reduce different costs which arise from volatile prices) the Central bank should adjust money supply in response to exchange rate fluctuations since changes in both money supply and exchange rate affect the country's inflation. In other words, monetary policy should be endogenous to the exchange rate.

Estimation of the influence of the present monetary policy on PTE has practical implications for development of further monetary policy in order to achieve more stable economic situation in Russia. Also, if monetary policy decreases PTE, but has a lower effect on necessities that on luxuries, in order to support the poor the government should implement stronger contractionary policy than in the case when the effect of monetary policy on PTE is higher for necessities than luxuries.

4.2 Literature review

4.2.1 Theories of exchange rate PTE

The benchmark of the theory of exchange rate pass-through is Purchasing Power Parity, which states that pass-through of exchange rate on domestic prices ought to be complete (implying PTE of 100 per cent) and no arbitrage opportunities may exist in the long run, formally:

$$P = P^{*} \times E$$

where P – domestic price level, $P*$ – foreign price level (assumed to be constant), E – exchange rate, measured in units of the domestic currency per unit of the foreign currency.[2] But even in the simplest models assuming PPP, inter-country differences in PTE of exchange rate on domestic prices may exist. In a *large economy* the inflationary effect of depreciation of domestic currency is counteracted by a decline in world prices (due to decreased world demand), which tends to decrease the observed PTE, whereas in a *small economy* PTE should be complete. Also, this theoretical model is based on several assumptions which do not hold in the real world, e.g. the assumptions of perfect competition and absence of transaction costs. Isard (1977) was one of the first who questioned the possibilities of international arbitrage to decrease the difference between prices of a good in different countries to the level of transportation costs.

A number of theories were proposed to explain why PTE is incomplete in real life. The Obstfeld and Rogoff (2000) model assumes presence of transportation costs, which increase prices of imported goods and preclude their perfect substitutability for the competing domestic goods. A related argument is that the costs of imported inputs constitute only a small part of the cost of a final good, but the majority of costs being attributable to non-traded services, such as marketing and distribution. Several authors (Bergin and Feenstra, 2001; Bergin, 2001; Corsetti and Dedola, 2001; Bachetta and Wincoop, 2002) argue that PTE may be below 100 per cent even if prices are fully flexible, but markets are imperfectly competitive, which may create incentives for optimal price discrimination or strategic pricing. Finally, if the imported good is an intermediate good, which has locally produced substitutes priced in domestic currency, the local producer may replace the imported input by the domestic one in response to exchange rate changes. Obsfeld (2001) terms this 'expenditure-switching effect', which depends on the degree of substitutability between local and imported goods.

4.2.2 Empirical evidence

However compelling are the above explanations, discrimination between them is not straightforward, not least because empirical evidence of PTE is quite heterogeneous. Most existing research is concentrated on the effects of exchange rate changes on *import prices* (Goldberg and Knetter (1997) provide a detailed survey). Several works study PTE on *producer and consumer prices* (e.g. Woo, 1984; Feinberg, 1986, 1989; Parsley and Popper, 1998; McCarthy, 2000); some more consider its relationship to the export prices (e.g. Klitgaard, 1999; Dwyer, Kent and Pease, 1993). Most authors concentrate on PTE across industries and products, as well as its dependence on macroeconomic policy measures, such as monetary policy, as discussed in the next subsection.

Almost all studies report that exchange rate PTE on national prices is incomplete and varies greatly across countries, industries and other parameters under investigation. Most works are based on the American markets because of their size and superior quality of the data (Menon (1995) describes results of 43 such papers). Quite a few authors analyse PTE on other OECD countries, such as the EU (e.g. Hufner and Schoder (2002), Fouquin et al. (2001)), Australia (Menon (1996), Dwyer, Kent and Pease (1993)), Japan (Tokagi and Yoshida (2001)); as well as developing countries, such as Korea (Lee, 1997), Taiwan (Liu, 1993), Chile (Garcia, Jose and Jorge, 2001), Belarus (Tsesliuk, 2002) and Ukraine (Kuzmin, 2002). Some papers study inter-country differences in PTE for developed countries (e.g. McCarthy (2000), Hufner and Schoder (2002)). Darvas (2001) and Dubravko and Marc (2002) are two of several papers which study PTE in some developing countries, where the effect appears to be larger than for the developed ones. Empirical results also imply that PTE is heterogeneous across countries: thus, Dwyer, Kent and Pease (1993) concluded that pass-through on import prices is higher that that on export prices in short run in Australia, while the tendency appears to be opposite for Japan (Takagi and Yoshida, 2001).

Research on PTE at the *industry level* was mostly concentrated on studying pricing strategies and behaviour of mark-ups (the difference between the selling price and the cost of goods sold) in response to changes in an exchange rate. A theoretical basis for most of these studies was the work of Dornbusch (1987), which appeals to the arguments from industrial organisation. Specifically, it explains the differences in PTE by market concentration, degree of import penetration and substitutability of imported and local goods. For instance, if profit-maximising firms have significant market power in a given industry, PTE is expected to be high in spite of other factors (Phillips (1988)). On the contrary, if firms aim to maximise their market share instead of profits, PTE will be lower (Hooper and Mann (1989), Ohno (1990). Moreover, if opportunities to discriminate between markets exist, then the situation of *'pricing-to-market'* may occur, which will lead to different PTE in different segmented markets (Krugman (1987), Gagnon and Knetter (1992)).

Goldberg and Knetter (1997) reported that PTE on import prices is lower in more segmented industries, where producers have more opportunities for third-degree price discrimination. Yang (1997) estimated, that PTE is positively related to the degree of product differentiation (i.e. negatively related to the degree of substitutability of goods) and negatively depends on the elasticity of marginal costs with respect to output. Also, PTE is affected by the degree of returns to scale in production of imported goods (Olivey (2002). On the basis of these principles Feinberg (1986, 1989) concluded that PTE on prices of national producers is higher in industries, which are less concentrated and which have higher import share. These conclusions have been occasionally challenged; e.g. Menon (1996) found that PTE negatively depends on quantitative restrictions (quotas) for imports, foreign control (presence of multinational corporations), concentration, product differentiation and import share in total sales, and positively depends on substitutability between imported and domestic goods.

4.2.3 Influence of monetary policy on PTE

According to the principle of money neutrality an increase in money supply causes a proportional increase in domestic prices. This effect co-exists with the exchange rate pass-through. Expansionary monetary policy provokes devaluation of home currency, what makes extra pass-through in home prices, but, on the other hand, monetary policy in many countries is aimed at achieving price stability and is adjusted to exchange rate fluctuations to reduce PTE.[3] This means that monetary policy is endogenous to the exchange rate.

Following economic logic and findings of other authors (Parsley and Popper (1998), Devereux and Yetman (2003)), monetary policy should be taken into account while estimating PTE, as it was shown that omission of this variable results in biased estimates of pass-through. Empirical evidence from the American market supports the theory that monetary policy is aimed at minimisation of price volatility and, therefore, decreases PTE. This conclusion was derived by Parsley and Popper (1998), who estimated the influence of monetary policy on PTE on prices of 32 consumer goods and services.

4.3 Theoretical model

The theoretical model of monetary policy influence on PTE was proposed by Parsley and Popper (1998).

Suppose that the price of a particular good is determined in the following way: in each period, *t*,

$$p_{it} = E\{f_i[e_t, m(g_t), z_{it}]I_t\} \tag{1}$$

where p_{it} is the price of the *i*-th good; e_t is the nominal exchange rate in terms of foreign currency units per domestic currency unit; monetary policy, $m(g_t)$, is implemented using some instruments, g_t; z_{it} summarises all other factors that affect the individual price; and I_t represents the information available when the price is determined.

Then the underlying responsiveness of individual and aggregate prices to the exchange rate can be characterised as follows:

$$\gamma_i = \frac{\partial E\{f_i[e_t, m(g_t), z_{it}]\ I_t\}}{\partial e}, \quad and \quad \gamma = \int_0^1 \alpha_i \gamma_i di \tag{2}$$

When monetary policy is unrelated to exchange rate movements, these parameters, γ_i and γ, can be estimated directly. In practice, measuring the impact of exchange rate changes on domestic prices may be complicated by the actions of the Central bank. The monetary policies of many countries respond to changes in the exchange rate, even if only implicitly. That is, often $\frac{dm(g_t)}{de} \neq 0$. This means that monetary policy is endogenous to the exchange rate. In such cases, the exchange rate affects prices in two ways. It affects prices directly, through the parameters γ_i and γ, and it affects prices indirectly through its influence on monetary policy,

$$\frac{\partial p_{it}}{\partial m(g_t)} \frac{dm(g_t)}{\mathrm{d}e_t} \quad and \quad \frac{\partial p_t}{\partial m(g_t)} \frac{dm(g_t)}{\mathrm{d}e_t} \tag{3}$$

Ignoring the role of monetary policy will bias measures of the underlying responsiveness of prices to exchange rate changes. This problem affects estimates of the responsiveness of both individual prices and the aggregate price index. If monetary policy during domestic currency depreciation is ignored, the effects of the exchange rate on prices may appear smaller than the underlying effects.

The same will be true if we assume that monetary policy can moderate price fluctuations not only by offsetting the effect of changes in the exchange rate, but also by influencing the exchange rate itself. In such a case we assume that both monetary policy and the exchange rate are endogenous to each other. Such a situation is relevant for the Russian economy, where the Central bank maintains the exchange rate in a corridor by changing its reserves and money supply. Again, if monetary policy during depreciation of domestic currency is ignored, the effect of the exchange rate on domestic prices may appear smaller than the true PTE. This would mean that monetary policy is aimed at reducing pass-through and price volatility.

This theory was supported by data for the American market in the work of Parsley and Popper.

4.4 Empirical analysis

4.4.1 Data

All data used in this research are time series with monthly frequency and cover time span from the beginning of 1995 until the end of 2002. All indices are transformed to the base period January 1995 and are expressed in natural logarithms. The main sources of data are Official Statistics of Rosstat (State Statistical Committee of Russian Federation) and International Financial Statistics (IFS). Data are available from the authors upon request.

Dependent variables

National Producer Price Index (LN_PPI). Detailed structure includes indices for the following industries: energy, oil, ferrous and non-ferrous metals, chemical industry, petrochemical industry, machinery, construction materials, textile, food processing and wood industry. The primary data on price indices are taken from Rosstat Statistical Annual Report, 2003. On aggregate level PPI is presented in International Financial Statistics, 2003, series code 92263XXZF.

National Consumer Price Index (LN_CPI). Detailed structure of CPI includes food (FOOD), goods (GOODS) and services (SERV). The primary data of CPI and its components are taken from Rosstat Statistical Annual Report, 2003. On aggregate level CPI is taken from International Financial Statistics, 2003, series code 92264XXZF.

Explanatory variables

Nominal Effective Exchange Rate Index (LN_NEERI). The exchange rate is measured as the number of units of trade weighted foreign currencies per unit of domestic currency (Russian rouble). An increase in

NEERI means appreciation of the rouble. The primary source of data is International Financial Statistics, 2003, series code 922..NECZF. Figure 4.1 below demonstrates time profile of the three variables central for our research. The outlier in the 12/97 originates from IFS statistics.

Price of Oil (*LN_OIL*). Price of 'UK Brent' serves as a proxy for the price of Russian oil 'Urals' (which is more relevant for our analysis), since the price of 'Urals' is not available for the whole time period, but on the available sample the prices correlate with coefficient 0.96. Monthly time series are provided by International Financial Statistics, 2003, code 11276AAZZF.

Money Supply (*LN_MONEY*). Aggregate money supply (M1) from International Financial Statistics 2003, code 92234..ZF..

Real Consumption (*LN_RCONS*). Serves as a proxy for real GDP because monthly data on real GDP is not supplied in Russia. The source of data: Rosstat Statistical Annual Report 2003.

All data have been tested for stationarity. We used ADF test with the specification chosen according to Dolado, Jenkinson, Sosvilla-Rivero (1990) procedure. The choice of augmentation was done according to 'general to specific' procedure proposed by W. Charemza (1997), which starts with reasonably large number of lags and is followed by iterative elimination of insignificant ones until only the significant lags are left in the model. As was expected, the test rejected

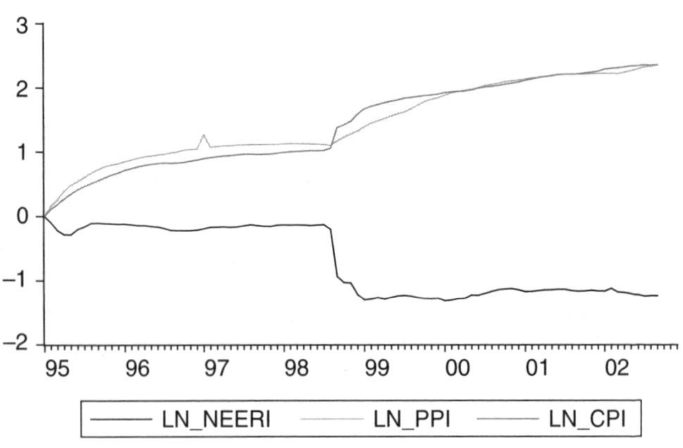

Figure 4.1 Time profiles of NEERI and national price indices

the stationarity hypothesis for all data in favour of non-stationary with the level of integration 1 (I(1)). We cannot totally rely on this test since it could confuse a structural break with a unit root. But the Phillips–Perron test for structural breaks confirmed our results. Moreover, the same conclusion about non-stationarity was obtained in the papers described in section 2, which deal with longer and more stable data of western economies.

4.4.2 Methodology and results

4.4.2.1 Different term of PTE

To estimate different term PTE we apply a two-step procedure of constructing an Error Correction Model (ECM). In the first step we estimate the following specification using Johansen co-integration analysis with 3–4 lags as usually the major adjustments occur within this time period in Russia:

$$LN\_P_t = \alpha_0 + \alpha_1{}^{*} LN\_NEERI_t + \alpha_2{}^{*} LN\_MONEY_t + \alpha_3{}^{*} LN\_RCONS_t + \alpha_4{}^{*} LN\_OIL_t + \varepsilon_t \quad (4)$$

where LN_P_t is the dependent variable under investigation: national CPI, PPI or their components in logs. We find that co-integration exists for all price indices,[4] what enables us generate stationary residuals ε_t.

In the second step we construct a modified ECM of the following specification using the residuals found above with one lag, which takes into account long run adjustments:

$$\Delta\left(LN\_P_t\right) = \sum_{i=0}^{5}\alpha_{1i}{}^{*}\,\Delta\left(LN\_NEERI_{t-i}\right) + \sum_{i=0}^{2}\alpha_{2i}{}^{*}\,\Delta\left(LN\_MONEY_t\right) + \alpha_3{}^{*}\,\Delta\left(LN\_RCONS_t\right) + \alpha_4{}^{*}\,\Delta\left(LN\_OIL_t\right) + \alpha_5{}^{*}\,AR(1) + \alpha_6{}^{*}\,\varepsilon_{t-1} + \nu_e \quad (5)$$

where $\hat{\alpha}_{10}$ is the estimate of one-month PTE and $\sum_{i=0}^{k}\hat{\alpha}_{1i}$ with k = 2 and 5 are the estimates of three-month and six-month PTE respectively. The coefficient of ε_{t-1} shows convergence.

The number of NEERI and money supply lags was chosen according to the 'general to specific' procedure of iterative elimination of insignificant lags. Lags after the 5th for LN_NEERI and after the 2nd for LN_MONEY were insignificant for all price indices. Also, if we look at the correlation of exchange rate and inflation with different leads, we see that the highest correlation exists with inflation in the following five months (see Table 4.1). Consumer prices in Russia react to exchange rate changes faster than producer prices, and the overall pattern of correlation of consumer and producer prices is similar to that in Brazil and Poland (correlation coefficients of 0.97 and 0.92 respectively (Dubravco and Marc, 2002)). In addition, in these three countries the highest correlation exists with inflation in the current period and it is close to one.

Since lags after the 5th are all insignificant, we interpret the period of about half a year as a long run for price adjustments. Also, we see that consumer prices react to exchange rate changes somewhat faster than producer prices. In terms of this correlation of consumer prices Russia can be compared with Brazil and Poland (corresponding correlation coefficients are –0.97 and –0.92 respectively (Dubravco and

Table 4.1 Correlation of exchange rate with inflation in the current and the following 12 months

	CPI	PPI
d(ln_p)	−0.87	−0.20
d(ln_p(11))	−0.21	−0.21
d(ln_p(+2))	−0.16	−0.16
d(ln_p(+3))	−0.28	−0.13
d(ln_p(+4))	−0.22	−0.19
d(ln_p(+5))	−0.08	−0.18
d(ln_p(+6))	−0.03	−0.11
d(ln_p(+7))	−0.04	−0.08
d(ln_p(+8))	−0.01	−0.09
d(ln_p(+9))	0.01	−0.09
d(ln_p(+10))	−0.03	−0.09
d(ln_p(+11))	0.00	−0.12
d(ln_p(+12))	−0.01	−0.15

Marc (2002)), as in these three countries the highest correlation exists with inflation in the current period and it is close to one.

Since we cannot reject the hypothesis that the first differences of I(1) variables are stationary, we estimate the ECM by Ordinary Least Squares method. We test two sets of hypotheses for all price indices:

1) *Short run PTE (1 month)*:

H_0: $\hat{\alpha}_{10} = 0$ (No PTE)
H_1: $\hat{\alpha}_{10} \neq 0$ (PTE exists)

2) *Long run PTE (6 months by assumption)*:

$$H_0: \sum_{i=0}^{5} \hat{\alpha}_{1i} = -1 \text{(Complete PTE)}$$

$$H_1: \sum_{i=0}^{5} \hat{\alpha}_{1i} > -1 \text{(Complete PTE)}$$

The results of the estimation of PTE on consumer prices are presented in Table 4.2. The statistically significant values are marked in bold. Pluses in the second column stand for confirmed co-integration.

We see that PTE in one month is significant for all consumer prices, what rejects the null hypothesis. This means that the effect of exchange rate on prices really exists even in one month. To test

Table 4.2 Estimates of different run PTE: consumer prices

Price index (in logarithms)	Co-integration	Pass-through elasticity 1 month	3 months	6 months
CPI	+	**−0.42**	**−0.40**	**−0.40**
t-statistics		−32.01	−10.06	−5.24
Food	+	**−0.45**	**−0.45**	**−0.56**
t-statistics		−25.43	−8.68	−6.33
Goods	+	**−0.55**	**−0.48**	**−0.29**
t-statistics		−34.88	−10.55	−3.16
Services*	+	**−0.05**	−0.06	−0.08
t-statistics		−3.15	−1.31	−0.96

Note: * Insignificant PTE at least in one period.

Table 4.3 t-statistics for testing long-run PTE: consumer prices

Price index	t-statistics
CPI	−7.5
Food	−4.89
Goods	−11.83
Services	−11.5

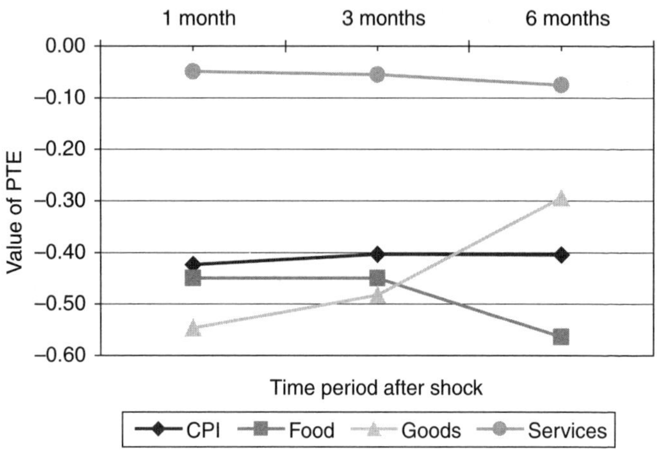

Figure 4.2 Term structure of PTE on consumer prices

whether six-month PTE is complete we perform the t-test of the null hypothesis for the cumulative effect of the six months PTE. The t-statistics are reported in Table 4.3.

Thus we may reject the null hypothesis about complete PTE in six months on all consumer prices, implying that Purchasing Power Parity does not hold in Russia. Further, all consumer prices except those for services are highly exchange rate elastic and the most remarkable adjustment occurs within the first month after the exchange rate change. Prices for services do not highly depend on exchange rate, which is natural for non-tradable goods. The term structure of PTE on consumer prices is presented on Figure 4.2.

These results suggest a number of conclusions can be made. First, the aggregate CPI adjusts to exchange rate changes for 40 per cent during half a year and the full adjustment (even some overshooting) occurs within the first month. Second, goods prices react faster than others in the first month and adjust for 55 per cent. But the highest pass-through elasticity in six months is observed for food prices, which adjust for 56 per cent in half a year. Third, prices for services are exchange rate inelastic and the PTE accounts for only 8 per cent in half a year and is statistically insignificant since services are non-traded goods.

These findings come in line with the results for Western economies presented in Table 4.4 (borrowed from Hufner and Schroder (2002), who use a similar econometric technique).

Tables 4.2 and 4.4 suggest that the PTE in Russia is much stronger than in European countries, confirming that Russia is a small economy, which is highly dependent on foreign markets.[5] Stronger PTE in Russia can also be explained by a relatively high import share of consumer goods, gradual depreciation of the rouble and less competitive Russian economy. If we compare PTE in Russia with that for other developing countries, estimated by Dubravco and Marc (2002), the strength of pass-through on consumer prices is similar to Hungary (−0.54) and Turkey (−0.56). Hence, we can make a general conclusion that PTE in developing countries is stronger than in the developed ones, and Russia is not an exception.

The same analysis applied to producer prices estimates by industries is presented in Table 4.5. Again, the statistically significant values are marked in bold; pluses in the second column stand for existing co-integration. The null hypothesis for one-month PTE is rejected for all producer prices except energy prices. Independence of energy prices can easily be explained by monopolisation and high

Table 4.4 Estimates of PTE for European countries

	After 6 months	**After 12 months**
France	0.01	0.07
Germany	0.07	0.08
Italy	0.06	0.12
Netherlands	0.12	0.11
Spain	0.09	0.08

Table 4.5 Estimates of different run PTE: producer prices

		Pass-through elasticity		
Price index (in logarithms)	**Co-integration**	**1 month**	**3 months**	**6 months**
PPI	+	−0.11	−0.20	−0.23
t-statistics		−2.50	−3.10	−3.66
Construction materials	+	−0.04	−0.09	−0.12
t-statistics		−4.40	−3.42	−2.36
Chemistry	+	−0.10	−0.21	−0.23
t-statistics		−5.07	−4.62	−2.87
Energy*	+	−0.03	−0.08	−0.17
t-statistics		−1.20	−1.41	−1.88
Ferrous metals*	+	−0.05	0.03	0.10
t-statistics		−3.04	0.60	0.93
Food processing	+	−0.26	−0.37	−0.50
t-statistics		−20.09	−10.42	−7.86
Fuel*	+	−0.08	−0.18	−0.22
t-statistics		−2.09	−1.75	−1.23
Machinery	+	−0.12	−0.17	−0.24
t-statistics		−9.88	−4.64	−3.44
Non-ferrous metals	+	−0.22	−0.59	−0.77
t-statistics		−5.85	−9.19	−9.57
Petrochemistry	+	−0.05	−0.05	−0.17
t-statistics		−3.95	−1.21	−2.17
Textile	+	−0.13	−0.27	−0.32
t-statistics		−14.31	−8.72	−5.86
Wood	+	−0.06	−0.24	−0.41
t-statistics		−6.02	−9.53	−8.56

Note: * Insignificant PTE at least in one period.

regulation of this industry. Although in the long run, PTE in this industry is small but significant. It follows that PTE is significant for most producer prices even in one month.

Long run PTE is significant for all producer prices except ferrous metals and fuel industries. Insignificant PTE in ferrous metals can be a result of wide use of long-term contracts in this industry. Absence of PTE in the fuel industry is due to monopolisation and regulation of prices. To test if PTE in six months is complete, we performed another t-test reported in Table 4.6. This table shows that PTE on prices in all

Table 4.6 t-statistics for testing long-run PTE: producer prices

Price index	t-statistics
PPI	−12.83
Construction materials	−17.6
Chemistry	−9.63
Energy	−9.22
Ferrous metals	−11
Food processing	−8.33
Fuel	−4.33
Machinery	−10.86
Non-ferrous metals	−2.88
Petrochemistry	−10.38
Textile	−11.33
Wood	−11.8

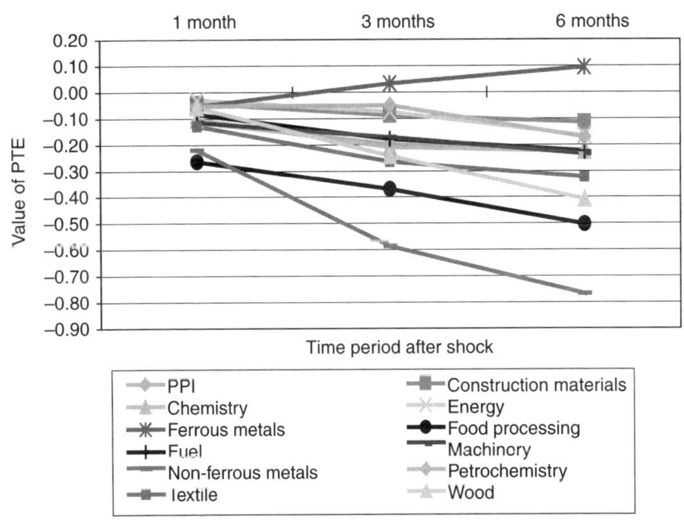

Figure 4.3 Term structure of PTE on producer prices

industries is incomplete in the long run, implying that producers are unable to fully transfer to their prices the cost changes occurred by exchange rate changes.

Term structure of PTE on producer prices is presented in Figure 4.3. We see that the maximum one-month PTE is on food prices – 26 per cent, while the maximum PTE in six months is on non-ferrous metals prices – 77 per cent. The minimum one-month PTE is 3 per cent in energy industry, which is monopolised and regulated, while the minimum six-month PTE is in ferrous metals and equals +10 per cent and insignificant. The remarkable difference between PTE in ferrous and non-ferrous metals industries can be explained by different market structures. Ferrous metals are usually OTC traded using long-term contracts, while non-ferrous metals are traded on an exchange where prices adjust very quickly.

These arguments imply we can divide all industries into two groups:

1) industries with long-run PTE higher that that of PPI (>23 per cent) – food processing, machinery, non-ferrous metals, textile and wood industries. These industries use quite high share of imported inputs.
2) industries with long-run PTE lower that that of PPI (<23 per cent), but still significantly different from zero – materials for construction, energy, chemistry and petrochemistry. These industries use local raw materials and are export-oriented.

The conclusion about different PTE for import and export industries comes in line with results of Dwyer, Kent and Pease (1993) for the Australian market. They also find that prices in import industries are more exchange rate elastic than prices in export-oriented ones.

It can be noticed that PTE on producer prices is significantly lower than that on consumer prices. This can be explained by the fact that consumer prices include import prices, which should be very exchange-rate elastic. Moreover, producer prices adjust to exchange rate changes more slowly than consumer prices, with some time lags.

If we look at food prices, we can notice that consumer prices are more elastic than producer prices. There are two reasons for this. First, consumer prices include prices of imported food. Second, wholesale and retail markets are organised differently.

4.2.3 Influence of monetary policy on PTE

As monetary policy in a country is often aimed at targeting inflation, it may decrease influence of exchange rate changes on prices when exchange rates are highly volatile. As argued above, and following

Parsley and Popper, we now incorporate monetary policy variable into the model developed in the previous section.

Our test is based on comparison of the estimated elasticities with and without monetary policy in order to determine the influence of this latter on PTE and inflation. In order to estimate PTE without monetary policy we again use ECM of the following specification for CPI and PPI:

$$LN\_P_t = \alpha_0 + \alpha_1 * LN\_NEERI_t$$

$$+ \alpha_3 * LN\_RCONS_t + \alpha_4 * LN\_OIL_t + \psi_t \quad (6)$$

$$\Delta\left(LN\_P_t\right) = \sum_{i=0}^{5} \theta_{1i} * \Delta\left(LN\_NEERI_{t-i}\right)$$

$$+ \alpha_3 * \Delta\left(LN\_RCONS_t\right) + \alpha_4 * \Delta\left(LN\_OIL_t\right)$$

$$+ \alpha_6 * AR(1) + \alpha_7 * \psi_{t-1} + \xi_e \quad (7)$$

The obtained estimates are compared with the estimates from the previous section in order to determine the behaviour of monetary policy. If the 'biased' PTE is smaller than the 'true' one $(|\sum_{i=0}^{k}\theta_i| < |\sum_{i=0}^{k}\alpha_i|)$, this will mean that monetary policy is aimed at reducing price fluctuations and PTE in Russia. If the opposite situation is true $(|\sum_{i=0}^{k}\theta_i| > |\sum_{i=0}^{k}\alpha_i|)$,this will mean that monetary policy has some aims other than controlling inflation and it increases PTE and, hence, increases price volatility in Russia.

The results of the estimation are the following. While estimation of co integration equation (1) produced the coefficient of exchange rate equal to −0.61 for CPI and −0.73 for PPI and monetary policy had a remarkable effect on CPI (coefficient −0.40) and almost no effect on PPI (coefficient −0.09), estimation of co-integration equation (3) without monetary policy produced coefficient of exchange rate equal to −1.03 for CPI and −0.85 for PPI, what means that PTE increased by absolute value greater for CPI (for which monetary policy is significant) than for PPI (insignificant monetary policy). So we conclude that omission of monetary policy leads to biased estimates of PTE,

Table 4.7 Estimates of PTE without monetary policy

Price index (in logarithms)	Co-integration	Pass-through elasticity 1 month	3 months	6 months
CPI	+	−**0.42**	−**0.41**	−**0.44**
t-statistics		−31.40	−9.17	−5.87
PPI	+	−**0.11**	−**0.21**	−**0.28**
t-statistics		−2.03	−3.02	−3.22

and that monetary policy in Russia in the long run increases the exchange rate PTE on prices. This last result is at odds with Parsley and Popper findings, who found out that omission of monetary policy leads to lower PTE, implying that monetary policy in the USA is aimed at diminishing PTE.

Short run 'true' PTE on CPI and PPI are presented in Tables 4.2 and 4.4 correspondingly. The estimates of the 'biased' PTE without taking into account monetary policy are presented in Table 4.7. This table again shows that monetary policy leads to stronger PTE on CPI and PPI, but in periods longer that one month. An interpretation is that during the studied period monetary policy in Russia did not smooth exchange rate fluctuations and their consequences on prices.

What is the aim of monetary policy then? Recall that before the crisis of 1998, government budget deficit was financed by state bonds (GKO) which led to accumulation of government debt to domestic and foreign investors. When the government defaulted on GKO, demand for the national currency from the side of foreign investors fell remarkably, what resulted was a sharp depreciation of the rouble on FOREX market. The direct effect of this depreciation was a significant rise of domestic prices (high PTE during the crisis). Therefore, the Russian economy needed more money for transactions at higher prices and financing the budget deficit, which resulted in money emission reflected in the statistical data. This type of monetary policy (expansion during rouble depreciation) explains why our findings contradict those of Parsley and Popper and others, and why monetary policy in Russia does not eliminate PTE, but, on the contrary, makes it stronger.

4.5 Conclusion

In this paper we study exchange rate PTE on domestic consumer and producer prices in Russia and the influence of government monetary policy on PTE for the period from January 1995 until December 2002.

We find that PTE on all prices studied in this work is incomplete even in the long run, which proves the irrelevance of Purchasing Power Parity in Russia. On the other hand, even one-month PTE is significant for most prices.

PTE on consumer prices is quite high and equals approximately 50 per cent, which corresponds to the results for other developing countries and is higher than PTE in developed countries. This characterises Russia as a small economy, which is highly dependent on shocks in the world markets. Therefore, in order to decrease price volatility, monetary policy in Russia should be endogenous and should eliminate the effect of exchange rate changes on prices, if the exchange rate is fully flexible, or the exchange rate should be in a corridor.

Almost all PTE on consumer prices occurs during one month, which supports the idea of flexible prices in Russia.

Among the studied consumer prices, prices of food and goods are highly exchange rate elastic while prices of services do not react to exchange rate changes. This can be explained by the fact that services can be an example of non-traded goods.

PTE on CPI is higher than that on PPI and CPI adjusts more quickly that PPI, which adjusts with some time lags. This is partially explained by the presence of imported goods in CPI, PTE on which should be high.

Prices in different industries of the Russian economy have different PTE. Low PTE is observed in industries with insignificant import shares (raw materials) and in highly regulated industries (e.g. energy). Companies, which work in competitive industries with low PTE and which have high imports are subject to high exchange rate risk, which should be managed properly. High PTE is observed in those industries which are closely connected with world markets and use a significant amount of imported intermediate goods (e.g. production of food and textile).

Estimation of PTE without taking into account monetary policy shows that monetary policy in the studies period did not eliminate PTE, but, on the contrary, made it stronger, which contradicts the results for western economies. This is explained by monetary expansion during the crisis of 1998, which was required in order to perform transactions at higher prices. When the Russian economy stabilises, the Central Bank of Russia should adopt other tactics and should aim its monetary policy at reducing price volatility and maintaining inflation rate constant.

These results may be interesting for the development of inflation and exchange rate policies as we have shown that it is impossible to manipulate inflation solely through changes in money supply when exchange rate is flexible and has an additional effect on domestic prices. If the aim of the government is to target inflation rate, then monetary policy should be endogenous (should adjust to exchange rate changes) since consumer prices are highly exchange-rate elastic during periods of Rouble depreciation.

Notes

1. In this paper we do not study PTE on import prices since the import price index is unavailable.
2. It should be noted that The Law of One Price has an economic sense only for import prices and not for all domestic prices in an economy, since there is no theoretical reason why exchange rate should completely pass through onto the prices of domestically produced goods.
3. For example, the European Central Bank has cited the possible inflationary effects of the weak euro as one factor behind its tightening of monetary policy in 2000 (May 2000 issue of the ECB Monthly Bulletin).
4. Results of these and all subsequent estimations are available from the authors upon request.
5. Higher PTE implies more flexible prices. Our results do not contradict the informational theory of financial disturbances expansion, which asserts that in less-developed economies maturities of contracts are shorter, than in developed, so prices are more volatile.

References

Bacchetta P., Wincoop E. (2002). 'Why Do Consumer Prices React Less Than Import Prices to Exchange Rates?' *NBER working paper # w9352*.

Bergin, Paul R. (2001). 'One Money One Price. Pricing to Market in a Monetary Union'. Department of Economics, University of California, Davis, manuscript.

Bergin, Paul R. and Robert C. Feenstra (2001). 'Pricing-to-Market, Staggered Contracts and Real Exchange Rate Persistence'. *Journal of International Economics*, 54: 333–359.

Charemza W.W. and Deadman D.F. (1999). 'New Directions in Econometric Practice: General to Specific Modeling, Cointegration and Vector Autoregression'. UK: Edward Elgar Publishing, 2nd edition.
Corsetti G., Giancarlo, and Dedola L. (2001). 'Macroeconomics of International Price Discrimination'. University of Rome III, manuscript.
Darvas Z. (2001). 'Exchange Rate Pass-Through and Real Exchange Rate in EU Candidate Countries'. Discussion paper, *Economic Research Center of the Deutsche Bundesbank*, May 2001.
Devereux M. and Yetman J. (2003). 'Monetary Policy and Exchange Rate Pass-through: Theory and Empirics', Hong Kong Institute for Monetary research, working paper.
Dolado J., Jenkinson T. and Sosvilla-Rivero S. (1990). 'Cointegration and Unit Roots'. *Journal of Economic Survey*, 4: 249–73.
Dornbusch R. (1987). 'Exchange Rates and Prices'. *American Economic Review*, 77: 93–106.
Dubravko M. and Marc K. (2002). 'A Note on the Pass-through from Exchange Rate and Foreign Price Changes to Inflation in Selected Emerging Market Economies'. *BIS Papers* #8: 69–81.12.
Dwyer J., Kent C. and Pease A. (1993). 'Exchange Rate Pass-Through: The Different Responses of Importers and Exporters'. Reserve Bank of Australia Research, Discussion Paper 9304.
Feinberg, Robert M. (1986). 'The Interaction of Foreign Exchange and Market Power Effects on German Domestic Prices'. *Journal of Industrial Economics*, 35: 61–70.
Feinberg, Robert M. (1989). 'The Effects of Foreign Exchange Movements on U.S. Domestic Prices'. *Review of Economics and Statistics*, 71: 505–11.
Fouquin M., Khalid Sekkat K., Mansour M., Mulder N. and Nayman N. (2001). 'Sector Sensitivity to Exchange Rate Fluctuations'. #11, CEPII.
Gagnon J.E. and Knetter M.M. (1992). 'Markup Adjustment and Exchange Rate Fluctuations: Evidence from Panel Data on Automobile Exports'. *NBER working paper #4123*.
Garcia C., Jose R. and Jorge E. (2001). 'Price Inflation and Exchange Rate Pass-Through in Chile'. *Central Bank of Chile working paper # 128*.
Goldberg P. and Knetter M. (1997) 'Goods Prices and Exchange Rates: What Have We Learned?' *Journal of Economic Literature*, 35 (3): 1243–1272.
Hooper P. and Mann C. L. (1989). 'Exchange Rate Pass-Through in the 1980s: The Case of U.S. Imports of Manufactures'. *Brookings Papers on Economic Activity*, 1: 297–337.
Hufner F. and Schoder M. (2002) 'Exchange Rate Pass-through to Consumer Prices: a European Perspective'. Centrum for European Economic Research, Discussion paper #0220.
Isard P. (1977). 'How Far Can We Push the Law of One Price?' *American Economic Review*, 67(5): 942–48.
Klitgaard T. (1999). 'Exchange Rates and Profit Margins: The Case of Japanese Exporters'. *Federal Reserve Bank of New York Economic Policy Review*, 5(1): 41–54.
Krugman, Paul M. (1987). 'Pricing to Market When the Exchange Rate Changes'. in Sven W. Arndt and J. David. Richardson, eds *Real-Financial*

Linkages Among Open Economies, Cambridge, MA and London: MIT Press, pp. 49–70.

Kuzmin (2002). 'Study of the Exchange rate Pass-Through to Import Prices in the Ukraine'. Proposal for EERC Workshop, July 2002.

Lafleche T. (1996). 'The Impact of Exchange Rates Movements on Consumer Prices'. *Bank of Canada Review*, Winter: 21–32.

Lee J. (1997). 'The Response of Exchange Rate Pass-through to Market Concentration in a Small Economy: the Evidence from Korea'. *The Review of Economics and Statistics*: 142–145.

Liu B.J. (1993). 'Cost Externalities and Exchange Rate Pass-through: Some Evidence from Taiwan'. in Takatoshi I. and Krueger A. eds, Macroeconomic Linkage, Chicago, IL: University of Chicago Press, p. 35.

McCarthy J. (2000). 'Pass-through of Exchange Rates and Import Prices to Domestic Inflation in Some Industrialised Countries'. Federal Reserve Bank of New York Staff Reports 111.

Menon J. (1995). 'Exchange Rate Pass-Through'. *Journal of Economic Surveys*, 9 (2): 197–231.

Menon J. (1996). 'The Degree and Determinants of Exchange Rate Pass-Through: Market Structure, Non-tariff Barriers, and Multinational Corporations'. *Economic Journal*, 106: 434–44.

Obstfeld, M. (2001). 'International Macroeconomics: Beyond the Mundell–Fleming Model'. *NBER working paper 8369*.

Ohno K. (1990). 'Export Pricing Behaviour of Manufacturing: a US – Japan Comparison'. International Monetary Fund Staff papers, 36: 550–579.

Olivey G. (2002). 'Exchange Rates and the Prices of Manufacturing Products Imported into the United States'. *New England Economic Review* (1st quarter, 2002), pp. 3–17.

Parsley D. and Popper H. (1998). 'Exchange Rates, Domestic Prices and Central Bank Actions: Recent US Experience'. *Southern Economic Journal*, 64 (4): 957–972.

Phillips R.W. (1988). 'The Pass-Through of Exchange Rate Changes to Prices of Imported Manufactures'. *A.N.U. Centre for Economic Policy Research Discussion Paper #197*.

Takagi S. and Yoshida Y. (2001). 'Exchange Rate Movements and Tradable Goods Prices in East Asia: an Analysis Based on Japanese Customs Data'. *1988–1999 IMF Staff Papers*, vol. 48, # 2, pp. 266–288.

Tsesliuk S. (2002). 'Exchange Rate and Prices in an Economy with Currency Substitution: the Case of Belarus'. MA Thesis, *EERC, Kiev*, p. 2.

Woo, Wing T. (1984). 'Exchange Rates and the Prices of Non-food, Non-fuel products'. *Brookings Papers on Economic Activity*, 2: 511–30.

Yang, J. (1997). 'Exchange Rate Pass-Through in U.S. Manufacturing Industries'. *Review of Economics and Statistics*, 79: 95–104.

5

Disaggregated Econometric Models to Forecast Inflation in Hungary

*Viktor Várpalotai**

5.1 Introduction

The Magyar Nemzeti Bank (Central Bank of Hungary, henceforth MNB) introduced an inflation-targeting monetary regime in June 2001. In a very simplified way, the purport of an inflation-targeting regime is the following: the monetary authority declares an inflation target for the future, next, it compares this target with its own forecasts of future inflation based on currently available information, and finally it revises monetary conditions, in order to eliminate any potential discrepancies between the announced target and its forecasts.[1]

As in inflation targeting-regimes, the monetary policy is mainly based on inflation forecasts; it is crucial to have reliable forecasts at the central banks. In practice, when a central bank wants to implement a 'reliable inflation forecast' it must consider two issues: (1) what kind of inflation to target, (2) how to forecast inflation. (1) It is common to define inflation as a change in consumer prices index (henceforth CPI). However, the theoretic background of choosing CPI as a measure of inflation is not so well elaborated, but it is relatively easy to measure and to communicate to the public.[2] Actually, the MNB uses CPI in its target as well. (2) As Pagan and Robertson (2002) argue, forecasting for policy purposes should be based on a pluralistic approach. Their argument for model variety is straightforward: a pluralistic approach might reduce uncertainties inheriting in each forecast. So it is not surprising that many central banks put a lot of effort into building inflation forecasting tools. For instance, Hornok and Jakab (2002) reviewed the inflation forecasting systems of five Central European central banks and found that four out of five reviewed central banks have more than one model to forecast inflation.[3] Among other central banks, the MNB also employs several models, however, as Pagan and Robertson (2002) stress, it is always useful to build a new one which uses methods different to former models.

The remainder of the paper is structured as follows. In the first section I present some other inflation-forecasting model currently used by the MNB in a nutshell. In the second section I describe the framework of the new disaggregated cost pass-through based inflation-forecasting model. It is accompanied by methodological issues on how to estimate 'smooth' coefficients in a distributed lag model. Next, I briefly present the estimation results and some ex-ante model forecast. Finally, I draw some conclusions.

5.2 Inflation forecasting models used by the MNB

In the last few years three main inflation forecasting models were built in the MNB:[4]

1) Partial equations;
2) Quarterly Projection Model;
3) Inflation forecasting system based on specialist information.

Each of them is disaggregated, however, at different levels. The MNB's official inflation projections, which are summarised in a fan-chart published in the MNB's Quarterly Report on Inflation, are created using a combination of these methods. Below I describe the main features of these three models.

1. Partial equations are used for forecasting inflation in three groups: tradable and non-tradable goods and services and

processed foods. These three categories together correspond to 60 per cent of the total CPI basket. The three equations determining the developments of the prices of these goods and services are written in error correction form, i.e. the model captures both the short-term dynamics and the adjustment to the long-term equilibrium. The inflation of tradable goods is modelled via a purchasing power parity rule with HUF/EUR exchange rate and prices of tradable goods in Germany augmented by a trend real appreciation of 0.35 per cent per year. The processed food inflation is derived from an equilibrium relationship among processed food prices and the other two main cost factors: unprocessed food prices and wage costs. Finally, the inflation of non-tradable goods is derived from an equilibrium relationship among the non-tradable/tradable inflation gap, household consumption and tradable productivity based on the Balassa–Samuelson effect and a demand side effect. The parameters of these equations are partly estimated and partly calibrated.

2. The Quarterly Projection Model (N.E.M) developed at the Magyar Nemzeti Bank (see Jakab et al., 2004) is a new-Keynesian, macro econometric model: it is supply-determined in the long run, but demand side with sluggish adjustment mechanism determines the variables in the short term. The N.E.M. model is a medium scaled model, comprising of 24 estimated behavioral equations extended with 206 accounting identities. In the model the CPI index is calculated as a weighted average of the GDP deflator, import prices endogenously determined in the model and prices of unprocessed foodstuffs, motor vehicle fuels, the administered prices, indirect taxes given exogenously.
3. The inflation forecasting system based on specialist information decomposes the CPI basket into 27 different subgroups yielding a higher degree of disaggregation compared to partial equation approach and the N.E.M. model. In this system, the exogenous variables (like wages, oil price, exchange rate, German prices) are the most important determinant of prices. This system is written in an input-output table form, where the parameters are calibrated according to the 1988 Input-Output matrix. The main advantage of this approach is that it is relatively easy to adjust the forecast by discretional information like changes in excise

duty system or in the regulation of VAT, nevertheless, the dynamics of price development plugged in the model lacks any empirical justification.

5.3 The disaggregated cost pass-through based inflation forecasting model

5.3.1 Framework of the model

The model explains the developments of consumer prices by changes in their cost factors. In other words, it treats prices as being ultimately determined by costs. This approach is applicable within the set of marketed goods of the consumer basket, which has competitive market structure ensuring a close relationship between prices and cost over both the short and long term causing only temporary changes in mark-up on factor costs. However, there exists other sets of goods and services in the CPI basket, whose administered prices are determined by discretionary decision taken by the central government or local authorities (non-marketed goods).[5] For this completely different way of price setting, the administered prices are not modelled in this paper.

I modelled the temporary changes in mark-up on factor cost of the marketed goods with an error correction approach distinguishing short from long term adjustment using monthly data. According to the standard two-stages method, I separated the problem of identifying the long-term equilibrium cost structures from that of identifying the short-term dynamics of cost pass-though adjustment toward the equilibrium.

As among other cost factors, I use the exchange rate and the foreign prices as cost factors, as well, relating this approach to exchange rate pass-through literature. This expression is generally used to refer to the effects of exchange rate changes on one of the following: (1) import and export prices, (2) consumer prices, (3) investments and (4) trade volumes. The incompleteness of exchange rate pass-through into consumer prices is a common wisdom of the empirical analysis.[6] The model gives implicitly an explanation of this phenomena decomposing the prices of traded good into different cost factors among which the foreign prices denominated in domestic currency represents only a part of the costs. Therefore, even if (as I assume) the exchange rate pass-through is complete at the level of cost factors, the prices of other (non-traded) cost factors lacks this adjustment, yielding an incomplete pass-through in the consumer prices of traded goods.

5.3.1.1 *Identifying cost structures (Long run equilibrium)*

The prices of marketed goods represented in the consumer basket are assumed to be determined by various cost elements, such as labour costs, energy, basic materials, farm crops, imports, as well as other goods and services which themselves are included in the consumer basket, such as flour in the case of bread, textiles in connection with clothing, etc. Furthermore, it is assumed that each cost elasticity is constant and, therefore, over the long term prices are determined by the following Cobb-Douglas type function below:

$$P_{i,t} = \left(A_i e^{\lambda_i t} C_{1,t}^{\gamma_{i,1}} C_{1,t}^{\gamma_{i,2}} \cdot \ldots \cdot C_{n_i-1,t}^{\gamma_{i,n_i-1}} C_{n_i,t}^{(1-\gamma_{i,1}-\gamma_{i,2}-\ldots-\gamma_{i,n_i-1})} \right) H_t \eta_{i,t}, \tag{1}$$

where $P_{i,t}$ is the consumer price index of the i good in t, $C_{j,t}$ is the price index of the j cost element in t, $\gamma_{i,j}$ is the cost elasticity of j cost element on price of i good, A_i is the scaling factor normalising costs to price, λ_i is the growth rate of productivity, so the term $e^{\lambda_i t}$ captures the changes in productivity, H_i is the profit margin assumed to be proportional to total costs, and finally $\eta_{i,t}$ is the error term with mean one.

It is worth noting that the price index of the cost factors is measured in 'natural units' (index of monthly average wages, price index of 1 kWh of electricity, price index of flour, etc.). That is why the term A_i is included in the function (1), where A_i transforms the cost indices, expressed in various units into a (consumer) price index.

The λ_i parameter of productivity change is expected to be a negative a priori, as, if there is an improvement in productivity, then the increase in consumer price index can be lower than the appropriate cost indices would predict. However, positive λ_i is not unexplainable either: this corresponds to a market on which one can (temporarily) earn an increasing profit margin. The sums of cost elasticities ($\gamma_{i,j}$) are restricted to 1, in order to ensure price homogeneity, i.e. if each cost factor prices increases by 1 per cent, then the final price of the goods increases by 1per cent supposing an unchanged mark-up. A further restriction is that each $\gamma_{i,j}$ parameters of cost elasticity should be positive.

For the calibration and econometric estimation, the logarithmic form of the cost function (1) has been used:

$$p_{i,t} = a_i + \lambda_i t + \gamma_{i,1}c_{1,t} + \gamma_{i,2}c_{2,t} + \ldots + \gamma_{i,n-1}c_{n_i-1,t}$$
$$+ (1 - \gamma_{i,1} - \gamma_{i,2} \ldots - \gamma_{i,n_i-1})c_{n_i,t} + h_i + \varepsilon_{i,t}, \quad (2)$$

where small case letters denote the logarithm of correspondent variables and price indexes and $\varepsilon_{i,t}$ is the error term with zero mean.[7]

To fill this framework, some further steps have to be taken. First, dependent variables $p_{i,t}$ have to be defined. The source data is the disaggregated CPI index statistics containing 160 components released by Central Statistical Office (CSO). 143 out of 160 CPI components have been identified as marketed goods;[8] the remaining 17 components have been categorised as non-marketed goods, as their prices are regulated. However, in order to keep the model tractable, I have made some aggregation creating 43 groups from the 143 individual components. This aggregation has yielded more homogeneous groups whose relative weights are more balanced.[9]

Secondly, the cost factors have to be selected for each of 43 aggregated groups. For nearly each group, I assume that cost factors include transportation, electricity, natural gas and wages.[10] For (internationally) traded goods, I use the price of the correspondent foreign goods denominated in domestic currency as a cost factor, as well.[11] As foreign prices, I use the weighted price indices of euro area countries released by Eurostat.For all products the price of the Brent crude oil has been selected as a factor cost but for motor fuel.[12] In some cases, some of the 43 aggregated groups of CPI index served as a cost factor of other groups (e.g. flour is a cost factor of bread, sugar in case of sweets, clothing materials in case of clothing, etc.). The Figure 5.1 provides some insight into a diversity of pass-through and some spillover effects.[13]

The grey area represents the set of goods whose prices are determined simultaneously. The arrows denote the directions of cost pass-through.

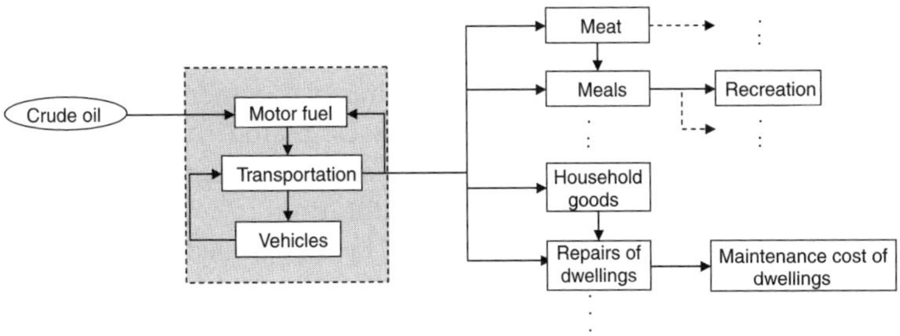

Figure 5.1 A set of cost pass-through and spillover channels in the model

Note: The grey area represents the set of goods whose prices are determined simultaneously. The arrows denote the directions of cost pass-through.

In the case of aggregated consumer prices, the appropriate handling of taxes poses problems. On the one hand, the price of each product and service in the CPI basket includes value added tax (VAT). Of course, goods might have different VAT contents. In 2005, in Hungary there exist three VAT rates: 0per cent, 15 per cent and 25 per cent. VAT rates have remained unchanged in the past years, except one major change in classification in January 2004.[14] Thus, if this type of tax is considered as a fixed ratio of costs, it only means a scaling problem, which can be resolved with the a_i scaling factor. On the other hand, the excise content of some goods of the CPI basket (e.g. tobacco, coffee, motor fuel and oils) has changed several times over the past years. As excise duty accounts for a large portion of the consumer prices of such goods,[15] any change in it might influence consumer prices considerably.[16] Therefore, these excise duties were removed from the consumer price of motor fuel, and the resulting series has been modelled by its cost factors.[17]

After having identified cost factors of each dependent variable, the next step has been to parameterise equations of type (2). It has been done by both estimation and calibration. For calibration, I used weights borrowed from judgments of MNB's experts that were originally derived from Input-Output tables of Hungary. Estimates have been calculated by using ordinary least squares methods.[18] As from a theoretical point of view, only positive $\gamma_{i,j}$ cost weights are plausible, which is not guaranteed by the standard econometric estimation of the equation (2), therefore an iterative process has been carried out. I have replaced the estimated value of $\gamma_{i,j}$ by weight suggested by experts' judgments, when the estimated $\gamma_{i,j}$ had incorrect (negative) signs or the absolute value seemed extremely high/low. After each replacement, I re-estimated the model until each $\gamma_{i,j}$ parameter had both positive sign and acceptable magnitude. A further consideration of calibration has been that the weights of those cost factors which had been included in each group of goods (e.g. transportation, electricity and gas) be roughly equal everywhere.

The sample periods have been selected in order to use only 'quiet' periods from the point of view of pricing. The reason behind this has been that long-term equilibrium weights can be easier detected in data during such periods. Thus, the period from January 1995 and December 1995 (or even later when it needed) was excluded from our sample, as an austerity package was introduced in March 1995, which has triggered a big jump in the CPI inflation. I also tested for structural breaks after May 2001, as a possible consequence of introducing new monetary policy framework. However, these breaks have been rejected.

As a consequence of these processes, the majority of cost factors' weights have been calibrated and only a few have been estimated.[19] For the complete list of final parameters see Appendix.

5.3.1.2 *Identifying cost pass-through (Short run dynamics)*

In accordance with the error correction approach, once long-run equilibrium has been parameterised, the task is to define short-run dynamics. As is customary, short-run dynamics consistent with long-run equilibrium can be written as follows:

$$\Delta p_{i,t} = \lambda_i + \gamma_{i,1} B_{i,1}(L)\Delta c_{1,t} + \gamma_{i,2} B_{i,2}(L)\Delta c_{2,t} + \ldots + \gamma_{i,n_i-1} B_{i,n_i-1}(L)\Delta c_{n-1,t}$$

$$+ (1 - \gamma_{i,1} - \gamma_{i,2} \ldots - \gamma_{i,n_i-1}) B_{i,n}(L)\Delta c_{n,t} - \phi_i \varepsilon_{i,t-1} + \xi_{i,t}, \qquad (3)$$

where Δ is difference, L is the lag operator, $\varepsilon_{i,t-1}$ is the residual of long-term equation i, ξ_i is the error term of the short-term equation and γ_i is the estimated/calibrated cost weights of the long-term equation. The $B_{i,j}(L)$ polynomials have the form

$B_{i,j}(L) = b_{i,j,0} + b_{i,j,1}L + b_{i,j,2}L^2 + \ldots + b_{i,j,q_{i,j}}L^{q_{i,j}}$, where the degree of the polynomials (length of lag) is $q_{i,j}$, and where the sum of parameters is 1 for every i and j. ($\sum_{k=0}^{q_{i,j}} b_{i,j,k} = 1$). A $B_{i,j}(L)$ polynomial represents the dynamics of the cost pass-through of relevant cost factors. Despite the fact, that (3) is a standard approach, the common estimation techniques like OLS cannot be adapted in this case. The reason for this is that cost pass-through processes have (at least) four characteristics that render the standard econometric techniques inapplicable to estimate parameters in equation (3).

1. Cost pass-through is a slow gradual process, market competition being unable to enforce immediate price adjustments. There might be several reasons for this. For instance, if there is a change in a price of a cost factor, it takes considerable time to affect the consumer prices, as it has to spillover through the chain of production and sale starting at producers or importers continuing with wholesalers and ending at retailers. Another reason might be the existence of long-term contracts or a relatively low frequency of price revision. A further factor that decelerates this process is that some goods serve as input for other goods, so a series of spillover effect has to occur before changes appear in the final consumer prices. Therefore, it is safe to assume that the cost pass-through might be a several-year-long process, where it might be that in the first months or quarters no price effect is discernible.
2. Although, the pass-through might be slow for some cost factor, it does not mean that the speed of pass-through is equally slow for each cost factor. Contrarily, it is reasonable that a change in a cost factor will show up in consumer prices relatively more rapidly than others will. For example, changes in the price of crude oil will manifest in motor fuel prices as quickly as a week or two; by contrast, the price of transport, which regards motor fuel as a cost factor, is very likely not to respond to changes in the price of crude oil instantly. Different market structures are likely to be responsible for these differences in the speed of the pass-through effect: any rise in costs is likely to pass-through quickly in a monopolistic market; similarly, a higher frequency of price revision will result in a faster pass-through.

3. The coefficients of cost changes should be non-negative ($b_{i,j,k} \geq 0$). This requirement can be explained by the expected characteristic of cost pass-through. The hypothesised process of cost pass-through is a path of price changes which would be discernible in the case of a one-off change in the price of a cost factor ceteris paribus. This path is assumed to reflect that one-off increase (decrease) in costs leads to gradual monotonic increase (decrease) in price without any break or reverse price movements (e.g. over-shooting).[20]
4. If the cost pass-through is a gradual process, then coefficients of cost changes might be interdependent. This means that, if the change in prices at period $t + j$ triggered by a change in costs in period t is small, there cannot be a sudden large change neither in the subsequent $t + j + 1$ period nor in the preceding period $t + j - 1$. If, for example, the speed of pass-through is slow in one period, it will also remain slow in the subsequent period; if it is relatively fast in a given period, it will also remain fast in the subsequent period. Consequently, the coefficients of the lag polynomials change only gradually.

Due to these four characteristics, I am faced with the following problems of estimation. First, the slowness of the pass-though would require estimating several lagged parameters.[21] Second, it would be difficult to interpret either the negative values appearing in estimated lag parameters or the hectic changes in lag coefficients from one period to the other. One might suggest that the parameter ϕ_i of the error correction is able to partially handle these problems, as, provided that it is small enough, the pass-through will be gradual and slow in the model. Furthermore, it might be enough to use only the first few lags with non-negative parameters of acceptable size. However, this is not an acceptable compromise, as the speed of cost pass-though might be different for each cost factor. Furthermore, putting aside the lag terms, the error-correction model implies identical speed of pass-through for each cost factor, and, unfortunately, predicts the highest change in prices one period after the shock occurs. Summarising the problems to be solved, one faces the following problems: one should use estimation techniques which guarantee the non-negativity of lag parameters, allows smooth gradual change in $b_{i,j,k}$ only, but which is flexible enough to capture diverse shape of pass-through process without estimating too many parameters.

5.3.2 Econometric issues: Distributed lag estimator derived from smoothness priors

I applied a non-parametric technique in order to estimate flexible pass-through profiles. I used smoothness prior approach developed by Shiller (1973) which, in fact, is a Bayesian estimator. For the sake of brevity, here I present only the way how the posterior mean has been estimated. A step by step introduction to this approach can be found in Shiller's paper. Equation of short run dynamics (3) has been estimated by defining a smoothness criterion for the estimated $b_{i,j,k}$ parameters, using $w_{i,j}$ a priori weights, in the form of:

$$\sum_{j=1}^{n_i} w_{i,j} \sum_{k=2}^{q_{i,j}-1} \left((b_{i,j,k} - b_{i,j,k-1}) - (b_{i,j,k} - b_{i,j,k+1}) \right)^2 \tag{4}$$

which is a term quantifying the 'punishment' for the variability in parameters $b_{i,j,k}$.

This smoothness criterion and the constraints for the non-negativity and appropriate sum of the parameters have been used to modify the standard ordinary least square estimation. As a result, the pass-through profiles (and the other parameters) have been estimated via solving the following quadratic programming problem:

$$\min_{\beta}(\mathbf{y} - \mathbf{X}\boldsymbol{\beta})'(\mathbf{y} - \mathbf{X}\boldsymbol{\beta}) + \boldsymbol{\beta}'\mathbf{S}\boldsymbol{\beta}$$

$$\text{s.t. } \mathbf{A}\boldsymbol{\beta} = \mathbf{d}$$

$$\boldsymbol{\beta}_{low} \leq \boldsymbol{\beta} \leq \boldsymbol{\beta}_{up}, \tag{5}$$

where $\mathbf{y}$ denotes vector of the prices changes ($\Delta p_{i,t}$), $\mathbf{X}$ the matrix of the explanatory variables ($\Delta c_{j,t}$ lagged change in cost variables, error correction term and constant vector), $\boldsymbol{\beta}$ is the vector of the coefficients $b_{i,j,k}$ to be estimated, including the constant parameter λ_i and error correction parameter ϕ_i. **S** is the smoothness criterion written in matrix form (4). It is worth noting the matrix **S** depends on $w_{i,j}$ a priori weights solely. In the restriction $\mathbf{A\beta} = \mathbf{d}$, **A** and **d** denote the matrix and vector of the restrictions respectively constraining the sum of the distributed lag parameters to equal one. Finally, $\boldsymbol{\beta}_{low}$ and $\boldsymbol{\beta}_{up}$ are the lower and upper constraints ensuring non-negative lag coefficients and a non-positive parameter for the error correction parameter.[22]

5.4 Empirical results and the predictive accuracy of the model

For the estimation I used a sample from January 1996 to December 2004. In the first step I used the iteration process described in section 2.2. to identify cost elasticity for each marketed goods aggregated into 43 subgroups. The results of this iterative estimation-calibration process are shown in the Appendix, where I present the tables of final coefficients. In the second step, after a couple of iterations, I have succeeded in calibrating the weights $w_{i,j}$ to produce sufficiently smooth cost pass-through profiles for each of the 43 goods and services then I solved the appropriate quadratic programming problem.[23] As this paper could not aim to give a full presentation of the estimated distributed lag coefficients, I have enclosed the graph of estimated cost pass-through profile system of 'repairs of dwellings' only obtained after the appropriate calibration of parameters $w_{i,j}$. The Figure 5.2 shows the pass-through of the costs of repairs of dwellings, showing lag structures $B_i(L)$.[24]

It is clear from the chart that the speeds of pass-through of the various cost factors are different. In this case, dwelling maintenance articles exhibited the fastest pass-through, in contrast to wages, which start to pass through after a six-month (wages in construction sector) and one-year lag (wages in market services sector) only.

The overall picture of estimated cost pass-through profiles has delivered some interesting findings about the speed of price adjustment. For cost factors, which are basic materials like crude oil, the average speed of adjustment is very high, more precisely; the half-lives of price adjustment are between 1–4 months. Regulated prices like electricity,

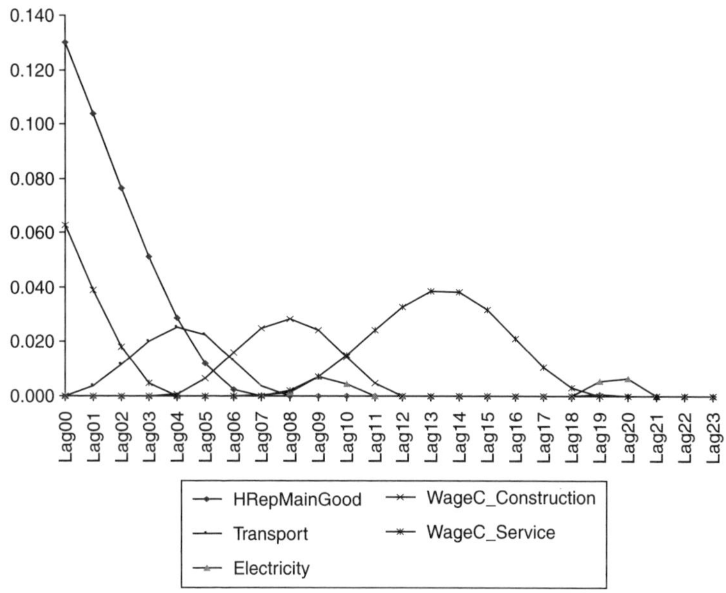

Figure 5.2 Estimated cost pass-through profiles ($b_{i,j,k}$) for 'repairs of dwellings'

natural gas, etc. pass-through more slowly, the half-lives are in a range of 3–10 months. According to the estimates, the wages induce the slowest price adjustment yielding a half-life range of 5–16 months. Interestingly, in the case of imported goods, I found different pass-through for exchange rate and foreign prices. Except for a few cases, a change in a foreign goods price measured in foreign currency shows up faster then a change in nominal exchange rate. This can be seen as a signal that foreign good price changes are more important to market participants than changes in the exchange rates. It is not surprising after all, as the variance of exchange rate is much larger then that of foreign goods' prices.

As the model has been constructed primarily for forecasting purposes, one should test how precisely the model is able to predict inflation. To illustrate this, I have made several out of sample simu-

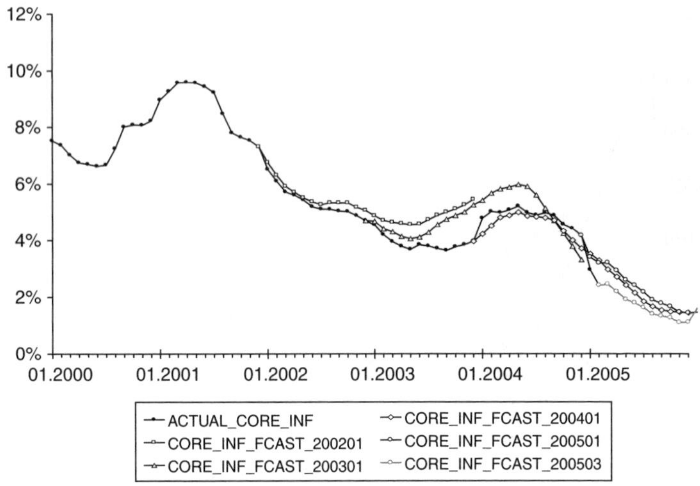

Figure 5.3 Actual versus out of sample model forecast

lations starting from 2001 to 2005, each of them starting in January except the last one that starts from March 2005. The long-run and short-run parameters of the models were estimated using only these shortened sample periods, and dynamic simulations have been run taking the exogenous variables, such as wages, agricultural prices, exchange rates, import prices, crude oil price and regulated prices as given.

In Figure 5.3, ACTUAL_CORE_INF denotes the actual, and CORE_INF_FCAST_yyyyqq the simulated year-on-year core consumer price indices.

To measure the predictive accuracy of our model I also calculated the *RMSE* (root mean squared errors) and MAE (mean average errors) indicators for periods January 2000–December 2004. Both of them show a similar pattern. For the short horizon the forecast errors are minimal but they increase with the longer forecast horizon. Interestingly, this increase is not monotonic as there is some decrease at longer horizon. Considering MAE indicators, it seems that the model tends to slightly over-predict the future inflation. After two-years experience, it has become clear that the overall

Table 5.1 Predictive accuracy of the model

	1Q Ahead	2Q Ahead	3Q Ahead	4Q Ahead	5Q Ahead	6Q Ahead	7Q Ahead	8Q Ahead
RMSE	0.29	0.41	0.44	0.47	0.51	0.55	0.53	0.50
MAE	0.08	0.15	0.21	0.29	0.30	0.32	0.34	0.29

Note: Numbers were calculated from the actual and the predicted year-on-year indices of CPI for periods Janary 2000 December 2004.

forecasting ability of the model is reasonably good. Analysing the forecasts at the disaggregated level one can reveal that the less variance the actual series have the more precise forecasts the model delivers. Nevertheless, forecasts of non-tradable goods and services are always surpassingly precise.

I compared our model performance with other models' forecasts, as well. However, the direct comparison is impossible: each model uses different information set (e.g. exogenous variables) and, this is the main reason, the MNB publishes only one official forecast that comprises all model forecasts and expert information about future inflation. Therefore I could compare the model forecasts only with MNB inflation forecasts. For calculation I generated new model simulations where the forecasted values of exogenous variables were set according to those that MNB used in its correspondent inflation forecast.

Figure 5.4 reveals that the patterns of *RMSEs* are very similar, but on three horizons (2, 4, 5 quarter ahead) the disaggregated inflation forecasting model slightly beats MNB's official inflation forecasts. However, one must be very cautious with this interpretation as the differences are minimal and presumably not significant.

5.5 Conclusions

I provided an insight to inflation forecasting models used by the MNB. Briefly, I reviewed three inflation-forecasting models which were developed earlier at the MNB. The main focus of the paper was to present the disaggregated cost pass-through based econometric inflation forecasting model, which has been developed recently. This model is the first one both in the literature and in the practice of a central bank which uses Bayesian smoothness prior to

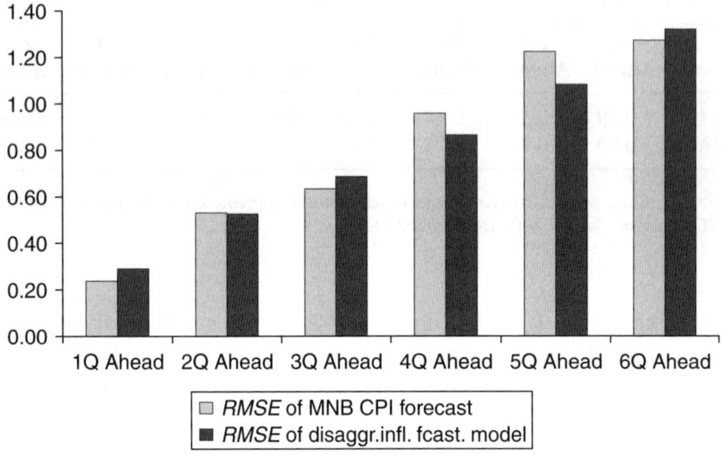

Figure 5.4 *RMSE*s of MNB official inflation forecasts vs. disaggregated inflation forecasting model

capture the slow price adjustment process in order to forecast consumer prices.

The pass-through processes estimated on Hungarian monthly data delivered some interesting findings about the speed of price adjustment. The fastest consumer price adjustment is triggered by the change in basic materials' prices, a slower adjustment has been detected in the case of a change in regulated prices, while the changes in wage costs effect consumer prices only with considerable lags. Another typical feature of pass-through profiles is that, with few exceptions, changes in foreign prices pass through into prices much sooner than the change in nominal exchange rate.

Beside these interesting findings, the forecasting ability of the model is reasonably good. It delivers especially good forecasts for non-tradable goods and services. Realising these favorable properties, the MNB has begun to use this model in its official inflation forecasting procedure.

Appendix

Long-run cost factor structures

The vast majority of cost factors were calibrated based on expert information and a few of them were estimated. This can be seen in Appendix 1, 2, 3 and 4 presented below that show the long-run cost factor structures of our model. The tables identify which cost factors were used for each group of goods and their weights. In the tables, each equation has three rows. The names of cost factors are presented in the first row. In the second row, the mark 'E' means that the given parameter was estimated, the mark 'R' appears when the parameter was estimated under restriction, in order to ensure that the sum of cost factor parameters equals to 1. Lastly, the final parameters used by the model can be found in the third row. The sample period of estimation is reported in the second column of the table. To make our tables more transparent, the estimated parameters are marked with a grey background. The trend and constant parameters were estimated in each equation.

Appendix 1

	Name of the CPI subgroups	Sample period				
					1	2
1	UnProcMeat		_Const	_Trend	TransPort	Electricity
	From	1996:01	B	B	0.050	0.025
	To	2004:12	−0.0637	0.0009	0.050	0.025
2	ProcMeat		_Const	_Trend	TransPort	Electricity
	From	1996:01	B	B	0.050	0.035
	To	2004:12	−0.8906	− 0.0003	0.050	0.035
3	Fish		_Const	_Trend	TransPort	Electricity
	From	1996:01	B	B	0.050	0.035
	To	2004:12	−3.9400	−0.0029	0.050	0.035
4	Egg		_Const	_Trend	TransPort	Electricity
	From	1996:01	B	B	0.050	0.025
	To	2004:12	−0.1420	−0.0001	0.050	0.025
5	Milk		_Const	_Trend	TransPort	Electricity
	From	1996:01	B	B	0.100	0.025
	To	2004:12	−0.5171	0.0016	0.100	0.025
6	MilkProd		_Const	_Trend	TransPort	Electricity
	From	1998:01	B	B	0.050	0.025
	To	2004:12	−0.4999	0.0008	0.050	0.025
7	VegetFat		_Const	_Trend	TransPort	Electricity
	From	1996:01	B	B	0.050	0.025
	To	2004:12	−4.3500	−0.0025	0.050	0.025
8	Flour		_Const	_Trend	TransPort	Electricity
	From	1996:01	B	B	0.050	0.025
	To	2004:12	−2.4725	−0.0021	0.050	0.025
9	BreadRolls		_Const	_Trend	Flour	TransPort
	From	1996:01	B	B	R	0.050
	To	2004:12	−2.1547	0.0008	0.370	0.050
10	Sugar		_Const	_Trend	TransPort	Electricity
	From	2001:07	B	B	0.050	0.025
	To	2004:12	−4.4401	−0.0016	0.050	0.025
11	Sweets		_Const	_Trend	Sugar	TransPort
	From	2001:01	B	B	0.250	0.050
	To	2004:12	−2.9865	−0.0009	0.250	0.050

Cost factors					
3	4	5	6	7	8
Gas	Labc_Sale	Agri_Meat			
0.025	0.150	0.750			
0.025	0.150	0.750			
Gas	Labc_Sale	Labc_Food	Agri_Meat		
0.035	0.150	0.100	0.630		
0.035	0.150	0.100	0.630		
Gas	Labc_Sale	Labc_Food	EU_Fish	huf_EUR	
0.015	0.150	0.150	0.600	0.600	
0.015	0.150	0.150	0.600	0.600	
Gas	Labc_Sale	Agri_Egg			
0.025	0.100	0.800			
0.025	0.100	0.800			
Gas	Labc_Sale	Agri_Milk			
0.025	0.200	0.650			
0.025	0.200	0.650			
Gas	Labc_Sale	Labc_Food	Agri_Milk		
0.025	0.100	0.100	0.700		
0.025	0.100	0.100	0.700		
Gas	Labc_Sale	Labc_Food	EU_Fat	huf_EUR	
0.025	0.100	0.400	0.400	0.400	
0.025	0.100	0.400	0.400	0.400	
Gas	Labc_Sale	Labc_Food	Agri_Wheat		
0.025	0.100	R	R		
0.025	0.100	0.421	0.379		
Electricity	Gas	Labc_Sale	Labc_Food		
0.100	0.100	0.100	R		
0.100	0.100	0.100	0.280		
Gas	Labc_Sale	Labc_Food	EU_Sugar	huf_EUR	
0.050	0.150	0.400	0.325	0.325	
0.050	0.150	0.400	0.325	0.325	
Electricity	Gas	Labc_Sale	Labc_Food	EU_Sugar	huf_EUR
0.100	0.050	0.250	0.250	0.050	0.050
0.100	0.050	0.250	0.250	0.050	0.050

Appendix 2

	Name of the CPI subgroups		Sample period					
						1	2	3
12	OtherCereal			_Const	_Trend	TransPort	Electricity	Gas
		From	1996:01	B	B	0.050	0.030	0.030
		To	2004:12	−4.6327	−0.0010	0.050	0.030	0.030
13	FreshVegetab			_Const	_Trend	TransPort	Labc_Sale	Agr_VegFruit
		From	1996:01	B	B	0.150	0.200	0.650
		To	2004:12	−0.6055	0.0016	0.150	0.200	0.650
14	PreservFood			_Const	_Trend	TransPort	Electricity	Gas
		From	1996:01	B	B	0.050	0.050	0.050
		To	2004:12	−3.5723	−0.0019	0.050	0.050	0.050
15	Meals			_Const	_Trend	TransPort	Electricity	Gas
		From	1997:01	B	B	0.050	0.050	0.050
		To	2004:12	−1.7275	0.0027	0.050	0.050	0.050
16	CoffeTea			_Const	_Trend	TransPort	Electricity	Gas
		From	1996:01	B	B	0.050	0.025	0.025
		To	2004:12	−4.0056	−0.0009	0.050	0.025	0.025
17	AlcBever			_Const	_Trend	Sugar	TransPort	Electricity
		From	1997:01	B	B	0.025	0.050	0.025
		To	2004:12	−4.9600	−0.0001	0.025	0.050	0.025
18	NonAlcBever			_Const	_Trend	Sugar	PreservFood	TransPort
		From	1999:04	B	B	0.025	0.050	0.100
		To	2004:12	−3.6802	0.0012	0.025	0.050	0.100
19	Tobacco			_Const	_Trend	TransPort	Electricity	Gas
		From	1996:01	B	B	0.025	0.025	0.025
		To	2004:12	−4.9758	0.0043	0.025	0.025	0.025
20	ClothMat			_Const	_Trend	TransPort	Electricity	Gas
		From	1998:01	B	B	0.100	0.100	0.100
		To	2004:12	−3.2267	−0.0034	0.100	0.100	0.100
21	Shoes			_Const	_Trend	TransPort	Electricity	Gas
		From	1996:01	B	B	0.050	0.025	0.025
		To	2004:12	−4.4292	−0.0002	0.050	0.025	0.025
22	Clothing			_Const	_Trend	ClothMat	TransPort	Electricity
		From	1997:01	B	B	0.100	0.050	0.025
		To	2004:12	−3.8654	0.0007	0.100	0.050	0.025

Cost factors					
4	5	6	7	8	9
Labc_Sale	Labc_Food	EU_BreadCere	huf_EUR		
0.250	0.350	0.290	0.290		
0.250	0.350	0.290	0.290		
Labc_Sale	Labc_Food	Frisszgyum	EU_OthFood	huf_EUR	Agr_Meat
0.200	0.200	0.100	0.330	0.330	0.020
0.200	0.200	0.100	0.330	0.330	0.020
Labc_Hotel	UnProcMeat	BreadRolls	PreservFood		
0.300	R	0.050	R		
0.300	0.034	0.050	0.466		
Labc_Sale	EU_CoffTeaCo	huf_EUR			
0.250	0.650	0.650			
0.250	0.650	0.650			
Gas	Labc_Sale	Labc_Food	EU_Beverage	huf_EUR	
0.025	0.200	R	R	R	
0.025	0.200	0.551	0.124	0.124	
Electricity	Labc_Sale	Labc_Food	Water	EU_Softdrink	huf_EUR
0.025	0.150	0.150	0.100	0.400	0.400
0.025	0.150	0.150	0.100	0.400	0.400
Labc_Sale	Labc_Food	EU_Tobacco	huf_EUR		
0.150	R	R	R		
0.150	0.385	0.390	0.390		
Labc_Sale	Labc_Cloth	EU_Textil	huf_EUR		
0.150	0.150	0.400	0.400		
0.150	0.150	0.400	0.400		
Labc_Sale	Labc_Cloth	EU_Shoe	huf_EUR		
0.150	0.190	0.560	0.560		
0.150	0.190	0.560	0.560		
Gas	Labc_Sale	Labc_Cloth	EU_Garment	huf_EUR	
0.025	0.150	0.050	0.600	0.600	
0.025	0.150	0.050	0.600	0.600	

Appendix 3

	Name of the CPI subgroups	Sample period			1	2
23	Underwear		_Const	_Trend	ClothMat	TransPort
	From	1996:01	B	B	0.200	0.100
	To	2004:12	−3.2600	0.0000	0.200	0.100
24	Furniture		_Const	_Trend	TransPort	Electricity
	From	1996:01	B	B	0.050	0.025
	To	2004:12	−4.1990	−0.0013	0.050	0.025
25	DurHousGood		_Const	_Trend	TransPort	Electricity
	From	1996:01	B	B	0.050	0.050
	To	2004:12	−4.5002	−0.0031	0.050	0.050
26	Vehicles		_Const	_Trend	TransPort	Electricity
	From	1996:01	B	B	0.050	0.025
	To	2004:12	−4.1529	−0.0033	0.050	0.025
27	DurRecreaGood		_Const	_Trend	TransPort	Electricity
	From	1996:01	B	B	0.050	0.050
	To	2004:12	−4.4181	−0.0047	0.050	0.050
28	CoalWood		_Const	_Trend	TransPort	Labc_Mining
	From	1998:06	B	B	0.200	0.100
	To	2004:12	−3.8647	0.0016	0.200	0.100
29	BPGas		_Const	_Trend	TransPort	Labc_Sale
	From	2001:01	B	B	0.050	0.050
	To	2004:12	−3.6275	0.0020	0.050	0.050
30	HRepMainGood		_Const	_Trend	TransPort	Electricity
	From	1996:01	B	B	0.050	0.025
	To	2004:12	−5.0591	−0.0031	0.050	0.025
31	HouseGood		_Const	_Trend	TransPort	Electricity
	From	1997:01	B	B	0.050	0.025
	To	2004:12	−4.6611	−0.0031	0.050	0.025
32	ChemGoods		_Const	_Trend	TransPort	Electricity
	From	1996:01	B	B	0.050	0.025
	To	2004:12	−4.4951	−0.0012	0.050	0.025
33	Uzemanyag_nt_ft		_Const	_Trend	TransPort	Electricity
	From	1999:01	B	B	0.050	0.025
	To	2004:12	−4.5680	−0.0026	0.050	0.025

Cost factors					
3	4	5	6	7	8
Electricity	Gas	Labc_Sale	Labc_Cloth	EU_UnderWear	huf_EUR
0.025	0.025	0.200	0.150	0.300	0.300
0.025	0.025	0.200	0.150	0.300	0.300
Gas	Labc_Sale	Labc_Wood	EU_Furniture	huf_EUR	
0.025	0.150	0.100	0.650	0.650	
0.025	0.150	0.100	0.650	0.650	
Gas	Labc_Sale	Lapc_Indust	EU_DurHousG	huf_EUR	
0.025	0.250	0.125	0.500	0.500	
0.025	0.250	0.125	0.500	0.500	
Gas	Labc_Sale	Lapc_Indust	EU_Car	huf_EUR	
0.025	0.175	0.175	0.550	0.550	
0.025	0.175	0.175	0.550	0.550	
Gas	Labc_Sale	Lapc_Indust	EU_DurEntG	huf_EUR	
0.025	0.200	0.200	0.475	0.475	
0.025	0.200	0.200	0.475	0.475	
Labc_Sale	EU_SolEnerg	huf_EUR			
0.150	0.550	0.550			
0.150	0.550	0.550			
EU_Gas	huf_EUR				
0.900	0.900				
0.900	0.900				
Gas	Labc_Sale	Lapc_Indust	EU_RepHouseG	huf_EUR	
0.025	0.400	0.400	0.100	0.100	
0.025	0.400	0.400	0.100	0.100	
Gas	Labc_Manuf	Labc_Sale	EU_RepHouse	huf_EUR	
0.025	0.300	0.300	0.300	0.300	
0.025	0.300	0.300	0.300	0.300	
Gas	Labc_Manuf	Labc_Sale	EU_Chemicals	huf_EUR	
0.025	0.250	0.250	0.400	0.400	
0.025	0.250	0.250	0.400	0.400	
Gas	Labc_Manuf	Labc_Sale	huf_USD	usd_OILB_m2	
0.025	0.150	0.100	0.650	0.650	
0.025	0.150	0.100	0.650	0.650	

Appendix 4

	Name of the CPI subgroups	Sample period				
					1	2
34	NewspBook		_Const	_Trend	TransPort	Electricity
	From	1996:01	B	B	0.100	0.050
	To	2004:12	−2.8317	−0.0011	0.100	0.050
35	RecreGFlow		_Const	_Trend	TransPort	Electricity
	From	1996:01	B	B	0.050	0.025
	To	2004:12	−4.6716	−0.0026	0.050	0.025
36	MaintCost		_Const	_Trend	RepairDwell	Disposal
	From	1996:01	B	B	0.125	0.162
	To	2004:12	−1.0646	−0.0005	0.125	0.162
37	RepairDwell		_Const	_Trend	HouseGood	TransPort
	From	1996:01	B	B	R	0.100
	To	2004:12	−1.4429	0.0027	0.661	0.100
38	TransPort		_Const	_Trend	Vehicles	Fuel
	From	1996:01	B	B	0.200	0.300
	To	2004:12	−3.1074	0.0023	0.200	0.300
39	RecreInland		_Const	_Trend	Meals	Electricity
	From	1996:01	B	B	0.100	0.050
	To	2004:12	−3.8563	0.0000	0.100	0.050
40	RecreAbroad		_Const	_Trend	Labc_Service	EU_Recreation
	From	1998:01	B	B	0.750	0.250
	To	2004:12	−5.6529	−0.0024	0.750	0.250
41	Repair		_Const	_Trend	DurHousGood	DurRecreaGooc
	From	1996:01	B	B	R	0.100
	To	2004:12	−1.6524	0.0053	0.523	0.100
42	CultService		_Const	_Trend	Electricity	Gas
	From	1996:01	B	B	0.050	0.050
	To	2004:12	−5.3138	0.0016	0.050	0.050
43	OtherService		_Const	_Trend	ChemGoods	Fuel
	From	1998:07	B	B	0.300	0.100
	To	2004:12	−2.8666	0.0004	0.300	0.100

Cost factors					
3	4	5	6	7	8
Gas	Labc_Sale	Labc_Wood	PPI_WoodPap		
0.050	0.150	R	R		
0.050	0.150	0.588	0.062		
Gas	Labc_Sale	EU_OthFlower	huf_EUR		
0.025	R	R	R		
0.025	0.547	0.353	0.353		
Water	Labc_Service	Sewer			
0.189	0.200	0.324			
0.189	0.200	0.324			
Electricity	Labc_Constr	Labc_Service			
0.025	0.150	R			
0.025	0.150	0.064			
Labc_Service					
0.500					
0.500					
Gas	Labc_Hotel	Labc_Service	EU_Recreation	huf_EUR	
0.050	0.300	0.300	0.200	0.200	
0.050	0.300	0.300	0.200	0.200	
huf_EUR					
0.250					
0.250					
TransPort	Electricity	Gas	Labc_Service		
0.050	0.025	0.025	R		
0.050	0.025	0.025	0.277		
Labc_Service					
0.900					
0.900					
Electricity	Gas	Labc_Service			
0.050	0.050	0.500			
0.050	0.050	0.500			

Notes

* Iam indebted to Zsolt Darvas, whose help was indispensable to construct the model. Also, I am grateful for every comment, recommendation and professional assistance that I received from the Economics Department staff of the MNB and from participants of the 2002 conference of the Economic Modeling Society and the 2005 conference of the European Economics and Finance Society. The remaining errors are those of the author.

1. Svensson (2000) calls this simple inflation control mechanism as 'strict inflation targeting'.
2. At least it is easier to measure CPI than other price index like, for instance, the GDP deflator.
3. Czech Republic, Hungary, Poland, Slovakia and Slovenia.
4. Those readers, who are interested in details, are referred to Hornok–Jakab–Reppa–Villányi [2002] paper, which delivers a full documentation of the inflation forecasting models constructed and used by the MNB.
5. There are 17 goods and services corresponding to 19per cent of CPI basket approximately: sewage disposal, meals at kindergartens, meals at schools, natural and manufactured gas, pharmaceutical products, local transport, rent, travel to work and school, miscellaneous travels, postal services, refuse disposal, gambling, purchased heat, telephone, TV fee, electricity and water charges.
6. See for example the survey paper of Menon (1995) and Glodberg-Knetter (1997).
7. These long-term co-integration-type estimates were estimated with the method of ordinary least squares. The prices of fuel, transport and vehicles are determined simultaneously in the model. Though such prices would have required the application of a different estimation method, however, it was neglected, as, eventually, each cost weight item in this simultaneous sub-system was calibrated.
8. These 143 marketed goods correspond to 81 per cent CPI basket approximately.
9. See Várpalotai (2003) for a detailed description of aggregation.
10. Transport, electricity, and natural and manufactured gas are also components of CPI themselves. Actually, it is their producer prices that would be needed. As they are unavailable, it is assumed that both producer and consumer prices develop identically.
11. Domestic prices of goods are defined exchange rate multiplied by their foreign price indices.
12. For additional details on motor fuel, see Várpalotai (2003).
13. Not the fullest diversity, of course, as price changes in transport pass-through to nearly every group of goods, triggering newer and newer spillover of price changes.
14. The horizon that is relevant from our point of view starts in January 1996.

15. In the case of motor fuels, for instance, excise content accounted for approximately 46 per cent of the final consumer price in July 2004.
16. As is wellknown in macroeconomics, the extent to which changes in excise duty can be 'passed through' to consumers depends on the price elasticity of the demand for and supply of the goods. It follows that if demand is almost completely inelastic (as it is supposed to be the case in, for example, the motor fuel market), then changes in taxes appear in the prices completely.
17. A similar method should have been adopted also in the case of (alcoholic) beverages, tobacco and coffee owing to the large excise content of these goods. However, the intricate regulation on excise duty entangles the calculation of the effective excise rate when a change occurs.
18. For the complete parameterisation, see the Appendix of Várpalotai (2003).
19. Finally, only 18 of the 268 cost factors included in the model have been estimated. Conversely, both constant and trend parameters have been estimated in each equation.
20. Though a few such negative parameters can certainly be attributed to overshooting, I ruled out this case from empirical investigation.
21. It means that when we have 5 cost factors with a 2-year pass-though horizon, this means estimating 5*24–5 = 115 lag parameters. Consequently, several decades of data would be required in this case even at monthly frequency to get reliable estimates.
22. For the exact declaration of vectors and matrices used in (5) quadratic problem, see the appendix of Várpalotai (2003).
23. It is worth mentioning that due to the long lags of some cost factors the effective sample was sometimes shortened by 2 years starting from January 1998.
24. Here the included cost factors are household repairs and maintenance goods, transport, electricity, wages of construction industry and market services.

References

Goldberg, P. K. and Knetter, M. [1997]: Goods prices and exchange rates: What have we learned?, *Journal of Economic Literature*, Vol. 35(3), pp. 1243–72.

Hornok, C. and Jakab, Z. [2002]: Forecasting Inflation: A Case Study on the Czech, Hungarian, Polish, Slovakian and Slovenian Central Banks. MNB Background Studies 2002/3.

Hornok, C., Jakab, Z., Reppa, Z. and Villányi, K. [2002]: Inflation Forecasting at the National Bank of Hungary. MNB mimeo.

Jakab, Z., Kovács, M., Párkányi, B., Reppa, Z. and Vadas, G. [2004]: The Hungarian Quarterly Projection Model (N.E.M.) – Non-technical summary. http://english.mnb.hu/Resource.aspx?ResourceID=mnbfile&resourcename=nem_summary_en

Menon, J. [1995]: Exchange rate pass-through. *Journal of Economic Surveys*, Vol. 9(2), pp. 197–231.

Pagan, A. and Robertson, J. [2002]: Forecasting for Policy. in: *A Companion to Economic Forecasting*, Edited By: Clements, M. and Hendry, D., Blackwell publishing.

Schiller, R. [1973]: A Distributed Lag Estimator Derived from Smoothness Priors. *Econometrica*, Vol. 41, pp. 775–778.

Svensson, L. E. O. [2000]: Open-Economy Inflation Targeting. *Journal of International Economics*, Vol. 50, pp. 155–183.

Várpalotai, V. [2003]: Disaggregated Cost Pass-Through Based Econometric Inflation-Forecasting Model for Hungary. MNB Working Paper 2003/4.

Part III

Exchange Rates Dynamics and Structural Shocks on Economies

6
An Open Economy Dynamic General Equilibrium Model Linking the Euro Area and the US Economy

Gregory de Walque and Raf Wouters

6.1 Introduction

Over the last decade, the 'New Open Economy Model' (NOEM) has become the standard model to analyse the behaviour of the exchange rate and the current account. This model is based on the optimising behaviour of the microeconomic units, firms and households, in a monopolistic competitive environment with nominal rigidities in the price and wage setting. Consumption and investment goods are aggregate baskets of domestic and foreign goods, which are considered as imperfect substitutes. Demand is allocated between these goods based on the real exchange rate. The current account is consistently explained by the intertemporal decisions on the one hand, that is the savings minus investment identity, and the intratemporal decisions, that is the allocation of demand depending on the relative price of the domestic and foreign goods, on the other hand. The exchange rate is determined by the uncovered interest rate parity condition. In the literature, these models have been used intensively to discuss the issue of optimal monetary policy and of international policy co-ordination.

Most of the work on the NOEM is highly theoretical and based on small stylised models. Recently a series of larger and more realistic open and two (or multi-) country models, based on these same principles, have been constructed within central banks.[1] These models include extensions in the form of more realistic nominal rigidities, capital accumulation with adjustment costs, labour markets, differentiated sectors, etc.

Ghironi (1999), Bergin (2004), Lubik and Schorfheide (2003) have started to estimate small scale NOEModels. Recent advances in Bayesian estimation techniques have made it feasible to estimate larger scale models. Smets and Wouters (2003a,b,c) applied these approaches to closed economy models for the Euro area and the *US* economy. The underlying model and the estimated coefficients show that both economies are very similar both in terms of underlying shocks, structure and monetary policy behaviour. Adolfson et al. (2004) recently applied very similar techniques to an open economy model for the Euro area. In this contribution, we extend previous work and present some preliminary results on an empirical two-country DSGE model for the Euro area and the *US*.

Section 2 of the chapter describes the model. Following the approach in Smets and Wouters (2002), we assume that the import prices are sticky and set according to the Calvo model. This implies that the pass-through of foreign price and exchange rate fluctuations is gradual but complete in the long run. The import and export decisions are characterised by adjustment costs in order to smooth the impact of relative prices on the allocation of demand. We also include oil in the model as a fraction of the consumption bundle and as an input in the production function. Finally, we adopt the assumption that international capital markets are imperfect, with the effect that the accumulation of net foreign assets affects domestic absorption.

The data and estimations are discussed in section 3. The estimation of an open economy model and more in particular the estimation of the intra-temporal elasticity of substitution between domestic and foreign goods creates a specific problem. The standard assumption in the NOEM literature is that this elasticity is larger than one and similar in nature to the substitution elasticity between individual goods. In macroeconomic import and export equations this elasticity is typically estimated with a large uncertainty and is often quite small, sometimes even insignificantly different from zero (e.g. Chinn, 2003; Anderton et al., 2004). Different values for the substitution elasticity over this range have very different implications for the functioning of the open economy model (cf. Corsetti et al., 2003). The reaction of the exchange rate to shocks is not continuous over this range of parameter values and around some critical parameter value between zero and one the exchange rate will be extremely volatile. This characteristic of the model makes the estimation outcome dependent on the starting values for the substitution parameter, as the parameter will never succeed in crossing the critical value. We will compare the estimation outcomes for two different starting values of the substitution elasticity and discuss the implications for the overall model behaviour.

Based on the model estimates, section 4 reviews the major implications of alternative shocks (productivity shocks, preference or spending shocks, monetary policy and exchange rate risk premium shocks and shocks originated in the rest of the world) on the exchange rate and the current account. The different impact of alternative types of technology shocks is an interesting issue in this context. Our results confirm the results of Benigno and Thoenissen (2002) in that positive productivity shocks and declining mark-ups, or the typical characteristics of the new economy, are unable to explain a major appreciation of the exchange rate. We also check in section 5 whether the estimated model is able to reproduce a series of stylised facts of the open economies as represented by the standard deviations, autocorrelations and correlations between the exchange rate, net exports, output and demand components. In its present state, the model has clearly some problems to replicate the observed international synchronisation in the cyclical output and aggregate demand components. It remains a topic for further research to analyse how much of the observed correlation between the output of the two major economies can be explained once we allow for a positive correlation between the domestic shocks that hit the two economies (which are assumed to be orthogonal in the estimation approach up to now). However, our model captures correctly the traditional open economy puzzle of the NOEM, i.e. the low and positive correlation between relative consumption and the real exchange rate.

Starting from the impulse-responses for the different types of shocks, the joint behaviour of the domestic variables and the typical open economy variables (the exchange rate and the net trade balance) will be informative to identify the contribution of the major shocks over this period. In particular, we can identify the major sources of exchange rate and current account developments. This is of interest since the literature on this issue delivered mixed results (Clarida and Gali, 1994; Bergin, 2004). In our model, shocks originating in the Uncovered Interest Rate Parity (hereafter UIRP) deviations turn out to be very important for explaining the short run volatility in the exchange rate, but fundamental shocks explain an important fraction of the long run swings. The trade balance is also affected by UIRP shocks over the medium run and by various supply shocks over longer horizons. We may also look at the importance of the different spillover or transmission mechanisms between these two major economies. The typical domestic shocks to productivity and preferences in the two economies have a significant effect on the trade balance, at least over a longer horizon, but their impact on the output of the foreign economy turns out to be largely compensated by offsetting wealth effects on the domestic demand components.

6.2 Model description

The model used in this contribution links the closed economy models for the Euro area and the *US* presented in Smets and Wouters (2003c). It is a two-country model with a small block for the Rest of the World, which is treated mostly as exogenous. There is some asymmetry in the model in that it is assumed that the goods of the Rest of the World and oil are priced in *US* dollar. The Euro-US dollar exchange rate therefore also applies to the trade of the Euro area with the Rest of the World. As a consequence the exchange rate has a potentially more important effect on the Euro area than it has on the *US* economy (for instance the pass-through will be more important for the Euro area than for the *US* economy). The *US* economy is modelled exactly as the *EU* one, while the Rest of the World economy, denoted R, is captured through a simplified structure.

6.2.1 Households

In each country, there is a continuum of households indicated by index $\tau \in [0,1]$, each one supplying a differentiated labour. The instantaneous utility function of each household depends positively on the consumption (C_t^τ) relative to an external habit variable (H_t^τ) and negatively on labour supply (l_t^τ):

$$U_t^\tau = \left(\frac{\left(C_t^\tau - H_t\right)^{1-\sigma_c}}{1-\sigma_c} + \varepsilon_t^L \right) \cdot \exp\left(\frac{\sigma_c - 1}{1+\sigma_l} \left(l_l^\tau\right)^{1+\sigma_l} \right) \tag{1}$$

$$\text{with } \varepsilon_t^L = \rho_L \varepsilon_{t-1}^L + \eta_t^L \text{ with } \eta_t^L \text{ an i.i.d.-Normal error term} \tag{2}$$

where σ_c is the inverse of the intertemporal elasticity of substitution and σ_l represents the inverse of the elasticity of work effort with respect to real wage. Equation (1) also contains ε_t^L, a preference shock to the labour supply. The external habit variable is assumed to be proportional to aggregate past consumption: $H_t = hC_{t-1}$. Each household maximises an inter-temporal utility function given by:

$$E_0 \sum_{t=0}^{\infty} \beta^t \cdot \varepsilon_t^b \cdot U_t^\tau \tag{3}$$

$$\text{with } \varepsilon_t^b = \rho_b \varepsilon_{t-1}^b + \eta_t^b \text{ with } \eta_t^b \text{ an i.i.d.-Normal error term} \tag{4}$$

where β is the discount factor and ε_t^b is a second preference shock affecting the discount rate that determines the intertemporal substitution decisions of households.

A household's total income consists of three components: labour income plus the net cash inflows from participating in state-contingent securities, the return on the capital stock diminished of the cost associated with variations in the degree of capital utilisation and the dividends derived from the imperfect competitive intermediate firms described in the domestic sector subsection below:

$$Y_t^\tau = (w_t^\tau l_t^\tau + A_t^\tau) + (r_t^k z_t^\tau K_{t-1}^\tau - \psi(z_t^\tau) K_{t-1}^\tau) + Div_t^\tau \tag{5}$$

The assumption of state-contingent securities implies that households are insured against variations in household specific labour income so that the first term in the total income is equal to aggregate labour income and the marginal utility of wealth is identical across households.

Households maximise their objective function subject to an intertemporal budget constraint which is given by

$$\frac{1}{R_t}\frac{B_t^T}{P_t} + \frac{1}{I_t \cdot R_t^*}\frac{B_t^{T*}}{S_t P_t} = \frac{B_{t-1}^T}{P_t} + \frac{B_{t-1}^{T*}}{S_t P_t} + Y_t^T - C_t^T - I_t^T \tag{6}$$

Households hold their financial wealth in the form of domestic bonds B_t^T and foreign bonds B_t^{T*}. Current income and financial wealth can be used for consumption and investment in physical capital. Bonds are one period securities with gross nominal rate of return R_t and $I_t \cdot R_t^*$ respectively for the domestic and foreign bonds. Imperfect integration of the financial market is introduced via I_t. Following Benigno (2001) and Laxton and Pesenti (2003), it represents a premium on foreign bonds holdings and is defined as

$$I_t = \Xi\left(\frac{B_t^{T*}}{S_t P_t}\right) + \varepsilon_t^S \tag{7}$$

with $\Xi(\cdot) > 0$, $\Xi(1) = 1$ and $\Xi' < 0$

$$\varepsilon_t^S = \rho_S \varepsilon_{t-1}^S + \eta_t^S \text{ with } \eta_t^S \text{ an i.i.d.-Normal error term} \tag{8}$$

so that the foreign interest rate faced by the households is increased by the premium when the domestic economy is a net borrower and reduced by the premium when it is a net lender. This guarantees that in steady state, there is no incentive to hold foreign bonds so that the steady state net foreign position is zero. The risk premium is affected by a time-varying shock ε_t^S which plays the role of an uncovered interest parity shock.

Maximising (3) subject to the budget constraint (6) with respect to consumption and holdings of bonds, yields the following first-order conditions:

$$E_t\left[\beta\frac{\lambda_{t+1}}{\lambda_t}\cdot\frac{R_t P_t}{P_{t+1}}\right] = 1 \tag{9}$$

$$E_t\left[\beta\frac{\lambda_{t+1}}{\lambda_t}\cdot\frac{S_t}{S_{t+1}}\frac{I_tR_t^*P_t}{P_{t+1}}\right]=1 \tag{10}$$

where λ_t is the marginal utility of consumption, which is given by:

$$\lambda_t=\varepsilon_t^b\cdot(C_t-H_t)^{-\sigma_c}\cdot\exp\left(\frac{\sigma_c-1}{1+\sigma_l}(l_t^\tau)^{1+\sigma_l}\right) \tag{11}$$

Equations (9) and (10) give the uncovered interest rate parity for the determination of nominal exchange rate:

$$\frac{R_t}{I_tR_t^*}=\frac{S_t}{S_{t+1}} \tag{12}$$

The labour supply and wage setting processes are modelled as in Smets and Wouters (2003a,b). Households are price-setters in the labour market and, following Calvo (1983), they can set optimally their wage with a probability $1-\xi_w$. With the complementary probability, their wage is partially indexed to the consumption price. Optimising households choose the nominal wage $\tilde{w}_t$ in order to maximise their intertemporal objective function (3) subject to the intertemporal budget constraint (6) and the following labour demand

$$l_t^\tau=\left(\frac{W_t^\tau}{W_t}\right)^{-\frac{1+\lambda_{w,t}}{\lambda_{w,t}}}L_t \tag{13}$$

where the aggregate labour demand and aggregate nominal wage are respectively

$$L_t=\left[\int_0^1(l_t^\tau)^{\frac{1}{1+\lambda_{w,t}}}d\tau\right]^{1+\lambda_{w,t}}\text{and } W_t=\left[\int_0^1(W_t^\tau)^{-\frac{1}{\lambda_{w,t}}}d\tau\right]^{-\lambda_{w,t}} \tag{14}$$

Shocks to the wage markup are assumed to be i.i.d.-Normal around a constant: $\lambda_{w,t}=\lambda_w+\eta_t^w$.

The investment, capital utilisation and capital accumulation decisions by the households replicate exactly Smets and Wouters (2003a,b). Variations in the capital utilisation and in investment are assumed to incur adjustment costs. A shock $\varepsilon_t^I=\rho_I\varepsilon_{t-1}^I+\eta_t^I$ (with η_t^I an i.i.d.-Normal error term) is introduced in the investment cost function.

6.2.2 The firms and price setting

6.2.2.1 The consumption and capital goods sectors

As displayed in the previous sub-section, two different final goods enter the model, one serving consumption purposes while the other is a physical capital good. Each of these goods is produced by a different sector and both final good sectors are perfectly competitive. Final goods are produced with a domestically produced good and an imported good which are both aggregated indexes of differentiated goods.

The final good consumed (resp. invested) in the *EU* economy is the composite of three goods, labelled *domestic* ($D_{c,t}$ or resp. $D_{i,t}$), *imports* ($M_{c,t}$ or resp. $M_{i,t}$) and *oil* ($o_{c,t}$ or resp. $o_{i,t}$). The c subscript stands for the consumption final good sector while the i subscript indicates the investment final good sector. In order to shorten the presentation, let us indicate the sector by a subscript s with $s \in \{c,i\}$.

The *domestic* and *imports* inputs are combined through a CES technology. As in Erceg, Guerrieri and Gust (2003) and Laxton and Pesenti (2003), the allocation of final domestic demand between the baskets of domestic and foreign goods depends on the relative price of the two goods and is subject to a reallocation adjustment cost. This adjustment cost implies that the reallocation between domestic and imported goods will happen only gradually, depending on the perceived persistence of the relative price changes.

$$\Omega_{s,t} = \left[\mu_s^{\frac{\rho_s}{1+\rho_s}} D_{s,t}^{\frac{1}{1+\rho_s}} + (1-\mu_s)^{\frac{\rho_s}{1+\rho_s}} (\phi_{s,t} M_{s,t})^{\frac{1}{1+\rho_s}} \right]^{1+\rho_s} \tag{15}$$

where $(1+\rho_s)/\rho_s$ is the elasticity of substitution between domestically produced and $\phi_{s,t}$ imported goods and reflects the adjustment cost. Parameter μ_s translates the preference for domestically made products. Note that $\mu_i < \mu_c$ so that the investment goods have a higher import content. The adjustment cost is assumed to take the form

$$\phi_{s,t} = \left[1 - \phi_s \left(1 - \frac{M_{s,t} / D_{s,t}}{M_{s,t-1} / D_{s,t-1}} \right)^2 \right] \tag{16}$$

The domestic final good S_t (with $S_t = C_t$ if $s = c$ and $S_t = I_t$ if $s = i$) is then produced from the intermediate good $\Omega_{s,t}$ and oil $o_{s,t}$ following a Leontieff technology with a fixed proportion θ_s of *oil*:

$$S_t = \min\{(1 - \theta_s)\cdot\Omega_{s,t}; \theta_s\cdot o_{s,t}\} \tag{17}$$

Each firm of the final good sector maximises its expected profit using a discount rate $\beta\,\Lambda_t$, with $\Lambda_{t+k} = \lambda_{t+k} / \lambda_t P_{s,t+k}$ where λ_t is the marginal utility of consumption and $P_{s,t}$ the final good price index. The producer of the final good chooses $D_{s,t}$ and $M_{s,t}$ in order to maximise the discounted profit

$$\max_{D_{s,t},\, M_{s,t}} \sum_{i=0}^{\infty} \beta^i \Lambda_{t+i}\left[P_{s,t+i}\, S_{t+i} - P_{t+i}^{D}\, D_{s,t+i} - P_{s,t+i}^{M}\, M_{s,t+i} - P_{t+i}^{o}\, o_{s,t+i}\right]$$

where P_t^D is the price index of the domestically produced good, $P_{s,t}^M$ the price index of the imported good and P_t^o the oil price.

Three subsectors are then left to model: a domestically produced intermediate good sector, an import sector for consumption goods and an import sector for capital goods.

6.2.2.2 The domestic intermediate good sector

The *domestic* good is produced from a continuum of intermediate goods y_t^j domestically produced and indexed j, with $j \in [0,1]$. The domestic good does not only serve domestic purposes but may also be exported, so that total domestic production Y_t is larger than the domestic demand of domestically produced good $D_{c,t} + D_{i,t}$. Assuming a CES technology,

$$Y_t = \left[\int_0^1 \left(y_t^j\right)^{1/1+\lambda_{p,t}} dj\right]^{1+\lambda_{p,t}} \tag{18}$$

where y_t^j is the quantity of intermediate good j used in the domestically produced good. Parameter $\lambda_{p,t}$ is stochastic and determines the time varying mark-up in the market of the domestically produced goods. It is assumed that $\lambda_{p,t} = \lambda_p + \eta_t^p$, with η_t^p i.i.d.-Normal. The shock η_t^p is interpreted as a 'cost-push' shock to the inflation equation. From the cost minimisation, one obtains the demand of each intermediate producer:

$$y_t^j = \left(\frac{p_t^j}{P_t^D}\right)^{-\frac{1+\lambda_{p,t}}{\lambda_{p,t}}} Y_t \tag{19}$$

and the index of the domestically produced good is

$$P_t^D = \left[\int_0^1 \left(p_t^j\right)^{-1/\lambda_{p,t}} dj\right]^{-\lambda_{p,t}} \tag{20}$$

Intermediate goods y_t^j are produced in a monopolistic competitive sector with a continuum of firms characterised with sticky prices. They are produced with a Cobb–Douglas technology nested in a Leontieff production function:

$$v_{j,t} = \varepsilon_t^a \cdot \left(\tilde{K}_{j,t}\right)^{\alpha} \cdot \left(L_{j,t} \cdot e^{\gamma \cdot t}\right)^{1-\alpha} \tag{21}$$

$$y_t^j = \min\{\omega \cdot v_{j,t}; (1-\omega) \cdot o_{j,t}\} - \Phi \cdot e^{\gamma \cdot t} \tag{22}$$

with $\varepsilon_t^a = \rho_a \varepsilon_{t-1}^a + \eta_t^a + \varepsilon_t^\gamma$ (η_t^a is i.i.d.-Normal) (23)

$$\varepsilon_t^\gamma = \rho_\gamma \varepsilon_{t-1}^\gamma + \eta_t^\gamma \ (\eta_t^\gamma \text{ is i.i.d.-Normal}) \tag{24}$$

where ε_t^a is a level productivity shock, ε_t^γ a growth rate shock, $\tilde{K}_{j,t} = z_t \cdot K_{j,t-1}$ the capital stock effectively utilised, $L_{j,t}$ an index of various types of labour hired by the firm, γ the constant rate of technological progress and Φ a fixed cost introduced to ensure zero profits in steady state. The fixed cost and variable capital utilisation assumptions smooth the reaction of employment and marginal costs following a shock. Variable $o_{j,t}$ is the oil necessary for the production process and parameter ω represents its share.

Cost minimisation implies

$$\frac{v_{j,t}}{o_{j,t}} = \frac{1-\omega}{\omega} \text{ and } \frac{W_t L_{j,t}}{r_{j,t}^k \tilde{K}_{j,t}} = \frac{1-\alpha}{\alpha} \quad \forall j \in [0,1] \tag{25}$$

and the marginal cost is given by

$$MC_t = (1 - \omega)\frac{W_t^{1-\alpha} \cdot \left(r_t^k\right)^{\alpha}}{\alpha^{\alpha}(1 - \alpha)^{1-\alpha} \cdot \varepsilon_t^a \cdot \varepsilon_t^{\gamma t(1-\alpha)}} + \omega\,\frac{P_t^o}{S_t} \tag{26}$$

The real marginal cost contains the cost of capital, the real wage and the real price of oil. Because the real wage for the firm is deflated by the domestic producer price, the real marginal cost will also contain a terms of trade effect if the wage is deflated by the consumer price index. The assumption of perfect mobility of capital between firms involves that the marginal cost is identical for all firms $j \in [0,1]$. Nominal profits for firm j are computed as

$$\pi_t^j = (p_t^j - MC_t)\left(\frac{p_t^j}{P_t^D}\right)^{-\frac{1+\lambda_{p,t}}{\lambda_{p,t}}} Y_t - MC_t \Phi e^{\gamma t} \tag{27}$$

In a Calvo pricing system with a probability $1 - \xi_p$ of re-optimising prices, the objective function of the firm j is

$$\max_{p_t^j} E_t \sum_{i=0}^{\infty} \left(\beta\xi_p\right)^i \Lambda_{t+i}\left(\tilde{p}_t^j \cdot \left(\frac{P_{t-1+i}^D}{P_{t-1}^D}\right)^{\gamma_p}\left(\pi_{t+i}\right)^{1-\gamma_p} - MC_{t+i}\right) y_{t+i}^j \tag{28}$$

where $\beta\Lambda_t$ is the discount rate and $\left(P_{t-1+i}^D / P_{t-1}^D\right)^{\gamma_p}\left(\pi_{t+i}\right)^{1-\gamma_p}$, the indexation device used in the economy. Note that firms set the same price in the domestic and the foreign market. In other words, the assumption of producer currency pricing for export goods is retained.

The nominal value added for firm j can be easily computed as

$$VA_t^j = y_t^j \cdot p_t^j - o_{j,t}\frac{P_t^o}{S_t} = y_t^j \cdot \left(p_t^j - \omega\frac{P_t^o}{S_t}\right) \tag{29}$$

where the second equality is obtained from the cost minimisation. Aggregating over j one gets

$$VA_t = Y_t \cdot \left(P_t^D - \omega\frac{P_t^o}{S_t}\right) \tag{30}$$

and the second term on the RHS of the last expression represents the value added deflator.

6.2.2.3 *Import sector*

As presented in the final goods section supra, the import sector is divided into two subsectors, one dealing with consumption goods (denoted by subscript *c*) and the other with capital goods (denoted by subscript *i*). In order to shorten the presentation, let us adopt the same notation as supra and denote import sectors by subscript $s \in \{c,i\}$.

Imports are made up from the output of two subsectors, one active in the *US* economy and the other in the Rest of the World. These goods are produced with the technology:

$$M_{s,t} = \left[\nu_s^{\frac{\iota_s}{1+\iota_s}} \left(M_{s,t}^{US} \right)^{\frac{1}{1+\iota_s}} (1+\nu_s)^{\frac{\iota_s}{1+\iota_s}} \left(\phi_{s,t}^{M} M_{s,t}^{R} \right)^{\frac{1}{1+\iota_s}} \right]^{1+\iota_s} \quad (31)$$

where it is considered that it is costly to adjust the proportion of inputs and the adjustment cost variable $\phi_{s,t}^{M}$ is as described in (16). Consumption goods importers seek to maximise the discounted profit

$$\max_{M_{s,t}^{US},\, M_{s,t}^{R}} \sum_{i=0}^{\infty} \beta^i \Lambda_{t+i} \left[P_{s,t+i}^{M} \cdot M_{s,t+i} - P_{s,t+i}^{M,US} M_{s,t+i}^{US} - P_{s,t+i}^{M,R} M_{s,t+i}^{R} \right] \quad (32)$$

where $P_{s,t}^{M}$ is the price index for imported consumption goods.

Each of the inputs ($M_{s,t}^{US}$ and $M_{s,t}^{R}$) are processed from a continuum of importing firms indexed by *l*, with $l \in [0,1]$. Importing firms operating in the $r \in \{US, R\}$ economy buy the homogeneous good Y_t^r produced in the *r* economy at the $P_t^{D,r}$ price in the producer currency and differentiate it, e.g. by brand naming. The differentiated good they produce is then sold on the domestic market at price $p_{s,t}^{M,l,r}$. It is assumed that importers can set optimally their price according to a random Calvo process with probability $(1 - \xi_m^s)$ and then $p_{s,t}^{M,l,r} = \tilde{p}_{s,t}^{M,l,r}$. Contrarily to what is assumed in the domestic sector, the share ξ_m^s of the importers who cannot optimise their price do not index it to the last period inflation (cf. Smets and Wouters, 2002).

Depending on the degree of nominal stickiness, the pass-through of the exchange rate will be slower or quicker. In the long run, the pass-through is complete. This assumption seems to give a realistic empirical description of the pass-through process as identified in detailed empirical tests. Most empirical studies indeed report only a partial pass-through in the short run, a pass-through that is also very different between countries and sectors, but in the long run the hypothesis of complete pass-through cannot be rejected in most cases (cf. for example Campa and Goldberg, 2002).

Nominal profits for firm l importing consumption goods from the $r \in \{US,R\}$ economy are computed as

$$\pi_{s,t}^{M,l,r} = \left(p_{s,t}^{M,l,r} - MC_{s,t}^{M,l,r}\right) \cdot m_{s,t}^{l,r} - MC_{s,t}^{M,l,r} \Phi_{s,m}^{r} \tag{33}$$

with $m_s^{l,r}$ is the quantity of the differentiated good l used in the composite good imported from country $r \in \{US,R\}, \Phi_{s,m}^{r}$ is a fixed cost and $MC_s^{M,l,r}$ its marginal cost defined as

$$MC_{s,t}^{M,l,r} = \frac{P_t^{D,r}}{S_t^r} \tag{34}$$

with S_t^r the r country currency units you can buy with one EU currency unit. When setting optimally their price, import firms face the following problem:

$$\max_{\tilde{p}_{s,t}^{M,l,r}} E_t \sum_{n=0}^{\infty} \left(\beta \xi_m^s\right)^n \left(\frac{\lambda_{t+n}}{\lambda_t P_{s,t+n}^{M,r}}\right) \left(\tilde{p}_{s,t}^{M,l,r} - MC_{s,t+n}^{M,r}\right) m_{s,t+n}^{l,r} \tag{35}$$

Assuming that the differentiated import goods are combined through a CES technology, we have

$$M_{s,t}^{r} = \left[\int_0^1 \left(m_{s,t}^{l,r}\right)^{\frac{1}{1+\lambda_{m,t}}} dl\right]^{1+\lambda_{m,t}} \tag{36}$$

and the demand faced by each importing firm is

$$m_{s,t}^{l,r} = M_{s,t}^{r} \cdot \left(\frac{P_{s,t}^{M,l,r}}{P_{s,t}^{M,r}}\right)^{-\frac{1+\lambda_{m,t}}{\lambda_{m,t}}} \tag{37}$$

Parameter $\lambda_{m,t}$ is stochastic and determines the time varying mark-up in the imported goods market. Shocks to the imported goods price mark-up are assumed to be i.i.d.-Normal around a constant.

Exports are simply the result of the *US* and Rest of the World import firms that are active on the domestic market:

$$X_t = M_{c,t}^{US,EU} + M_{c,t}^{R,EU} + M_{i,t}^{US,EU} + M_{i,t}^{R,EU}$$

6.2.3 Balance of payments

The current account relationship determines the accumulation of foreign assets B_t^*

$$\frac{1}{I_t \cdot R_t^*} \frac{B_t^*}{S_t P_t} - \frac{B_{t-1}^*}{S_t P_t} = \frac{P_t^D}{P_t} X_t - \frac{P_t^M}{S_t P_t} M_t - \frac{P_t^o}{S_t P_t} o_t$$

The trade balance is the difference between the real value of exports and the real value of imports and oil inputs. Oil intervenes both in the final good production and the intermediary domestic good production process, so that

$$o_t = \theta_c \cdot C_t + \theta_i \cdot I_t + \omega \cdot Y_t$$

The demand for oil is assumed to be proportional to total demand and total production: no substitution effects are allowed. The oil price feeds immediately into the consumer price without any rigidity, while the oil price affects the domestic output price gradually through the marginal production cost and the Calvo price setting assumption. As the domestic sales price only adjusts gradually to an increase in the oil price, the GDP deflator will initially decline following an increase in oil prices.

6.2.4 Market equilibrium

The final good market is in equilibrium if the production equals the demand by domestic consumers and investors, the government, and foreign import firms operating in the domestic country:

$$Y_t = D_{c,t} + D_{i,t} + G_t + X_t \tag{38}$$

Government spendings are assumed to be realised exclusively in domestic goods. They are introduced as an AR(1) shock with an i.i.d.-Normal residual: $\varepsilon_t^g = \rho_g \varepsilon_{t-1}^g + \eta_t^g$. The capital rental market is in equilibrium if the demand for capital expressed by the intermediate goods domestic producer equals the supply by the households. Equilibrium on the labour market is realised if the firm's labour demand equals the labour supply at the wage set by the households.

The interest rate is determined by a reaction function describing monetary policy decisions. At equilibrium in the capital market, the government debt is held by domestic or foreign investors at rate R_t.

6.2.5 The *US* economy and the rest of the world

The *US* economy is modelled similarly to the *EU* economy described above. The Rest of the World is modelled as a small third country that imports and exports goods to the United States and the Euro area. Its prices are expressed in dollars. In this respect, the representation of the Rest of the World does not require as much detail as the two other countries and only the variables describing exchanges between the third country and the two others will be considered.

Absorption (excluding government spending) in economy *R* as well as the price index of the domestically produced good in economy *R* is represented by an AR(1) process. In other words, both the Rest of the World demand and the Rest of the World production price are modelled as exogenous shocks:

$$C_t^R + I_t^R = \varepsilon_t^{DR} = \rho_{DR}\varepsilon_{t-1}^{DR} + \eta_t^{DR} \text{ with } \eta_t^{DR} \text{ an i.i.d.-shock} \tag{39}$$

$$P_t^R \equiv \varepsilon_t^{PR} = \rho_{PR}\varepsilon_{t-1}^{PR} + \eta_t^{PR} \text{ with } \eta_t^{PR} \text{ an i.i.d.-shock} \tag{40}$$

Both these shocks act as global shocks to the two other economies considered in the model. Domestic absorption $C_t^R + I_t^R$ is also validly represented by equations (15) to (17) and the import sector is similar to this described for the *EU* and *US* economies but for the (31) equation which becomes

$$M_{s,t} = \left[v_s^{\frac{\iota_s}{1+\iota_s}} \left(M_{s,t}^{EU} \right)^{\frac{1}{1+\iota_s}} (1 + v_s)^{\frac{\iota_s}{1+\iota_s}} \left(\varepsilon_t^{MR} \phi_{s,t}^{M} M_{s,t}^{US} \right)^{\frac{1}{1+\iota_s}} \right]^{1+\iota_s} \tag{41}$$

with $\varepsilon_t^{MR} = \rho_{MR}\varepsilon_{t-1}^{MR} + \eta_t^{MR}$ with η_t^{MR} an i.i.d.-Normal error term.

The latter shock represents an exogenous shift in the preferences of the Rest of the World with respect to *US* goods. Contrarily to the ε_t^{DR}

shock, this foreign demand shock does not affect symmetrically the *EU* and *US* economies.

6.2.6 The monetary policy

Monetary policy is governed by a generalised Taylor reaction rule. The interest rate reacts on current and lagged CPI inflation, output gap and the lagged interest rate. The output gap is defined as the natural output gap, i.e. the output level that would prevail in the flexible economy driven by the fundamental shocks to technology and preferences, and the actual or sticky price output level. The monetary reaction function in its linearised form is given by

$$\hat{R}_t = \rho\left(\hat{R}_{t-1} - \bar{\pi}_{t-1}\right) + (1-\rho)\left[r_k\left(\hat{\pi}_{c,t-1} - \bar{\pi}_{t-1}\right) + r_Y\left(\hat{Y}_{t-1} - \hat{Y}^p_{t-1}\right)\right]$$

$$+ r_{\Delta\pi}\left[\left(\hat{\pi}_{c,t} - \bar{\pi}_t\right) - \left(\hat{\pi}_{c,t-1} - \bar{\pi}_{t-1}\right)\right] + r_{\Delta Y}\left[\left(\hat{Y}_t - \hat{Y}^p_t\right) - \left(\hat{Y}_{t-1} - \hat{Y}^p_{t-1}\right)\right]$$

$$+ \bar{\pi}_t + \sigma_c\left(1-\rho\right)\varepsilon^\gamma_t + \eta^R_t$$

The parameter ρ captures the degree of interest rate smoothing and the reaction function includes a short run feedback from the current changes in inflation and the output gap. Two monetary policy shocks are considered: one is a temporary i.i.d.-Normal interest rate shock (η^R_t) and the other is a permanent shock to the inflation objective ($\bar{\pi}_t$) which is assumed to follow a random walk process ($\bar{\pi}_t = \bar{\pi}_{t-1} + \eta^\pi_t$). Note that a correction on the real interest rate is included to prevent unrealistic effects of a persistent growth rate shock.

6.2.7 Structural shocks summary

In order to apply the model for estimation on a series of 20 macroeconomic time series a whole set of independent structural shocks are added to the model:

1. the domestic economy shocks:
   level TFP shocks (equ. 23); growth rate TFP shocks (equ. 24); investment specific technology shocks (ε^I_t); public expenditure

shocks (ε_t^g in (38)); intertemporal preference shocks on consumption (equ. 4); labour supply shocks (equ. 2); permanent mark-up shocks in the consumption price; mark-up shocks in domestic prices (η_t^p in (18)), in wages (η_t^w in (13)) and in asset prices; monetary policy shocks ($\bar{\pi}_t$ in (43)); permanent inflation objective shocks (in (43));

the Rest of the World shocks (all persistent AR(1) processes close upthe Rest of the World demand shocks (equ. 39); preference shocks in the demand for Euro area or *US* good (equ. 42); shocks in the export price of the Rest of the World good (equ. 40); oil price shocks (ε_t^o); uncovered interest rate parity shocks (equ. 8);

6.3 Data and estimation

The model presented above has been estimated with a Bayesian full information approach following the applications in Smets and Wouters (2003a,b). The twenty macroeconomic time series used for estimation are 9-country specific variables plus the exchange rate (USD-EUR) and inflation in the oil price.[2] The 9country-specific series are the real GDP, consumption and investment expenditures, real wages, inflation in the CPI and the import deflator, the short term interest rate, the real trade balance and employment (or hours worked for the US).[3]

The estimation period is 1974:1–2003:4 so that it is consistent with the Smets and Wouters (2003c) exercise. A series of structural parameters is calibrated to reflect more or less the average historical values: e.g. the degree of openness is reflected in the share of foreign goods in aggregate demand. The import share of investment goods (0.4) is assumed to be higher than the import share of consumption goods (0.12). The oil content of final demand and production process are set at 0.35 per cent and 0.85 per cent respectively. The estimated parameters are displayed in Table 6.1.

The model parameters for the two economies are very similar confirming the results of Smets and Wouters (2003c). The number of open economy parameters is voluntarily kept small. The import sectors in both economies are assumed to share the same Calvo parameter, which determines the pass-through of exchange rate fluctuations to prices. The adjustment cost (resp. the substitution elasticity)

Table 6.1 Parameter estimates

		Prior distribution		Estimated mode (starting value > 0.6 for the elasticity of substitution) Laplace approximation 2643.1530		Estimated mode (starting value < 0.6 for the elasticity of substitution) Laplace approximation 2571.746	
	Type	Mean	Std. err.	Mode	Std.err.	Mode	Std.err.
Open economy							
import share adj. cost.	Normal	2.000	0.500	2.384	0.490	1.977	0.496
σ subst. (Home and For. goods)	Normal	1.500	0.500	1.210	0.061	0.216	0.062
calvo imp.	beta	0.750	0.050	0.859	0.013	0.819	0.013
ρ UIRP shock	beta	0.850	0.100	0.829	0.028	0.863	0.020
ρ ROW dem. shock	beta	0.850	0.100	0.891	0.049	0.989	0.005
ρ ROW price shock	beta	0.850	0.100	0.953	0.015	0.956	0.021
ρ ROW pref. shock	beta	0.850	0.100	0.983	0.004	0.991	0.004
ρ oil price shock	beta	0.850	0.100	0.958	0.014	0.958	0.015
UIRP shock	inv gamma	0.250	2.000	0.834	0.151	0.719	0.117
ROW dem. shock	inv gamma	0.250	2.000	2.469	0.184	2.509	0.165
ROW price shock	inv gamma	0.250	2.000	10.000	1.985	10.000	1.623
ROW pref. shock	inv gamma	0.250	2.000	6.365	0.467	5.375	0.348
oil price shock	inv gamma	0.250	2.000	0.178	0.011	0.178	0.011

Euro area							
ρ prod. shock	beta	0.850	0.100	0.999	0.000	0.978	0.008
ρ growth rate shock	beta	0.850	0.100	0.763	0.074	0.857	0.044
ρ cons.pref. shock	beta	0.850	0.100	0.915	0.016	0.937	0.010
ρ gov. spending shock	beta	0.850	0.100	0.992	0.004	0.988	0.005
ρ lab. supply. shock	beta	0.850	0.100	0.996	0.003	0.991	0.005
ρ investment shock	beta	0.850	0.100	0.927	0.028	0.901	0.025
invest. adj. cost	Normal	4.000	1.500	7.040	1.151	7.337	1.148
σ cons. utility	Normal	1.000	0.375	1.551	0.417	1.968	0.276
h consumption habit	beta	0.700	0.100	0.636	0.063	0.563	0.047
σ labour utility	Normal	2.000	0.750	2.336	0.629	2.357	0.625
fixed cost	Normal	1.250	0.125	1.475	0.093	1.512	0.087
capital util. adj. cost	Normal	0.200	0.075	0.366	0.062	0.332	0.062
calvo wage	beta	0.750	0.050	0.697	0.036	0.713	0.037
calvo prod. price	beta	0.750	0.050	0.930	0.011	0.931	0.009
calvo employment	beta	0.500	0.100	0.752	0.022	0.757	0.025
indexation wage	beta	0.750	0.150	0.399	0.134	0.416	0.131
indexation price	beta	0.750	0.150	0.415	0.111	0.410	0.115
r inflation	Normal	1.500	0.100	1.633	0.082	1.575	0.080
r d(inflation)	Normal	0.300	0.100	0.331	0.044	0.309	0.043
r lagged interest rate	beta	0.750	0.050	0.723	0.030	0.712	0.032
r output	beta	0.125	0.050	0.035	0.015	0.031	0.013
r d(output)	beta	0.063	0.050	0.086	0.029	0.113	0.035
trend	Normal	0.400	0.100	0.351	0.057	0.181	0.034
σ prod. shock	inv gamma	0.250	2.000	0.582	0.073	0.616	0.080
σ growth rate shock	inv gamma	0.050	2.000	0.094	0.022	0.087	0.017

Continued

Table 6.1 Continued

		Prior distribution		Estimated mode (starting value > 0.6 for the elasticity of substitution) Laplace approximation 2643.1530		Estimated mode (starting value < 0.6 for the elasticity of substitution) Laplace approximation 2571.746	
	Type	Mean	Std. err.	Mode	Std.err.	Mode	Std.err.
σ inflation obj. shock	inv gamma	0.050	20.000	0.154	0.016	0.131	0.016
σ cons. pref. shock	inv gamma	0.250	2.000	0.258	0.057	0.154	0.028
σ gov. spending shock	inv gamma	0.250	2.000	0.381	0.024	0.381	0.024
σ lab supply shock	inv gamma	0.250	2.000	2.096	0.432	2.301	0.476
σ investment shock	inv gamma	0.250	2.000	0.126	0.017	0.138	0.021
σ interest rate shock	inv gamma	0.250	2.000	0.113	0.013	0.112	0.013
σ equity premium shock	inv gamma	0.250	2.000	0.588	0.066	0.519	0.068
σ cons. price shock	inv gamma	0.250	2.000	0.218	0.018	0.201	0.016
σ import price shock	inv gamma	0.250	2.000	1.110	0.094	1.053	0.093
σ wage mark-up shock	inv gamma	0.250	2.000	0.252	0.020	0.248	0.018
US							
ρ prod. shock	beta	0.850	0.100	0.693	0.131	0.685	0.100
ρ growth rate shock	beta	0.850	0.100	0.996	0.005	0.989	0.010
ρ cons.pref. shock	beta	0.850	0.100	0.793	0.089	0.723	0.085
ρ gov. spending shock	beta	0.850	0.100	0.982	0.020	0.982	0.023
ρ lab. supply. shock	beta	0.850	0.100	0.983	0.007	0.981	0.007
ρ investment shock	beta	0.850	0.100	0.879	0.043	0.938	0.033

invest. adj. cost	Normal	4.000	1.500	6.698	1.947	6.507	1.217
σ cons. utility	Normal	1.000	0.375	0.770	0.208	0.802	0.140
h consumption habit	beta	0.700	0.100	0.708	0.076	0.749	0.050
σ labour utility	Normal	2.000	0.750	2.518	0.805	2.260	0.660
fixed cost	Normal	1.250	0.125	1.438	0.070	1.462	0.071
capital util. adj. cost	Normal	0.200	0.075	0.273	0.061	0.295	0.061
calvo wage	beta	0.750	0.050	0.809	0.047	0.777	0.039
calvo prod. price	beta	0.750	0.050	0.853	0.037	0.875	0.021
indexation wage	beta	0.500	0.150	0.453	0.243	0.424	0.145
indexation price	beta	0.500	0.150	0.334	0.132	0.369	0.149
r inflation	Normal	1.500	0.100	1.381	0.109	1.392	0.108
r d(inflation)	Normal	0.300	0.100	0.245	0.061	0.199	0.059
r lagged interest rate	beta	0.750	0.100	0.789	0.033	0.816	0.028
r output	Normal	0.125	0.050	0.001	0.117	0.001	0.039
r d(output)	Normal	0.063	0.050	0.190	0.037	0.202	0.036
trend	Normal	0.400	0.100	0.302	0.035	0.331	0.030
σ prod. shock	inv gamma	0.250	2.000	0.388	0.037	0.384	0.033
σ growth rate shock	inv gamma	0.050	2.000	0.106	0.040	0.105	0.031
σ inflation obj. shock	inv gamma	0.050	20.000	0.096	0.025	0.089	0.021
σ cons. pref. shock	inv gamma	0.250	2.000	0.793	0.410	1.587	0.684
σ gov. spending shock	inv gamma	0.250	2.000	0.550	0.035	0.549	0.035
σ lab supply shock	inv gamma	0.250	2.000	3.207	0.724	2.959	0.701
σ investment shock	inv gamma	0.250	2.000	0.196	0.041	0.165	0.030
σ interest rate shock	inv gamma	0.250	2.000	0.232	0.031	0.227	0.021
σ equity premium shock	inv gamma	0.250	2.000	0.567	0.227	0.655	0.119
σ cons. price shock	inv gamma	0.250	2.000	0.210	0.017	0.217	0.018
σ import price shock	inv gamma	0.250	2.000	1.434	0.108	1.080	0.098
σ wage mark-up shock	inv gamma	0.250	2.000	0.285	0.025	0.284	0.022

Note: * For the Inverted Gamma function, the degrees of freedom are indicated.

parameters determine the speed of adjustment (resp. the degree of substitutability) between domestic and foreign goods, but also between the goods imported by the Euro area from the *US* and the Rest of the World economies and this for the production of each of the final goods: investment and consumption. We suppose that these parameters are the same for both countries as well as for both final goods.

An important parameter for an open economy model is the elasticity of substitution between domestic and foreign goods. This parameter is crucial for understanding the reaction of the exchange rate to exogenous shocks and especially to understand the required volatility in the exchange rate. Because of the discontinuous and extreme reaction of the exchange rate around some critical value for this parameter between zero and one,[4] an iterative optimisation procedure will never succeed to cross this critical point for this parameter. Furthermore, existing empirical evidence on this parameter yields mixed results: at the micro level one might argue in favour of a high substitution elasticity, while at the macro level the typical estimates are sometimes far below one. Therefore, we consider in our estimation two different starting values for the substitution elasticity: one above the crucial value and one below. The marginal value of the estimated models will give an indication on the parameter value preferred by the data. In the next section alternative model validation criteria will be discussed. The estimation results are displayed in Table 6.1.

Not surprisingly, the two estimates for elasticity substitution of substitution are quite divers: 1.21 and 0.21. The adjustment cost parameter (2.38 and 1.98) is estimated a little higher than the prior (set at 2.00) for the case with high substitution elasticity. For the case with a lower substitution elasticity, the role of the adjustment costs is minimal and the posterior estimate is close to the prior.

The Calvo parameter for imported goods, determining the pass-through of the exchange rate is estimated to be fairly high (0.86 and 0.82 respectively for the high and low substitution elasticity estimations). The initial impact of the exchange rate on the import price is therefore relatively small. Bergin (2004) also estimates a high degree of pricing to market to fit the small pass-through effect. However, our estimation approach allows differentiating between the initial and the long run pass-through, which we assume to be perfect.

The remaining model parameters for the two economies are very similar confirming the results of Smets and Wouters (2003c). The following remarks apply to the estimated shocks:

- the domestic shocks are very similar to those in the closed economy models;
- the persistent processes for foreign demand, the relative preference, the ROW price level and the oil price are all estimated between 0.9 and 0.95 while the persistence parameter for the interest rate parity is estimated around 0.85;
- the i.i.d. mark-up shocks in consumption and import prices are relatively important and of a similar size as the mark-up shock in the domestic good prices in the closed economy models;
- some of the time series for the structural shocks have a relatively high correlation while in the estimation procedure they are assumed to be orthogonal. This result indicates that the number of shocks can probably be reduced by a different specification.

6.4 Impulse response functions for the shocks

The estimated model can be evaluated by looking at the plausibility of the structural impulse response functions of the different shocks and to analyse the implied decomposition of the historical data and the variance decomposition of the forecast errors of the model. In the next section we will concentrate on the capability of the models to reproduce a list of stylised facts in the data that are traditionally used in the NOEM literature. In this discussion, we take the model with the high substitution elasticity as the benchmark model and we will mention the important deviations that are obtained under the alternative low elasticity case.

6.4.1 Productivity shocks

In the model we identify three types of productivity shocks: level productivity shocks modelled as highly persistent AR(1) shocks in the level of Total Factor Productivity (TFP), growth rate productivity shocks in TFP modelled as persistent AR(1) shocks to the drift component of TFP and investment specific technology shocks which are persistent AR(1) shocks to the relative price of the investment goods. In the following discussion, we consider shocks affecting the Euro area economy.

6.4.1.1 Level shocks in TFP (see Figure 6.1)

This TFP shock expands temporarily the production frontier of the economy and lowers the marginal cost of production. Firms decrease their prices, but given the stickiness this will happen only gradually over time. Real wages and real income in general increase and consumption follow with some delay as a consequence of the habit persistence. Higher expected returns on capital stimulate investment. As the supply of the domestic good is increased, the relative price of these goods to the foreign price has to decline in order for demand to shift towards the domestic good. This means that the domestic economy will undergo a deterioration in the terms of trade or a real depreciation.

The estimated degree of substitution between domestic and foreign goods in our model is modest (1.21) and a persistent shock to the level of Total Factor Productivity (with an autocorrelation of 0.99) clearly results in an important depreciation of the exchange rate. The jump in the exchange rate does affect the retail import prices only gradually given the high degree of price stickiness in the importing sector. The stickiness in the domestic prices also implies that the

Variable list

C	: real consumption	EX	: real export
I	: investment	IY	: real import
L	: labour supply	NETTRADE	: trade balance
NFA	: current account	PCINF	: consumer price inflation (annualised)
PC	: CPI index	PIE	: domestic price inflation (annualised)
P	: domestic price index	PMINF	: import price inflation (annualised)
PM	: import price index	R	: nominal short term interest rate (annualised)
RS	: real exchange rate	TOT	: terms of trade
W	: real wage	Y	: real output

Note: In the following figures, the number 1 in variables name indicates that the variable relates to the Euro area while number 2 indicates that it relates to the *US* economy.

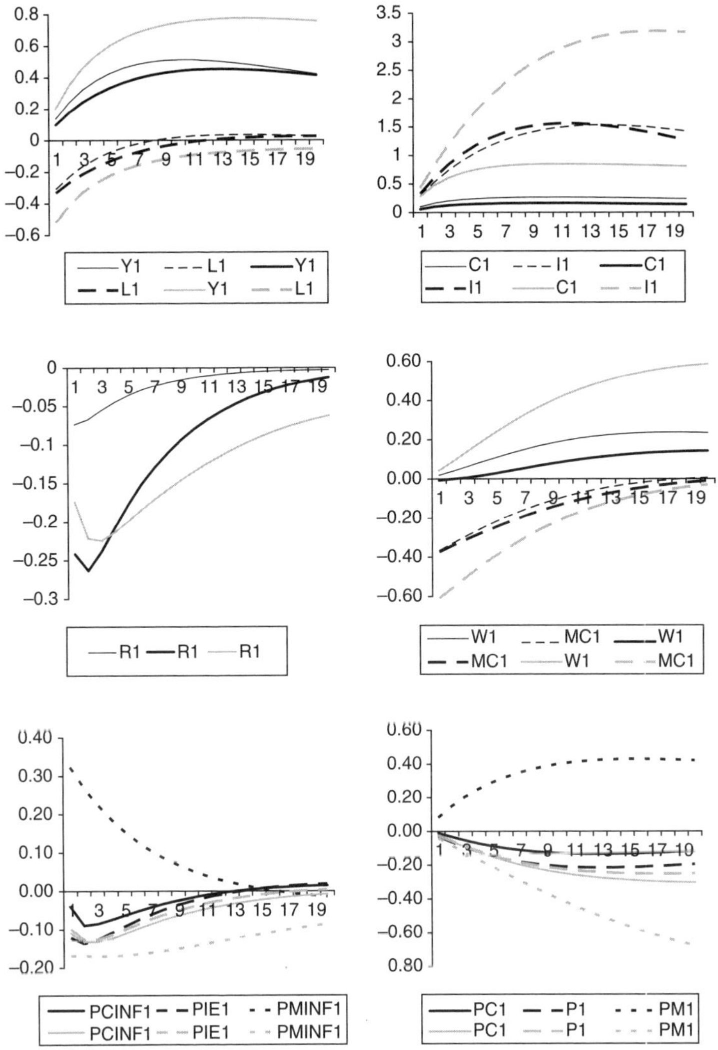

Figure 6.1 Continued

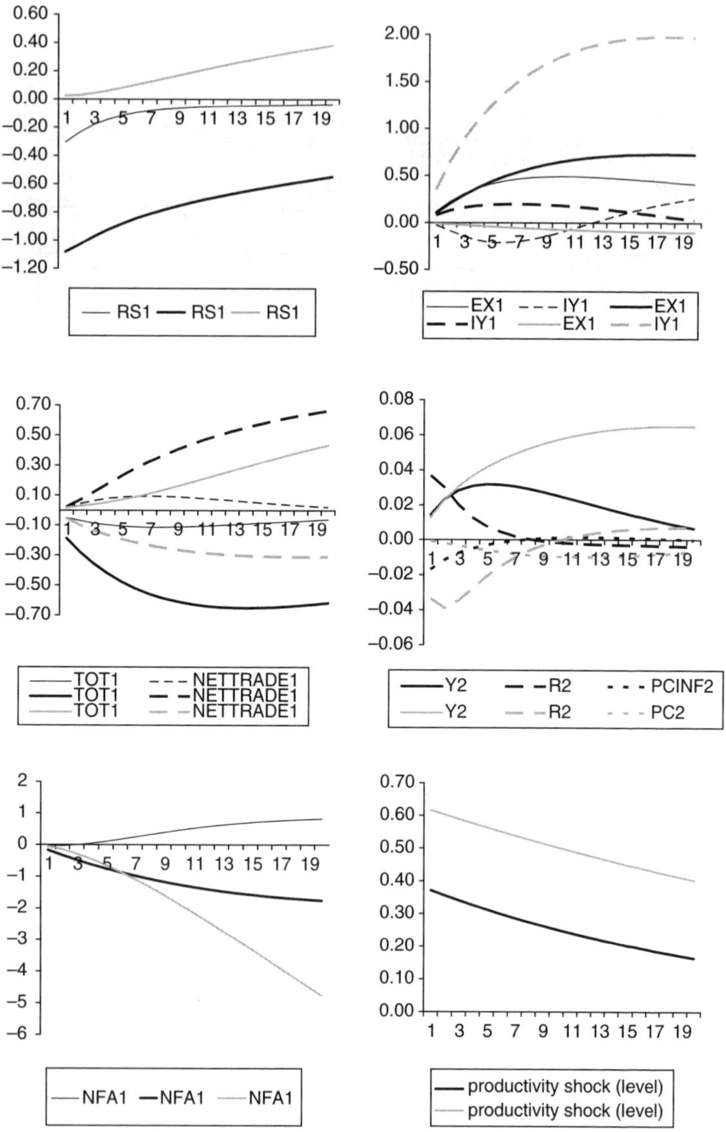

Figure 6.1 TFP productivity shock
(i) High elast. of subst. (1.21) (bold black lines)
(ii) Low elast. of subst. (0.21) (bold gray lines)
(iii) Very high elast. of subst. (11) (thin black lines)

domestic and export prices will only gradually fall following the decrease in the marginal cost. As these relative price adjustments take time and because there are adjustment costs in the reallocation of demand between domestic and foreign goods, exports and imports respond slowly as well. The result is a strong deficit in the current account mainly because the terms of trade deterioration dominates the net export effect initially. This deficit continues for several years and is stabilised finally through the positive real trade balance.

The important deterioration of the terms of trade also limits the expansion of domestic demand and especially consumption in an open economy context compared to a closed economy model. The terms of trade deterioration for the domestic economy and the gain for the *US* economy result in a sharing of the wealth effects between the two economies. The outcome is also a modest expansion in consumption expenditures in the *US*. On the other hand, the depreciation of the Euro and the resulting net trade effects imply that production in the *US* economy will expand less than demand.

The exact impulse response for the level productivity shock depends on a number of important parameters in the model. We know from the discussion on the effects of a productivity shock on employment in the closed economy models, that the impact of a productivity shock depends crucially on the assumptions about the monetary policy reaction to the shock, on the reaction speed of domestic demand and prices and on the nature of the productivity shock. The same parameters also have an impact on the open economy implications of the productivity shock. However in an open economy context, another crucial parameter for the productivity shock is the degree of price substitution between domestic and foreign goods.

In an open economy context, there is a tradition to differentiate between productivity shocks according to whether the shock affects productivity in the tradable or the non-tradable sector (see Benigno and Thoenissen (2002) for a recent discussion). Technology shocks in the tradable sector, which is often considered as price-taker on the international market, will lead to an expansion of exports and economic activity. This will exert upward pressure on domestic wages in both the tradable and the non-tradable sectors resulting in a relative price increase of non-tradables, which is equivalent in this setup to an appreciation of the real exchange rate for the domestic economy. This mechanism is underlying the typical Balassa–Samuelson effect.

Our model does not allow to distinguish between tradable and non-tradable sectors. However, the impact of a productivity shock in the production of the domestic good, which is modelled as an imperfect substitute for the foreign good, will depend strongly on the degree of substitution or in other terms on the degree of price-takership. To illustrate the impact of the substitution elasticity on the outcome of a productivity shock, we show the impulse response for a much higher substitution elasticity in Figure 6.1 (the parameter is set at 11 compared to the baseline estimate of 1.21 in Figure 6.1). The bold black lines represent the IRFs for the estimated substitution elasticity while the thin ones correspond to the alternative parameter. With a very high elasticity of substitution between the domestic and the foreign goods, a productivity shock in the domestic economy will lead to a small decline in the relative price and a relatively important expansion of activity causing also an important increase in the real wage and domestic costs. In this situation, the productivity shock approximates the result for a productivity shock in the tradable good sector. The productivity shock will lead to a smaller decline in the export price. Less deterioration of the terms of trade moderates the negative wealth effect and supports the expansion of domestic demand. In these circumstances the productivity shock will result in a less strong depreciation of the domestic currency: the increase in domestic costs will be higher while the increased supply of the almost perfectly substitutable domestic good will exert only a weak effect on its relative price.

A very different picture appears when we consider the version of the model with the very low estimated substitution elasticity. Corsetti, Dedola and Leduc (2003) recently discussed the importance of the intra-temporal substitution parameters to understand the exchange rate reaction following a productivity shock. For a high elasticity of substitution, the exchange rate reaction to shocks will remain modest because the resulting expenditures' switching effects will be large. Relative minor exchange rate movements will be able to restore the equilibrium in the trade balance. As the elasticity of substitution becomes smaller, it is clear that the required fluctuations in the exchange rate will tend to be higher. We know from the traditional and static Marshall–Lerner condition that the impact of the exchange rate on the current account will reverse for some critical value. A similar critical value exists in these dynamic and more complex open economy models. In our model, an exact value of the parameter is difficult to pin down as it will also depend on the degree and the speed of the pass-through of the exchange rate on the relative prices, the implied import shares of the final expenditures, etc. For values of the substitution elasticity approaching the critical value, the fluctuations in the exchange rate are extremely high. At the critical value the sign of the exchange rate response to shocks in the demand or the supply of domestic and foreign shocks will reverse. For very small values, the expenditures switching effects of the exchange rate are minimal and income and wealth effects will be dominant in the behaviour of the current account.

Grey lines in Figure 6.1 summarise the impact of the productivity shock in the model version with a low substitution elasticity. The exchange rate does not react on impact and appreciates somewhat in the long run. For slightly higher values of the substitution elasticity, the exchange rate appreciates on impact, but the estimation does not support this case. In the absence of a strong terms of trade deterioration, domestic consumption and real wages will react much stronger to the productivity shock. This response resembles more the closed economy outcome. Consumption in the foreign economy is supported much less as the exchange rate does not fulfil its role as a risk sharing device in this case.

6.4.1.2 Growth rate shocks in TFP (see Figure 6.2, grey lines)

The persistent nature of the productivity rise in the *US* economy over the last ten years suggests that the shock to the productivity process is probably affecting the growth rate rather than the level of the productivity process (see Erceg et al. (2003) for a discussion of these growth rate shocks and the role of learning about the nature of the TFP shock). The estimated model tries to identify both types of productivity shocks. The growth rate shock takes the form of an AR(1) shock to the drift component of the TFP process, and therefore generates a moderate increase in the growth rate expectation. The response of a positive growth rate shock in the Euro area is displayed in Figure 6.2.

For a growth rate shock, the exchange rate has initially to depreciate less compared to the level shock. Higher expected future growth in productivity generates a relatively important wealth effect and

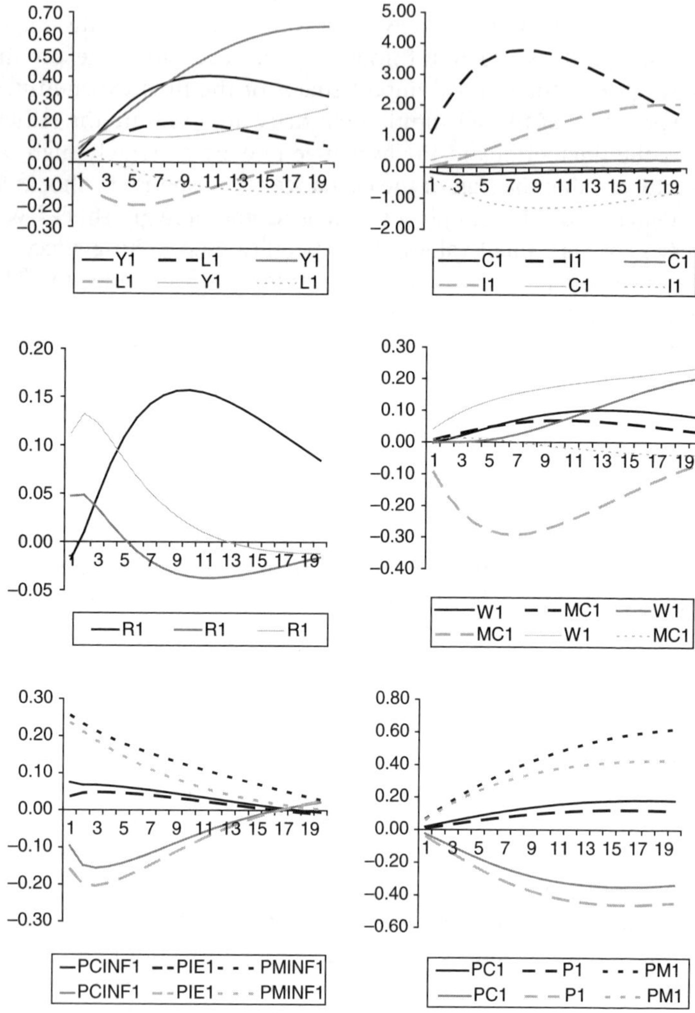

Figure 6.2 Continued

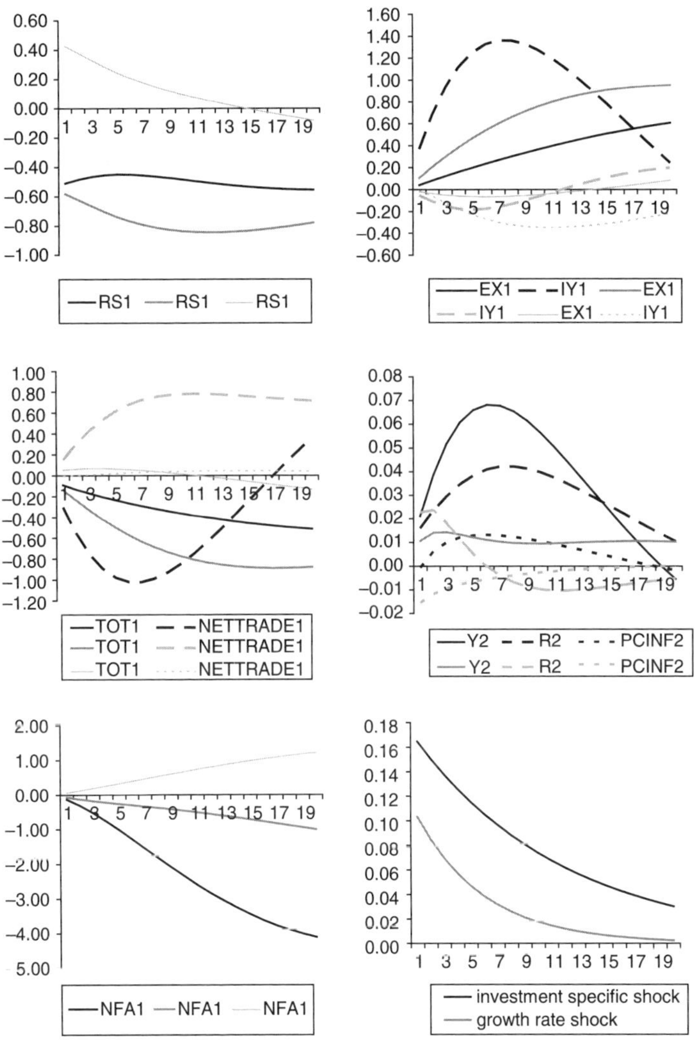

Figure 6.2 Investment specific technology shock (bold black lines) and growth rate shock in TFP

(i) Estimated: bold gray lines

(ii) Almost permanent: thin gray lines

stimulates domestic demand but the immediate supply effect remains very modest. In order to moderate the demand expansion, the interest rate has to increase to balance the expected growth effects. The impact on the real trade balance is positive as the expenditure switching effect seems to dominate the income effects and this limits somewhat the current account deficit for this shock. The spillover effects to the *US* economy are similar to those for the level shock: domestic demand in the *US* reacts positively mainly through the beneficial terms of trade effect but production is much less affected because of the negative substitution effect towards the cheaper foreign goods.

It is clear from Figures 6.1 and 6.2 that the exchange rate depreciation accompanying the growth rate shock is much less outspoken than for the level TFP shock. A growth rate shock in productivity is potentially able to generate an exchange rate appreciation. To illustrate this we show the impulse response for a more persistent growth rate (thin grey lines). With this quasi-permanent shock to the drift component (but with a lower standard deviation), the initial wealth and demand effect are further strengthened, and the result is a weak appreciation of the exchange rate. However, this shock does not induce a strong current account deficit.

6.4.1.3 Investment specific technology shocks (see Figure 6.2, black lines)

A third type of productivity shock that is identified in the model is the investment specific technology shock. This shock decreases the price of investment goods and makes it interesting for firms to invest and to increase the capital stock. In the short run, this shock resembles much more a demand shock than a supply shock. The higher import content of investment translates in an increase in imports and therefore in a deterioration in the trade balance. The strong deterioration of the trade balance contrasts with the level and growth rate shocks to TFP. The real interest rate will also react positively over time and the exchange rate depreciation will be less pronounced. In the absence of an important positive terms of trade effect, the current account will be strongly and persistently negative. The spillover effects on *US* output are more significant for this type of productivity shock as there is no offsetting movement in the domestic demand components.

Overall the results for the different types of productivity shocks point out that positive productivity shocks are not able to explain a strong appreciation of the exchange rate. Effects on the exchange rate remain rather modest for these supply shocks. Benigno and Thoenissen (2002) also questioned the role of productivity shocks in explaining recent exchange rate movements. Probably other models of technological progress, which take the form of product innovation rather than process innovation, would be able to generate a real appreciation of the exchange rate because their major impact is to generate an additional demand for the innovative economy. However, all the productivity shocks lead to a deterioration in the current account.

The impact of positive mark-up shocks is very similar to a negative productivity shock: higher mark-ups restrain supply and this will require an appreciation of the exchange rate. The terms of trade effect and the income effect again dominate the substitution effect and the current account will turn out positive. These results correspond also with Benigno and Thoenissen (2002).

6.4.2 Domestic demand shocks (see Figure 6.3, grey lines)

Domestic demand shocks lead to an important appreciation of the currency. This effect is very similar for an intertemporal preference shock in consumption and for a public expenditure shock. Higher demand implies that the relative price of the domestic goods with respect to foreign goods has to increase. The increase in the real interest rate also supports the appreciation of the exchange rate. Again the spillover effects on the *US* output are limited because the positive effects resulting from the net trade flows are offset by the negative terms of trade effect on domestic demand in the *US* economy.

6.4.3 Monetary policy shocks (see Figure 6.3, black lines)

The same mechanisms are at work for a monetary policy shock. Higher interest rates have a negative effect on domestic demand and as the UIRP holds (disregarding the small net foreign asset effect on the risk premium), the exchange rate appreciates. The exchange rate reaction implies an additional transmission mechanism of a monetary policy shock. The appreciation generates a negative contribution

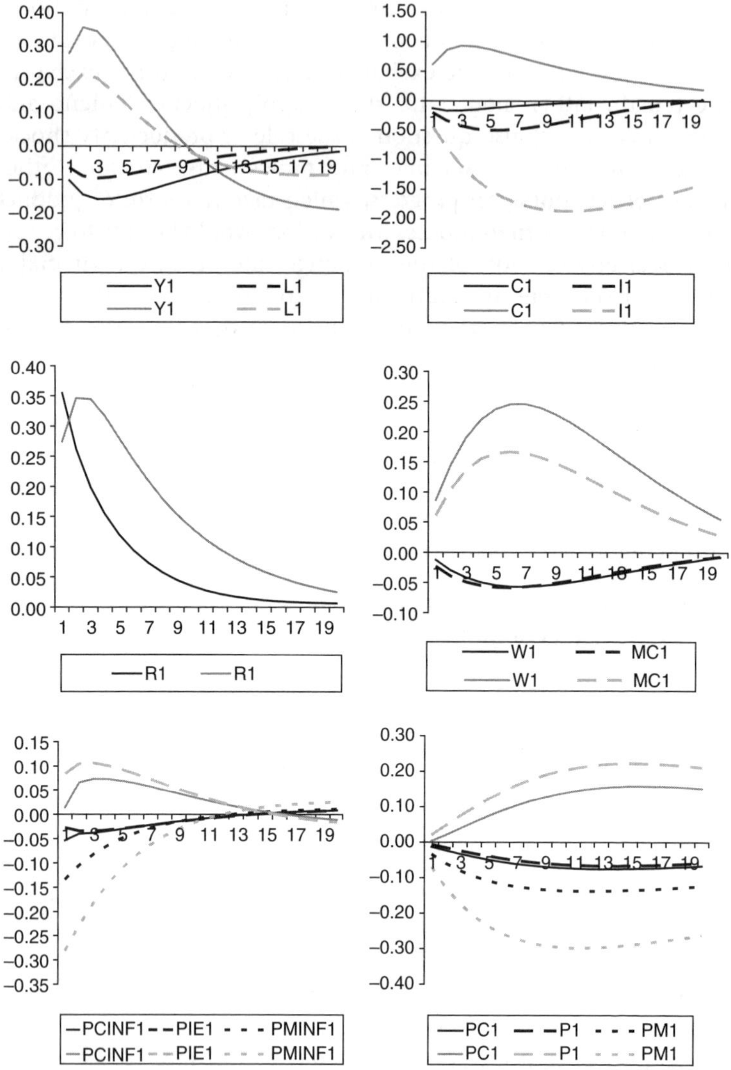

Figure 6.3 Continued

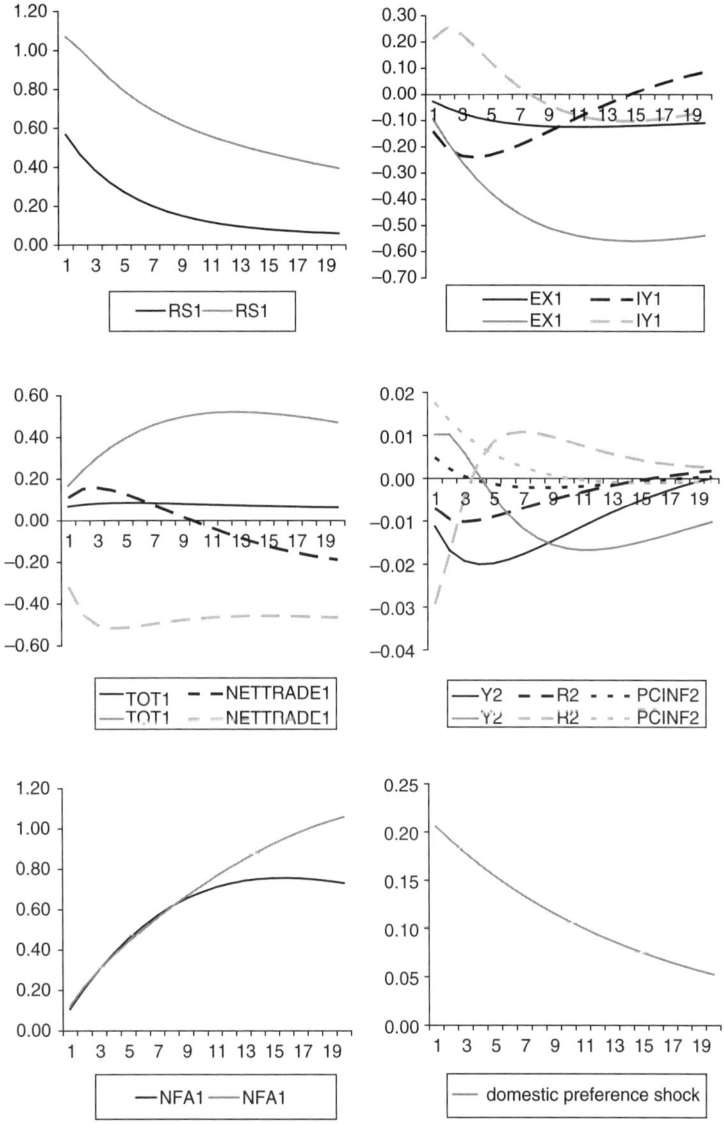

Figure 6.3 Monetary policy shock (black lines) and domastric intertemporal preference shock (gray lines)

of net exports to GDP. However, compared to the closed economy model, the terms of trade effect tends to weaken the transmission channel of interest rate shocks on domestic consumption.

6.4.4 Oil shocks (see Figure 6.4, black lines)

The oil price shock is estimated to have a standard error of 17 per cent with an autocorrelation of 0.95. The impact on GDP is around 0.15 per cent in the first and second year. Both consumption and investment decline after the shock. Consumption declines because of the monetary policy response but also because of the negative wealth effect following the term of trade loss of the oil importing economies. As we assumed that a fraction of oil imports is used immediately in final consumption and the other fraction is used as a production factor in domestic production, the pass-through of the oil price is quite complex in the model. The share of oil imports used in final consumption is assumed to be characterised by flexible prices, so that the consumption price adjusts immediately. On the other hand, oil is part of the production cost of domestic firms and the oil price will work gradually through the final sales price of domestic goods following the estimated stickiness of the domestic price setting. The joint impact implies that consumption prices will first adjust immediately due to the oil component in final consumption and then there will be some additional inflationary pressure through the domestic price component. The relative strength of these two channels depends on the share of oil imports that is used in consumption production. In this version, we assume that both shares are equal, but more fine-tuning is necessary. The pass-through in the domestic sales price will only be partial because domestic costs, and especially wages will at least partially compensate the increased oil costs. The relatively large immediate pass-through of the oil shock and the temporary nature of the estimated shock help to explain why there is no strong hump shaped reaction of inflation following the oil-shock.

The impact on the current account is negative because of higher costs of oil imports. The exchange rate of the Euro area reacts with a depreciation. This implies that domestic wealth and demand in the Euro area are further eroded, but on the other hand the real trade balance reacts slightly positively (see Jimenez-Rodriguez and Sanchez, 2004).

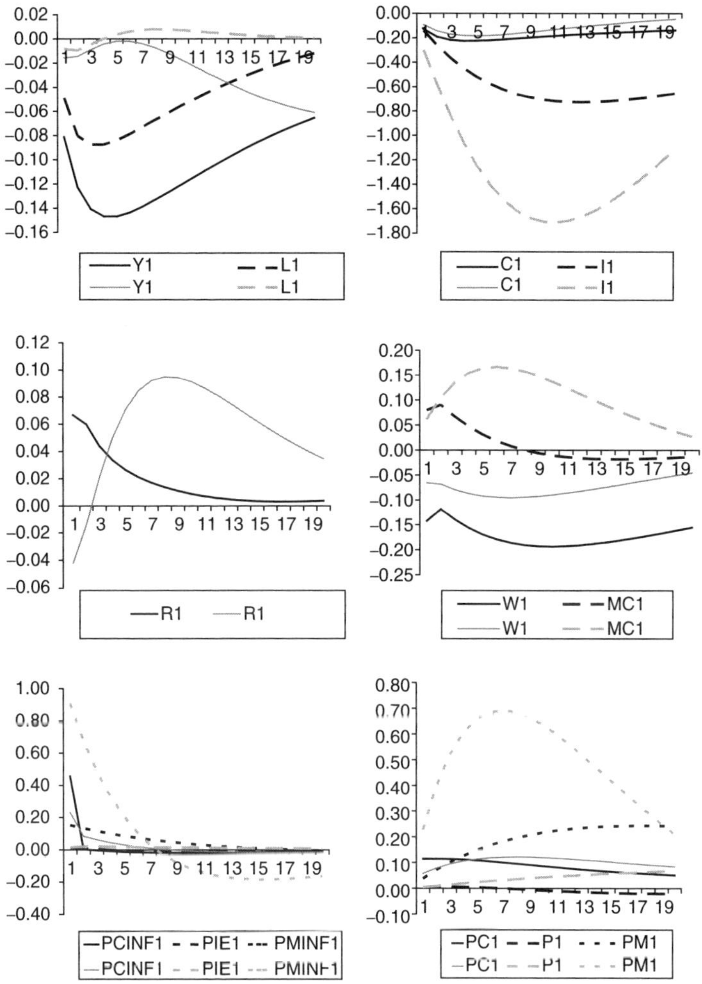

Figure 6.4 Continued

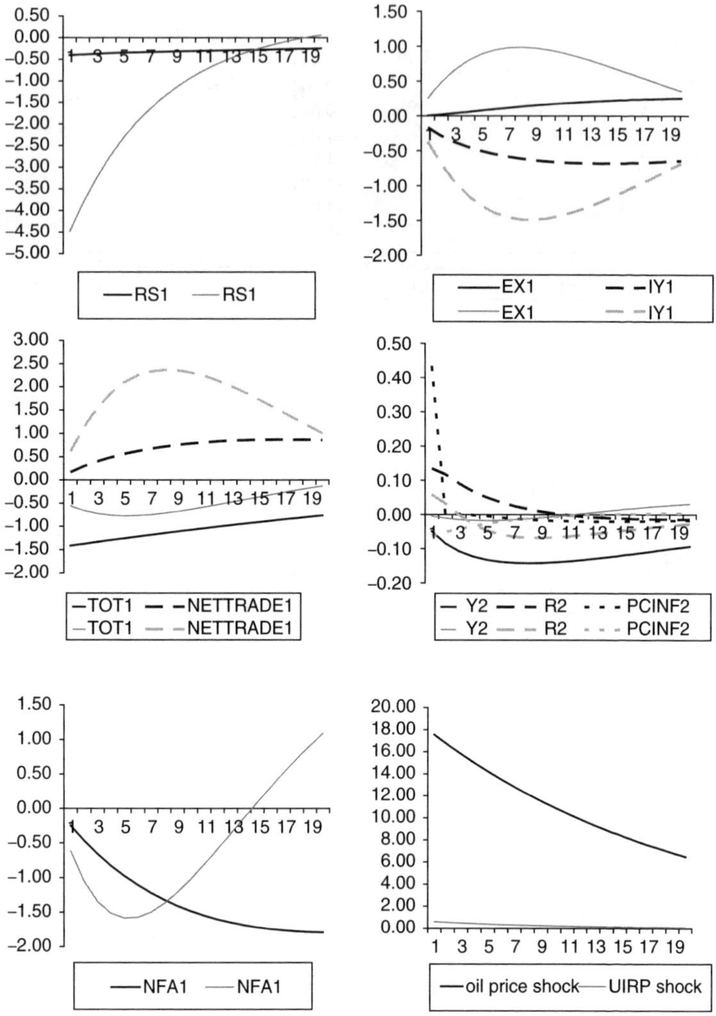

Figure 6.4 Oil shock (black lines) and UIRP shock (gray lines)

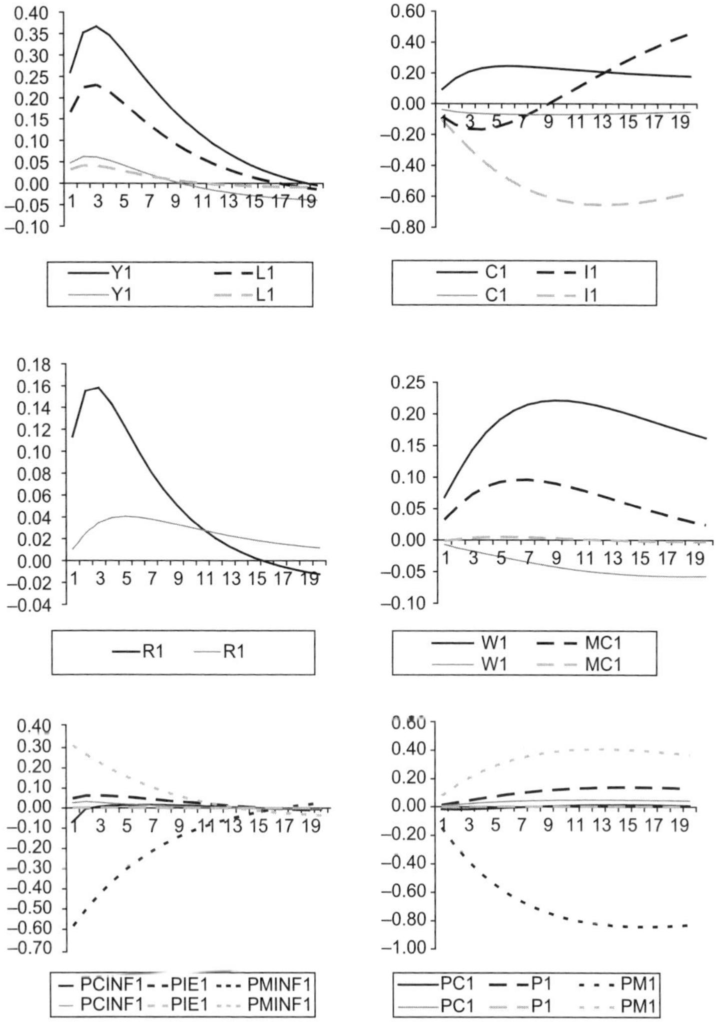

Figure 6.5 Continued

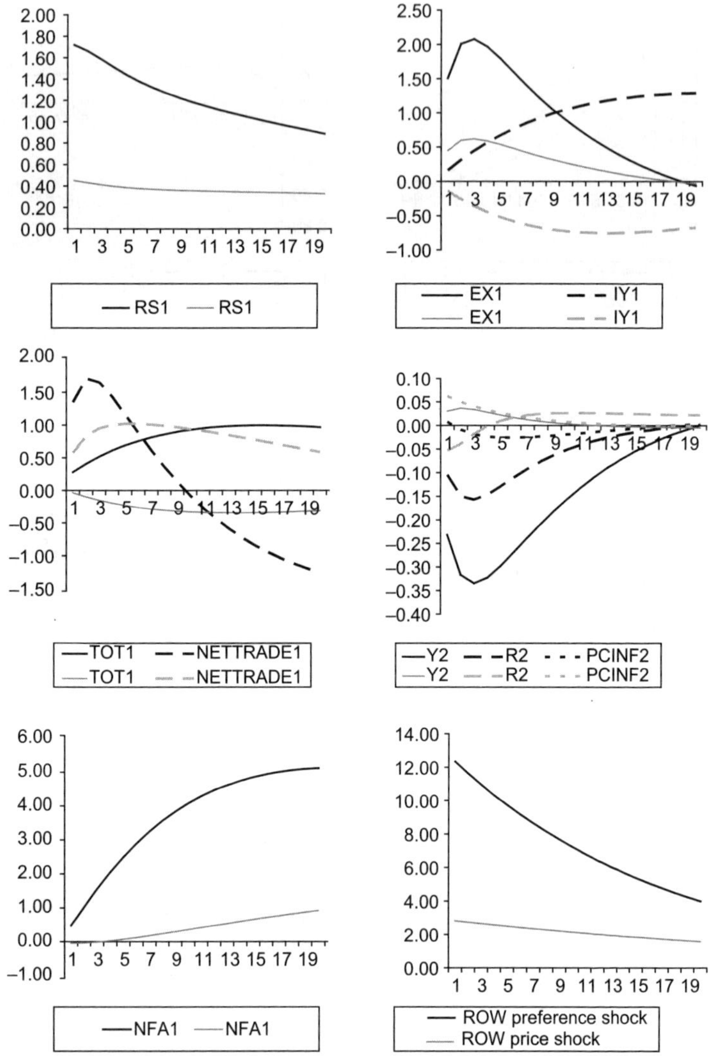

Figure 6.5 ROW preference shock (black lines) and ROW price shock (gray lines)

6.4.5 Uncovered interest rate parity shock to the exchange rate (see Figure 6.4, grey lines)

The large exchange rate depreciation leads to a strong increase in import prices. Although the exchange rate shock is typically overshooting on impact, the maximum response of import prices and consumer prices is only attained after more than one year. The depreciation causes a shift in demand toward domestic goods. But the deterioration in the terms of trade also generates a large negative wealth effect and reduces domestic demand. In addition real interest rate increases in order to reduce the inflationary effects. These negative effects on domestic demand seem to dominate the positive net trade effects in the estimated model. The current account follows the typical J-curve profile: initially the terms of trade dominate but after a few quarters the net trade balance results in a positive current account.

6.4.6 ROW shocks (see Figure 6.5)

An increase in the price of the Rest of the World (grey lines in Figure 6.5) differs strongly from an oil price shock because the competitive position of both the Euro area and the *US* economy improves vis-à-vis the ROW and exports are boosted. Exports react somewhat less in the Euro area because of the assumption that ROW prices are denoted in dollars so that the Euro appreciation is asymmetric relative to the dollar for this shock. On the other hand domestic consumption will decline relatively less in Europe through the extra terms of trade gains from the appreciation.

The ROW demand and preference shocks have very similar effects at least on the country that gains from the preference shift: higher exports and an appreciation will support domestic output and demand. The preference shock (black lines in Figure 6.5) has of course asymmetric effects on the two economies and the appreciation of the currency is much stronger in that case. This result under a high substitution elasticity contrasts sharply with the outcome under the alternative model with a low substitution elasticity. Under the alternative parameterisation (model with a low estimated substitution elasticity), the country benefiting from the preference shift undergoes depreciation and the wealth effect offsets the positive effects on domestic demand and redistributes the gains over the two economies.

6.5 Model validation by summary statistics

The marginal likelihood of the two models with a high and a low substitution elasticity indicate that the data clearly prefer a low substitution elasticity. This result is not totally unexpected given the empirical evidence from macroeconomic import and export equations. However, alternative model validation criteria can be considered in order to evaluate the performance of the model on different criteria. This might be especially relevant here because it is not possible to evaluate the marginal likelihood of the estimated DSGE models against alternative less restricted models such as the typical unrestricted or Bayesian VAR models which are not feasible here due to the high number of observables. One procedure, that is traditionally used to evaluate calibrated DSGE models, is to check whether the model is able to reproduce some stylised properties of the empirically observed data.

In Table 6.2 we summarise a series of statistics that describes some of the open economy characteristics observed in the data. The table is based on HP-filtered data and the real exchange rate is always expressed as the Euro in terms of *US* dollar. We also report the same statistics calculated for the two estimated models. The list of variables is similar to the one reported on Chari, Kehoe and McGrattan (2002).

The models generate a relatively high volatility in consumption and in net trade (measured by the log of the volume of export minus imports). The standard error of consumption in the models is considerable higher than the standard error of GDP, while the opposite holds in the data. The standard deviation of the net trade balance is twice as large as the one observed in the data. The typical open economy shocks clearly increase the volatility of consumption but not GDP because consumption and the trade balance tend to compensate each other. The stimuli of net trade are typically offset by adjustments in domestic demand. The volatility of investment is also increased by these shocks but not as strong as the volatility of consumption because the latter is much more sensitive to the wealth effects generated by the open economy shocks.

In the data the real exchange rate is found to be quite volatile and it behaves in a very persistent way. The models reproduce the standard deviation of the real exchange rate and the relative consumption price quite well. The nominal exchange rate fluctuations and the deviations from PPP are clearly the main cause of the real exchange rate movements. Surprisingly, the model with a low substitution elasticity does generate a lower volatility of the exchange rate. In terms of autocorrelations the models are able to match the data but for the real exchange rate. The relatively low correlation of the real exchange rate in the models can be explained by the typical overshooting reaction of the exchange rate in response to various shocks. This short-lived overshooting of the exchange rate implies a stronger mean-reverting and more predictable behaviour in the theoretical exchange rate. This systematic strong reaction of the exchange rate to shocks is clearly not observed with the same strength in the data.

The model also fails to generate a sufficiently high correlation between output and the main demand components of the two economies. The positive correlation between *US* and Euro area investment expenditures is totally absent in the two model versions, while the positive correlation between consumption is totally missing in the model with a low substitution elasticity. The spillover effects in our models are not strong enough to generate the observed synchronisation in the business cycle. The common impact of oil prices, world demand and world price shocks is not sufficiently powerful to generate a strong positive correlation over the cycle.

One element of the spillover effect is captured by the direct trade flows. In the data, we observe a strong negative correlation between output (and demand) and the net trade balance. The high elasticity of imports with respect to income is responsible for this observation. The model with a low substitution elasticity is able to replicate this negative correlation. In the case of a higher substitution elasticity, consumption is much less negatively correlated with net trade. This is related to the absence of a negative correlation between the net trade balance and the real exchange rate in the model with a high substitution elasticity. In this version of the model, a surplus in the trade balance initiates an appreciation of the exchange rate in order to restore the external balance in the long run. An appreciation and the implied terms of trade gain support domestic consumption. Hence, this equilibrating reaction of the exchange rate to the trade balance counterbalances the usual negative relation between the trade balance and consumption and the exchange rate. The low substitution economy does not has this problem because the equilibrat-

Table 6.2 Summary statistics

	Data		High substitution Model		Low substitution Model	
	US	Euro area	US	Euro area	US	Euro area
St.dev.						
GDP	1.61	1.02	1.48	1.25	1.45	1.19
Consumption	1.26	0.87	1.74	1.72	1.83	1.59
Investment	5.11	2.59	6.92	6.27	6.60	5.92
Employment	1.31	0.67	1.05	0.67	1.04	0.63
Net trade	0.42	0.46	0.82	0.83	0.72	0.71
Real exchange rate	7.65		7.59		6.26	
Relative consumption price	0.92		0.85		0.81	
Autocorrelation						
GDP	0.87	0.86	0.86	0.85	0.86	0.87
Consumption	0.87	0.83	0.89	0.88	0.89	0.87
Investment	0.92	0.88	0.93	0.94	0.93	0.94
Employment	0.88	0.96	0.79	0.92	0.80	0.93
Net trade	0.86	0.76	0.88	0.89	0.87	0.87
Real exchange rate	0.85		0.67		0.66	
Relative consumption price	0.93		0.91		0.90	

Cross correlations over countries									
GDP		0.48			0.13			0.21	
Consumption		0.37			0.18			−0.10	
Investment		0.41			−0.04			−0.09	
Employment		0.07			0.06			0.18	
Cross correlations within countries									
GDP-Net trade	−0.46		−0.35	−0.26		−0.03	−0.43		−0.38
Consumption-Net trade	−0.57		−0.61	−0.23		−0.24	−0.46		−0.56
Investment-Net trade	−0.52		−0.52	−0.77		−0.55	−0.82		−0.67
GDP-Real exchange rate	0.08		0.10	0.02		0.20	−0.04		0.09
Consumption-Real exchange rate	0.09		0.27	−0.05		0.25	−0.05		0.22
Investment-Real exchange rate	0.07		0.2	0.01		−0.07	−0.01		0.05
Net trade-Real exchange rate	0.25		−0.53	−0.03		−0.08	0.11		−0.23
Relative consumption-Real exchange rate		0.09			0.25			0.15	
Relative GDP-Real exchange rate		−0.02			0.12			0.10	

Note: HP-filtered data are used in the calculation of the historical and artificial statistics. The real exchange rate is the EUR-USD rate.

ing adjustment of the exchange rate to the net trade balance has the opposite sign and is therefore enforcing the negative correlation.

The NOEM are often criticised for being unable to generate the observed correlation between the real exchange rate and the relative consumption between countries (e.g. Chari et al., 2002). In the data, countries with high consumption (on the cyclical frequency) tend to appreciate. However in the NOEM with a standard calibration, a country-specific positive monetary shock or productivity shock will raise consumption while the real exchange rate will depreciate. The exchange rate acts as a risk-sharing device by redistributing the wealth effect over the two countries through the adjustment of the terms of trade. This general role of the exchange rate helps to understand the positive correlation between consumptions in the high substitution version. As explained in Corsetti, Dedola and Leduc (2003), substitution elasticities below the critical value are able to reverse this correlation. Also a preference shock driving consumption away from the standard equilibrium condition is able to generate correlations between relative consumption and the real exchange rate that are consistent with the data. In our case, neither of the two model versions has a problem with the correlation between the exchange rate and the relative consumption levels. The typical issue that occurs in highly stylised models which are often concentrated on monetary shocks or productivity shocks does not generate a problem in our more general model where various shocks, such as the uncovered interest rate shocks and the intertemporal preference shocks, imply deviations from the UIRP and therefore disconnect the strict linkage between relative consumption and the exchange rate.

6.6 The unconditional variance decomposition of the forecast errors

Table 6.3 summarises the results for the unconditional variance decomposition of the forecast errors for output, inflation, the real exchange rate and the trade balance based on the model estimates.

Unexpected short run output fluctuations are explained mainly by demand shocks, while the variance over the business cycles, i.e. over an horizon from 10 to 40 quarters, is mainly explained by supply shocks (productivity and labour supply). Labour supply shocks also take up some 10 to 15 per cent of the short run variance in output.

Table 6.3 Variance decomposition

Horizon	1 q.	4 q.	10 q.	10 y.	1 q.	4 q.	10 q.	10 y.
	Output euro area				Output US			
Domestic area shocks	0.709	0.763	0.868	0.960	0.006	0.006	0.005	0.003
TFP level	0.024	0.085	0.142	0.129	0.000	0.001	0.001	0.000
TFP growth	0.010	0.041	0.120	0.265	0.000	0.000	0.000	0.000
Inv. Techn.	0.004	0.052	0.109	0.076	0.001	0.002	0.003	0.001
Lab. Supply	0.106	0.223	0.293	0.396	0.001	0.001	0.001	0.000
Intert. pref.	0.191	0.133	0.054	0.032	0.000	0.000	0.000	0.000
Gov. Exp.	0.267	0.105	0.061	0.026	0.000	0.000	0.000	0.000
Dom.p. markup	0.023	0.044	0.032	0.009	0.000	0.000	0.000	0.000
Cons.p. markup	0.017	0.029	0.028	0.017	0.000	0.000	0.000	0.000
Wage markup	0.001	0.003	0.004	0.002	0.000	0.000	0.000	0.000
Asset p. markup	0.030	0.011	0.006	0.001	0.003	0.001	0.001	0.000
Interest rate	0.025	0.030	0.018	0.005	0.000	0.000	0.000	0.000
Inflation obj.	0.011	0.006	0.003	0.002	0.000	0.000	0.000	0.000
US shocks	0.017	0.022	0.015	0.005	0.841	0.878	0.921	0.968
TFP level	0.002	0.002	0.002	0.001	0.028	0.090	0.154	0.194
TFP growth	0.001	0.001	0.000	0.000	0.008	0.024	0.058	0.136
Inv. Techn.	0.005	0.010	0.007	0.002	0.036	0.094	0.106	0.049
Lab. Supply	0.003	0.003	0.002	0.000	0.085	0.184	0.249	0.417
Intert. pref.	0.001	0.000	0.000	0.000	0.151	0.122	0.058	0.019
Gov. Exp.	0.000	0.001	0.000	0.000	0.389	0.141	0.088	0.053
Dom.p. markup	0.000	0.000	0.000	0.000	0.012	0.032	0.028	0.010

Continued

Table 6.3 Continued

Horizon	**1 q.**	**4 q.**	**10 q.**	**10 y.**	**1 q.**	**4 q.**	**10 q.**	**10 y.**
	Output euro area				**Output US**			
Cons.p. markup	0.000	0.000	0.000	0.000	0.008	0.016	0.018	0.013
Wage markup	0.000	0.000	0.000	0.000	0.002	0.007	0.013	0.010
Asset p. markup	0.005	0.002	0.001	0.000	0.026	0.010	0.006	0.002
Interest rate	0.001	0.002	0.001	0.000	0.056	0.076	0.055	0.020
Inflation obj.	0.001	0.001	0.001	0.001	0.040	0.082	0.089	0.044
Open economy shocks	0.273	0.216	0.117	0.035	0.152	0.116	0.073	0.029
UIRP	0.001	0.000	0.000	0.003	0.000	0.000	0.000	0.001
Oil price	0.016	0.024	0.020	0.007	0.004	0.010	0.013	0.008
ROW demand	0.086	0.032	0.014	0.003	0.052	0.017	0.008	0.003
ROW price	0.006	0.004	0.002	0.002	0.002	0.001	0.000	0.000
ROW prefer.	0.165	0.155	0.082	0.021	0.095	0.087	0.052	0.017
	Consumer price inflation euro area				**Consumer price inflation US**			
Euro area shocks	0.884	0.894	0.905	0.914	0.001	0.001	0.001	0.001
TFP level	0.001	0.009	0.010	0.010	0.000	0.000	0.000	0.000
TFP growth	0.004	0.035	0.049	0.051	0.000	0.000	0.000	0.000
Inv. Techn.	0.002	0.008	0.011	0.013	0.000	0.000	0.000	0.001
Lab. Supply	0.001	0.001	0.001	0.001	0.000	0.000	0.000	0.000
Intert. pref.	0.000	0.007	0.011	0.011	0.000	0.000	0.000	0.000
Gov. Exp.	0.000	0.000	0.000	0.000	0.000	0.000	0.000	0.000
Dom.p. markup	0.459	0.409	0.372	0.315	0.000	0.000	0.000	0.000
Cons.p. markup	0.403	0.343	0.303	0.255	0.000	0.000	0.000	0.000
Wage markup	0.001	0.004	0.004	0.004	0.000	0.000	0.000	0.000

Asset p. markup	0.000	0.000	0.000	0.000	0.000	0.000	0.000	0.000
Interest rate	0.001	0.003	0.003	0.003	0.000	0.000	0.000	0.000
Inflation obj.	0.011	0.075	0.142	0.222	0.000	0.000	0.000	0.000
US shocks	0.004	0.005	0.004	0.004	0.893	0.923	0.941	0.951
TFP level	0.001	0.001	0.001	0.001	0.005	0.030	0.029	0.025
TFP growth	0.000	0.000	0.000	0.000	0.003	0.024	0.030	0.027
Inv. Techn.	0.000	0.000	0.000	0.000	0.001	0.003	0.004	0.005
Lab. Supply	0.000	0.000	0.000	0.000	0.000	0.000	0.000	0.000
Intert. pref.	0.000	0.000	0.000	0.000	0.000	0.004	0.004	0.004
Gov. Exp.	0.000	0.000	0.000	0.000	0.000	0.000	0.001	0.001
Dom.p. markup	0.000	0.000	0.000	0.000	0.445	0.346	0.274	0.222
Cons.p. markup	0.000	0.000	0.000	0.000	0.400	0.264	0.198	0.158
Wage markup	0.000	0.000	0.000	0.000	0.004	0.016	0.013	0.013
Asset p. markup	0.000	0.000	0.000	0.000	0.000	0.000	0.000	0.000
Interest rate	0.001	0.001	0.001	0.001	0.001	0.006	0.006	0.006
Inflation obj.	0.001	0.001	0.001	0.001	0.034	0.230	0.380	0.490
Open economy shocks	0.112	0.101	0.090	0.082	0.107	0.076	0.058	0.048
UIRP	0.022	0.024	0.021	0.020	0.002	0.004	0.003	0.003
Oil price	0.087	0.074	0.066	0.058	0.102	0.067	0.051	0.041
ROW demand	0.000	0.000	0.000	0.000	0.000	0.000	0.001	0.000
ROW price	0.000	0.001	0.001	0.001	0.002	0.003	0.003	0.002
ROW prefer.	0.002	0.002	0.002	0.002	0.000	0.001	0.001	0.001
	Trade balance euro area				**Trade balance US**			
Euro area shocks	0.106	0.147	0.188	0.336	0.026	0.037	0.042	0.157
TFP level	0.000	0.003	0.010	0.043	0.000	0.001	0.002	0.022
TFP growth	0.005	0.024	0.042	0.058	0.002	0.007	0.009	0.031

Continued

Table 6.3 Continued

Horizon	1 q.	4 q.	10 q.	10 y.	1 q.	4 q.	10 q.	10 y.
	Trade balance euro area				Trade balance US			
Inv. Techn.	0.021	0.069	0.078	0.100	0.006	0.016	0.018	0.040
Lab. Supply	0.000	0.003	0.019	0.084	0.000	0.001	0.002	0.039
Intert. pref.	0.023	0.027	0.025	0.026	0.006	0.007	0.007	0.013
Gov. Exp.	0.000	0.001	0.004	0.011	0.000	0.000	0.000	0.005
Dom.p. markup	0.001	0.001	0.000	0.002	0.000	0.000	0.000	0.001
Cons.p. markup	0.001	0.000	0.000	0.005	0.000	0.000	0.000	0.002
Wage markup	0.000	0.000	0.000	0.000	0.000	0.000	0.000	0.000
Asset p. markup	0.049	0.015	0.007	0.003	0.011	0.004	0.003	0.001
Interest rate	0.003	0.003	0.001	0.003	0.001	0.000	0.000	0.001
Inflation obj.	0.002	0.002	0.001	0.000	0.000	0.000	0.000	0.000
US shocks	0.051	0.080	0.089	0.142	0.162	0.219	0.227	0.142
TFP level	0.001	0.007	0.017	0.030	0.003	0.008	0.009	0.019
TFP growth	0.001	0.006	0.012	0.016	0.000	0.000	0.000	0.016
Inv. Techn.	0.025	0.050	0.038	0.033	0.075	0.140	0.149	0.066
Lab. Supply	0.000	0.002	0.008	0.031	0.006	0.009	0.010	0.014
Intert. pref.	0.004	0.005	0.003	0.001	0.010	0.008	0.007	0.001
Gov. Exp.	0.000	0.001	0.004	0.008	0.000	0.001	0.001	0.001
Dom.p. markup	0.002	0.003	0.002	0.001	0.000	0.001	0.002	0.001
Cons.p. markup	0.000	0.000	0.000	0.001	0.001	0.002	0.002	0.001
Wage markup	0.000	0.000	0.001	0.001	0.000	0.000	0.000	0.001
Asset p.markup	0.016	0.005	0.002	0.001	0.046	0.018	0.015	0.003
Interest rate	0.001	0.001	0.000	0.005	0.012	0.017	0.017	0.007
Inflation obj.	0.000	0.001	0.002	0.013	0.007	0.014	0.016	0.011

Open economy shocks	0.843	0.773	0.723	0.523	0.812	0.744	0.730	0.701
UIRP	0.085	0.298	0.433	0.209	0.030	0.086	0.102	0.104
Oil price	0.006	0.021	0.040	0.063	0.000	0.001	0.001	0.015
ROW demand	0.260	0.081	0.035	0.021	0.269	0.137	0.125	0.067
ROW price	0.076	0.100	0.095	0.048	0.104	0.168	0.183	0.421
ROW prefer.	0.416	0.273	0.120	0.182	0.408	0.353	0.320	0.094

	Real exchange rate			
Euro area shocks	0.156	0.193	0.245	0.357
TFP level	0.036	0.044	0.054	0.061
TFP growth	0.010	0.020	0.039	0.080
Inv. Techn.	0.008	0.010	0.016	0.039
Lab. Supply	0.033	0.041	0.052	0.085
Intert. pref.	0.035	0.040	0.044	0.041
Gov. Exp.	0.004	0.005	0.006	0.010
Dom.p. markup	0.005	0.006	0.005	0.004
Cons.p. markup	0.014	0.017	0.020	0.031
Wage markup	0.000	0.000	0.000	0.000
Asset p. markup	0.000	0.000	0.000	0.000
Interest rate	0.010	0.008	0.007	0.005
Inflation obj.	0.001	0.000	0.001	0.001
US shocks	0.129	0.134	0.146	0.167
TFP level	0.024	0.030	0.035	0.038
TFP growth	0.001	0.003	0.008	0.017
Inv. Techn.	0.000	0.001	0.002	0.007
Lab. Supply	0.014	0.016	0.019	0.031

Continued

Table 6.3 Continued

Horizon	1 q.	4 q.	10 q.	10 y.	1 q.	4 q.	10 q.	10 y.
	Real exchange rate							
Intert. pref.	0.005	0.003	0.002	0.001				
Gov. Exp.	0.003	0.004	0.004	0.006				
Dom.p. markup	0.003	0.005	0.004	0.003				
Cons.p. markup	0.009	0.010	0.012	0.017				
Wage markup	0.000	0.000	0.001	0.001				
Asset p. markup	0.000	0.000	0.000	0.000				
Interest rate	0.034	0.026	0.020	0.013				
Inflation obj.	0.035	0.037	0.037	0.032				
Open economy shocks	0.715	0.673	0.609	0.476				
UIRP	0.611	0.538	0.444	0.284				
Oil price	0.005	0.006	0.008	0.011				
ROW demand	0.003	0.005	0.006	0.007				
ROW price	0.006	0.008	0.011	0.018				
ROW prefer.	0.090	0.116	0.140	0.157				

Spillover effects from shocks in the *US* economy on the Euro area or the other way round do not explain a significant proportion of output fluctuations. However, exogenous demand shocks originating in the Rest of the World and preference shocks between *US* and Euro area goods do explain a significant short run fraction, but their impact is not very persistent and the contribution disappears mostly over an horizon longer than two years. The impact of these exogenous demand shocks is larger for the Euro area than for the *US* economy. Oil price shocks, exogenous terms of trade and exchange rate shocks do not have a strong impact on average on the variance of output. Overall their impact explains less than 3 per cent of output variance. The impact of monetary policy shocks is also small as it explains only 4 per cent of short run output variance in the Euro area and some 10 per cent to 15 per cent in the *US* economy. The higher contribution in the *US* economy is explained by the large interest rate shocks at the beginning of the eighties, which create an upward bias in the estimated variance of the interest rate shock. Finally the various mark-up shocks explain some 5per cent of output variance in the Euro area and some 7 per cent in the *US* economy.

Compared to the previous calculations for the closed economy models of the Euro area and the *US* economy (Smets and Wouters, 2003c), the relatively important contribution of exogenous foreign demand shocks goes at the cost of the domestic demand shocks and the monetary policy shocks. The shift from domestic demand shocks towards foreign demand shocks is the only major change in this decomposition exercise compared to the closed economy case.

The dominant factors behind the fluctuations in inflation are the price mark-up shocks in the short run and the inflation objective shocks in the long run. As discussed in de Walque, Smets and Wouters (2006), these price mark-up shocks can also be interpreted as productivity shocks in the flexible price sectors of the economy. Empirically it is difficult to separate between these two interpretations of the short run inflation volatility without more detailed sectorial information on inflation and relative prices. Oil shocks explain some 10per cent of the short run variance in inflation both in the *US* and the Euro area. The high degree of estimated stickiness implies that demand and supply shocks have only a very gradual and overall a limited impact on inflation.

The variance decomposition of the real exchange rate is interesting. The uncovered interest parity shock explains some 60 per cent of the one period forecast error variance. Although the shock is relatively persistent, the contribution decreases to 45 per cent at a 10-quarter horizon and 28 per cent at the 10-year horizon. Other shocks seem to explain a non-negligible share of the exchange rate variance. In the two economies, domestic shocks explain 29 per cent on impact and 52 per cent at the 10-year horizon. The supply shocks, productivity and labour supply together, explain half of this contribution with 12 per cent and 32 per cent. Monetary policy shocks contribute for less than 10 per cent to the real exchange rate variance. Of course their impact on the nominal exchange rate is much higher because in the long run PPP holds and the inflation objective is crucial for explaining the trends in price developments. The exogenous foreign demand shock and the preference shock between the Euro area and *US* goods explain the remaining fraction (from 10 per cent to 15 per cent).

The decomposition of the trade balance also provides some useful insights. Most of the short run variance in the trade balance is explained by the exogenous world demand and intratemporal substitution shocks (68 per cent on impact both in the Euro area and the *US* and 20 per cent over the ten year horizon in the Euro area versus 16 per cent in the *US*). The exchange rate shock has important effects on the net trade balance in the Euro area. The impact increases from 10 per cent at the shorter horizon towards a maximum of 43 per cent at the 10-quarter horizon. The much smaller effect for the *US* economy results from our assumption that the ROW prices are set in dollars. As a consequence, the *US* trade balance is influenced more by the exogenous ROW price shock.

This result confirms the findings in Bergin (2004), where the 'financial' exchange rate shock also explains a major proportion of the trade balance. All these effects are however largely offset by compensating wealth effects on domestic demand, and therefore their impact on final demand is much less important. Fundamental technology and preference shocks in the two economies are also important to explain the trade balance: from 10per cent at the short horizon, their contribution raises to 44 per cent in the Euro area and 27 per cent in the *US*.

A comparison of the exchange rate decomposition with previous studies is difficult because most of these papers are situated in the SVAR approach and therefore the analysis is limited to a small number of variables and shocks. Following Clarida and Gali (1994), the shocks are typically classified as nominal, demand and supply shocks and these shocks regroup our more detailed classification. They did not find a major role for supply shocks and nominal or monetary shocks were only important for the DEM and the JPY exchange rate. Applications on the Euro-dollar exchange rate are of course absent in the older literature.

6.7 Conclusion

The results we obtain for the exchange rate and the trade balance decomposition illustrate that the model is able to explain a significant proportion of the dynamics in these variables by structural shocks that have a clear economic interpretation. This is a promising result for future research. Furthermore, the model presented in this paper displays that adding shocks that lead to deviations from the UIRP allows to answer the criticism of Chari et al. (2002) that NOEM cannot reproduce the observed positive correlation between the relative consumption across countries and the real exchange rate. What is however less satisfactory is that spillover effects of foreign shocks to the domestic variables and correlation between outputs and demand components remain very small. These results are certainly partly due to the strong wealth effects in the model which arise mainly from the assumption of households having infinite horizons. However, the assumption that shocks are orthogonal plays for sure an important role and allowing for some correlation between productivity shocks would probably help to solve the problem.

Appendix

Data description

For the US, consumption, investment and GDP are taken from the US Department of Commerce – Bureau of Economic Analysis databank.

Real GDP is expressed in Billions of chained 1996 Dollars. Nominal Personal Consumption Expenditures and Fixed Private Domestic Investment are deflated with the GDP deflator. There are two inflation series which are the first difference of the log CPI and the log import deflator respectively. Hours and wages are taken from the Bureau of Labour Statistics (hours and hourly compensation for the NFB sector for all persons). Hourly compensation is divided by the CPI price deflator to get the real wage variable. Hours are adjusted to take into account the limited coverage of the NFB sector compared to GDP. The index of average hours for the NFB sector is multiplied with civilian employment (16 years and over). The aggregate real variables are expressed per capita by dividing with the population over 16. All series are seasonally adjusted. The interest rate is the Federal Funds Rate. The net trade variable is simply the difference between exportation and importation.

For the Euro area, all data are from the AWM database of the ECB (see Fagan et al., 2001). Investment includes both private and public investment expenditures. Real variables are deflated with their own deflator. Inflation variables are the first difference of the log CPI and the log import deflator. Real wages are obtained from the wage rate series divided by the CPI price deflator.

Consumption, investment, GDP, wages, hours/employment, and net trade are expressed in 100×log. Interest rate and inflation rates are expressed on a quarterly basis, as they appear in the model.

Notes

1. Examples of such models are Laxton and Pesenti (GEM – Global Economy Model at the IMF, 2003), Erceg, Guerrieri and Gust (SIGMA at the Federal Reserve Board, 2003), Benigno and Thoenissen (Bank of England, 2002), Murchison, Rennison and Zhu (Bank of Canada, 2004), Adolfson et al. (Riksbank, 2004), Kortelainen (Bank of Finland, 2002).
2. Following Shnatz, Vijselaar and Osbat (2003), the exchange rate for the years preceding the Euro has been computed as a synthetic index of the different European currencies' exchange rates with respect to the US Dollar. The oil price series is the price of the UK Brent in US Dollar.
3. For the Euro area, employment is used instead of hours worked. Since this variable responds more slowly to macroeconomic shocks than hours worked, it is considered as in Smets and Wouters (2003a) that only a constant fraction of firms is able to adjust employment to the desired total labour input.
4. On this point, see also Corsetti et al. (2003).

References

Adolfson, M., S. Laséen, J. Lindé and M. Villani (2004), 'Bayesian Estimation of an Open Economy DSGE Model with Incomplete Pass-Through', mimeo, Riksbank.

Anderton, R., di Mauro, F. and F. Moneta (2004), 'Understanding the Impact of the External Dimension on the Euro Area: Trade, Capital Flows and Other International Macroeconomic Linkages', ECB Occasional Paper Series, No. 12.

Benigno, P. (2001), 'Price Stability with Imperfect Financial Integration', mimeo, New York University.

Benigno, G. and C. Thoenissen (2002), 'Equilibrium Exchange Rates and Supply Side Performance', Bank of England Working Papers No. 156.

Bergin, P. (2004), 'How Well Can the New Open Macroeconomics Explain the Exchange Rate and Current Account?', NBER 10356.

Campa, J. and L. Goldberg (2002), 'Exchange Rate Pass-Through into Import Prices: a Macro and Micro Phenomenon', NBER Working Paper 8934.

Chari, V.V., Kehoe, P.J. and E.R. McGrattan (2002), 'Can Sticky Price Models Generate Volatile and Persistent Real Exchange Rates?', Review of Economic Studies, Vol. 69(3), pp. 533–563.

Chinn, M. (2003), 'Doomed to Deficits? Aggregate U.S. Trade Flows Re-examined', NBER Working Paper No. 9521.

Clarida, R. and J. Gali (1994),'Sources of Real Exchange Rate Fluctuations: How Important are Nominal Shocks?', Carnegie Rochester Conference Series on Public Policy, Vol. 41, pp. 1–56.

Corsetti, G., Dedola, L. and S. Leduc (2003), 'International Risk-Sharing and the Transmission of Productivity Shocks', EUI Working Paper ECO No. 2003/22.

de Walque, G., F. Smets and R. Wouters (2004), 'Price Schocks in General Equilibrium: Alternative Specifications', CESifo Economic Studies, Oxford University Press, Vol. 52(1), 153–176.

Erceg, J., L. Guerrieri and Christopher Gust (2003), 'SIGMA: A new Open Economy Model for Policy Analysis', mimeo.

Fagan, G., J. Henry and R. Mestre (2001), 'An Area-Wide Model (AWM) for the Euro Area', ECB Working Paper no 42.

Ghironi F. (1999), 'Towards New Open Economy Macroeconometrics', Mimeo Boston College.

Jimenez-Rodriguez, R. and M. Sanchez (2004), 'Oil Price Shocks and Real GDP Growth: Empirical Evidence for Some OECD Countries', ECB Working Paper no 362.

Laxton, D. and P. Pesenti (2003), 'Monetary Rules for Small, Open, Emerging Economies', Journal of Monetary Policy, Vol. 50(5), pp. 1109–1146.

Lubik, T.A. and F. Schorfheide (2003), 'Do Central Banks Respond to Exchange Rate Movements? A Structural Investigation', Mimeo Johns Hopkins University, University of Pennsylvania.

Murchison, S., Rennison, A. and Z. Zhu (2004), 'A Structural Small Open-Economy Model for Canada', Bank of Canada, Working Paper 2004–4.

Schnatz, B., F. Vijselaar and C. Osbat (2003), 'Productivity and the ("Synthetic") Euro-Dollar Exchange Rate', ECB Working Paper no 225.

Smets, F. and R. Wouters (2002), 'Openness, Imperfect Exchange Rate Pass-Through and Monetary Policy', Journal of Monetary Economics, 49(5), 947–981.

Smets, F. and R. Wouters (2003a), 'An estimated Dynamic Stochastic General Equilibrium Model of the Euro Area', Journal of the European Economic Association 1(5), 1123–1175.

Smets, F. and R. Wouters (2003b), 'Shocks and Frictions in US business cycles: a Bayesian DSGE Approach', mimeo, European Central Bank.

Smets, F. and R. Wouters (2003c), 'Comparing Shocks and Frictions in US and Euro Business Cycles: a Bayesian DSGE Approach', forthcoming in Journal of Applied Econometrics.

7
Liberalisation Shocks and Real Exchange Rates Appreciation in the Transition Economies

Christos Papazoglou

7.1 Introduction

The initial real depreciation of the exchange rate and the subsequent real appreciation that took place constituted a stylised fact that occurred during the early stages of transformation in almost all transition economies of Central and Eastern Europe. Table 7.1 provides supporting evidence from a sample of transition economies in Central and Eastern Europe, concerning the subsequent behavior of the real exchange rate. According to this information, it is apparent that the real exchange rate followed an appreciating trend across all transition economies after the initial depreciation.[1]

The removal of the price controls together with the presence of a monetary overhang led to a sudden increase in inflation at the outset of the reform process. This, in conjunction with the return to currency convertibility and the increased demand for foreign assets, particularly cash, was primarily responsible for the sizable nominal exchange rate depreciation which, in turn, led to the initial real depreciation. Over time, however, the real exchange rate followed an appreciating trend in most transition economies, irrespective of the exchange rate regime. This real appreciation can be largely attributable both to the stabilisation effort as well as to the transformation process. First, with respect to stabilisation, the real appreciation can be perceived as a return to equilibrium, following the initial depreciation and overshooting caused by the nominal shocks, as the macroeconomic conditions

Table 7.1 Real effective exchange rate in selected transition (CPI based, 1992 = 100)

	1993	1994	1995	1996	1997	1998
Bulgaria	155.3	141.5	158.8	136.6	166.8	194.8
Czech Republic	116.3	122.2	126.3	134.6	135.8	146.9
Hungary	108.9	107.0	102.4	105.6	109.7	108.3
Poland	107.3	108.2	117.1	127.4	130.4	137.8
Romania	150.7	155.9	136.8	148.5	175.0	177.8
Russia	150.0	250.0	273.5	333.8	352.8	312.3
Slovakia	105.4	106.5	109.5	109.1	114.6	112.1
Ukraine	43.8	62.1	74.3	87.6	99.2	96.8

Source: IMF.

started improving. Second, the productivity gains resulting from the transformation process itself, as captured through liberalisation and structural reform measures, also contributed to the real exchange rate appreciation. In this latter case the trend of the real rate primarily reflects appreciation in the equilibrium real exchange rate.[2]

The scope of this paper is to provide a theoretical framework capturing the role of liberalisation with respect to the behaviour of the real exchange rate by employing a dynamic macroeconomic model of a representative transition economy operating under a flexible exchange rate regime. The basic characteristics of a typical transition economy, which are embodied into the workings of the real as well as the financial sectors, refer to the following three main features: The co-existence of a state as well as a private sector in the product market; the long-run endogeneity of output; and the underdevelopment of the financial sector. Also, the analysis assumes secular inflationary conditions as being more appropriate to actual prevailing experience of these countries.[3]

The model is used in order to examine the dynamic adjustment of the economy to two specific disturbances, which are related to the liberalisation process. The first refers to an increase in the core inflation reflecting the impact of price controls removal, while the second considers a fall in the demand for money function as a result of financial liberalisation.

The paper is set out as follows. The specification of the model is described in Section 2, while Section 3 includes the solution to dynamics. The impact of an increase in core inflation is examined in Section 4. Section 5 considers the effect of a liberalisation shock in the money market. Finally, Section 6 includes the concluding remarks of the analysis.

7.2 The model

As we stated the analysis incorporates into the real and financial markets some of the basic features of a transition economy. In particular, the product market is divided into two sectors, a private one that works under conditions of a market economy and as a result it responds to market forces and a state sector still following the practices of central planning.[4] In particular, the economy is assumed to produce one good part of which is produced by the private sector and the rest by the old state sector.[5] The price of the domestic good and its inflation rate are endogenous, as well as the output produced by the private sector. The part of output produced by the state sector is assumed not to respond to market forces and as a result is exogenously set. Moreover, aggregate output is taken to be endogenous and not fixed at the full employment level due to the existence of idle and/or under-utilised resources. In addition, the price of the imported good and its inflation rate is taken to be exogenous. Finally, with respect to money markets, the domestic economy is not fully integrated with the rest of the world. That is, the economy is assumed to have an underdeveloped financial market with less than perfect capital mobility. Given these assumptions, the specification of the model, in which all variables are expressed in logarithms, is quite standard and described below.

Equation (1a) describes product market equilibrium for the private sector, where aggregate demand for the domestic good varies positively with real income and the relative price but inversely with the real rate of interest $(r - p^*)$:

$$Y_m = b_1 Y - b_2\left(r - p^*\right) + b_3 c$$

$$0 < b_1 < 1,\ b_2 > 0,\ b_3 > 0 \tag{1a}$$

where,

Y = real domestic output,

Y_m = real domestic output produced by the private sector,

r = domestic nominal rate of interest,
p^* = expected rate of inflation of the domestic price level P,
c = relative price of foreign to domestic goods.

The second equation defines the relative price c:

$$c = P_f + E - P \tag{1b}$$

where,
P = domestic price level (in terms of domestic currency), expressed in logarithms,
P_f = price of imported good (in terms of foreign currency), expressed in logarithms,
E = logarithm of current exchange rate (measured in units of the domestic currency per unit of foreign currency).

Equation (1c) states that part of output is produced by the private sector and the rest by the state sector, with the relative shares being θ and $(1 - \theta)$ respectively: $Y = \theta Y_m + (1 - \theta)\overline{Y}_G$

$$0<\theta<1 \tag{1c}$$

where, Y_G = real domestic output produced by the state sector, assumed fixed.

This means that, the larger the θ, the greater the private sector which, in turn, implies that the transformation process has proceeded more vigorously. As mentioned, the output produced by the state sector is fixed.

Equation (1d) represents a Phillips type relation that links domestic inflation to private output fluctuations and to exogenous rate of core inflation π. The core inflation is taken to be exogenous and captures the initial impact of price liberalisation Due to the assumption of a fixed output level for the state sector, inflation is related to privately produced output. In particular:

$$p = \gamma Y_m + \pi \quad \gamma>0 \tag{1d}$$

where, $p = \dot{P}$, which denotes the actual rate of inflation of P and π = core inflation.

Equation (1e) describes money market equilibrium:

$$M - P = a_0 + a_1 Y - a_2 r$$
$$a_0 > 0,\ a_1 > 0,\ a_2 > 0 \tag{1e}$$

where, M = logarithm of the domestic nominal money supply and a_0 = shift factor.

The real money stock depends positively on real income and negatively on the domestic nominal interest rate. Note, a_0 represents a liberalisation-shock parameter. That is, the effect of liberalisation on the financial sector is associated with a reduction in demand for money, which is captured though a decline in a_0.

Equation (1f) reflects balance of payments equilibrium under a flexible exchange rate regime:

$$\delta_1(r - r_f - e^*) - \delta_2 Y + \delta_3 c = 0$$

$$\delta_1 > 0, \delta_2 > 0, \delta_3 > 0 \tag{1f}$$

r_f = foreign nominal rate of interest, exogenous to the domestic economy,
e^* = expected rate of exchange depreciation.

In particular, capital account balance, captured by the first term, and current account balance, captured by the latter two terms, must add up to zero. The capital account balance depends positively on the expected interest rate differential, while the current account varies inversely with the domestic real income and positively with the real exchange rate.

The two exponential variables p^*, e^* are assumed to satisfy the rational expectations hypothesis, which in the absence of uncertainty, imply perfect foresight. This condition, described by equations (1g) and (1h), requires the expected rates of inflation and exchange depreciation respectively to coincide with the corresponding actual rates:

$$p^* = p \tag{1g}$$
$$e^* = e \tag{1h}$$

The final two equations determine the dynamics of the system:

$$\dot{M} = \mu \tag{1i}$$

$$\dot{c} = p_f + e - p \tag{1j}$$

$\mu \equiv \dot{M}$ = rate of domestic nominal monetary expansion, taken to be exogenous,

$$p = \dot{P}, e = \dot{E}, p_f = \dot{P}_f:$$

lower case letters denote rates of change, i.e. p denotes the actual rate of domestic inflation of P, p_f is the actual rate of foreign inflation and e is the rate of exchange depreciation.

The first, (1i), specifies a simple rule for monetary policy which fixes the rate of growth of the domestic money supply. This, then, means that at any instant of time the nominal stock of money is predetermined. The last equation, (1j), describes the evolution of the real exchange rate c, and is simply the time derivative of (1b).

The model is better analysed when expresses in real terms. To do this, we define the real stock of money h as

$$h \equiv M - P \tag{2}$$

and reduce the system (1a)–(1j), by doing the necessary substitutions as well, to the following set of equations:

$$\frac{1}{\theta}[Y - (1 - \theta)\overline{Y}_G] = b_1 Y - b_2\left(r - p\right) + b_3 c \tag{3a}$$

$$p = \frac{\gamma}{\theta}[Y - (1 - \theta)\overline{Y}_G] + \pi \tag{3b}$$

$$h = a_0 + a_1 Y - a_2 r \tag{3c}$$

$$e = r - r_f - \eta Y + \tau c \qquad \eta \equiv \frac{\delta_2}{\delta_1} > 0, \tau \equiv \frac{\delta_3}{\delta_1} > 0 \tag{3d}$$

$$\dot{h} = \mu - p \tag{3e}$$

$$\dot{c} = p_f + e - p \tag{3f}$$

Note that we arrived at equation (3b) by initially solving (1c) for Y_m which is then substituted into (1d). Also equation (3d) came from equation (1f) after solving for e. Turning to the evolution of the system, we assume that, at all points other than those where the exchange rate undergoes jumps in response to unanticipated disturbances, the real exchange rate and the real stock of domestic money evolve continuously and can be taken as predetermined. The four equations (3a)-(3d) yield the short run solutions for the four variables in terms of c,h. Substituting these solutions into (3e) and (3f), the dynamic adjustment of the system is determined.

The steady-state equilibrium is reached by setting $\dot{h} = \dot{c} = 0$ in (3e) and (3f). More specifically, the steady-state equilibrium values, denoted by tildes, are given by:

$$(\frac{1}{\theta} - b_1)\tilde{Y} = -b_2(\tilde{r} - \tilde{p}) + b_3\tilde{c} + \frac{(1-\theta)}{\theta}\bar{Y}_G \tag{4a}$$

$$\tilde{p} = \frac{\gamma}{\theta}[\tilde{Y} - (1-\theta)\tilde{Y}_G] + \pi \tag{4b}$$

$$\tilde{h} = a_0 + a_1\tilde{Y} - a_2\tilde{r} \tag{4c}$$

$$\tilde{e} = \tilde{r} - r_f - \eta\tilde{Y} + \tau\tilde{c} \tag{4d}$$

$$\tilde{p} = p_f + \tilde{e} = \mu_0 \tag{4e}$$

Using the above equations we determine the long-run equilibrium values for Y, p, r, h, e, c. Note that, μ_0 is the exogenous long-run rate of the domestic nominal monetary expansion.

7.3 The general solution of the system

For the evolution of the economy over time to be determined we must reduce the system (3a)–(3d) to a pair of autonomous differential equations in c, h. First, however, we must solve for the short-run solutions of Y, p, e and r. These solutions are given by the following expressions,

$$Y = \frac{b_3a_2}{\Delta}c - \frac{b_2}{\Delta}a_0 + \frac{a_2b_2}{\Delta}\pi \tag{5a}$$

$$e = \frac{\tau\Delta + b_3(a_1 - \eta a_2)}{\Delta}c + \frac{(1/\theta - b_1) + b_2(\eta - \gamma/\theta)}{\Delta}a_0 + \frac{b_2(a_1 - \eta a_2)}{\Delta}\pi \tag{5b}$$

$$p = \frac{\gamma b_3a_2}{\theta\Delta}c - \frac{\gamma b_2}{\theta\Delta}a_0 + \frac{(1/\theta - b_1)a_2 + a_1b_2}{\Delta}\pi \tag{5c}$$

$$r = \frac{b_3a_1}{\Delta}c + \frac{[(1/\theta - \mathrm{b}_1) - \gamma\mathrm{b}_2/\theta]}{\Delta}a_0 + \frac{b_2a_1}{\Delta}\pi \tag{5d}$$

where $\Delta \equiv a_2(1 - \theta b_1 - \lambda b_2)/\theta + a_1 b_2$, which is taken to be positive. Substituting (5a)–(5d) into (4e) and (3f), the dynamics of the economy are written as follows,

$$\begin{bmatrix} \dot{c} \\ \dot{h} \end{bmatrix} = \begin{bmatrix} q_{11} & q_{12} \\ q_{21}/\theta & q_{22}/\theta \end{bmatrix} \begin{bmatrix} c \\ h \end{bmatrix} + \begin{bmatrix} g_{11} & g_{12} \\ g_{21} & g_{22} \end{bmatrix} \begin{bmatrix} \pi \\ a_0 \end{bmatrix} \tag{6}$$

where

$$q_{11} = \frac{\tau\Delta + b_3(a_1 - \eta a_2) - \gamma a_2 b_3/\theta}{\Delta}$$

$$q_{12} = -\frac{(1/\theta - b_1) + \eta b_2}{\Delta} < 0$$

$$q_{21} = -\frac{\gamma a_2 b_3}{\Delta} < 0 \quad q_{22} = -\frac{\gamma b_2}{\Delta} < 0$$

$$g_{11} = a_2 q_{12} < 0 \quad g_{12} = -q_{12} > 0$$

$$g_{21} = -\frac{(1/\theta - b_1)a_2 + a_1 b_2}{\Delta} < 0, g_{22} = -\frac{q_{22}}{\theta} > 0 \tag{7}$$

It can be shown that $q_{11}q_{22} - q_{12}q_{21} = -\left[\gamma(\tau b_2 + b_3)/\Delta\right]$, which means that the equilibrium is a saddlepoint with roots $\lambda_1 < 0$ and $\lambda_2 > 0$.

The general solution to the system is obtained by integrating (6), assuming that μ, k and a_0 remain constant. We consider only the stable solution which simplifies to

$$c = -A\frac{q_{12}}{q_{11} - \lambda_1}\exp(\lambda_1 t) - \frac{1}{\lambda_1\lambda_2}q_{12}\pi \tag{8a}$$

$$h = A\exp(\lambda_1 t) + \frac{1}{\lambda_1\lambda_2}[(q_{11} - a_2\lambda_1\lambda_2)\pi + \lambda_1\lambda_2 a_0] \tag{8b}$$

The stable arm is obtained by eliminating $A\exp(\lambda_1 t)$ between equations (8a) and (8b). In particular the stable locus may be expressed as,

$$c = -\frac{q_{12}}{q_{11} - \lambda_1}h + \frac{q_{12}}{q_{11} - \lambda_1}[\frac{1}{\lambda_2}(1 - a_2\lambda_2)\pi + a_0] \tag{9}$$

This locus is positively sloped since $q_{12} < 0$ and $q_{11} - \lambda_1 = \lambda_2 - q_{22}/\theta > 0$. Equation (9), together with the short-run solutions given by (5a)–(5b), form the basis for our analysis of the two disturbances under consideration.

7.4 Increase in core inflation

The increase in core inflation primarily reflects the impact of price liberalisation. In the long run, an increase in π cannot affect the inflation rate, since the latter is tight to the monetary growth rate, and as a result output must decrease in order to offset the upward pressure on inflation. The fall in output requires a real exchange rate appreciation for product market equilibrium. The nominal interest rate may fall or increase depending on the relative effects of Y and c on the external sector. Finally, the real money stock is more likely to decrease because of the fall in the demand for money following the output decline. Note that, the size of the market sector affects the results quantitatively but not qualitatively. In particular, the existence of a state sector reduces the fall in output and the real exchange rate as well as the impact on r and h.

Turning to the short-run, we take the differential of (9) with respect to π in order to ascertain the instantaneous effect of an increase in core inflation on the real exchange rate. In particular,

$$\frac{dc_0}{d\pi} = \frac{q_{12}}{\lambda_2(q_{11} - \lambda_1)}\left(1 - a_2\lambda_2\right) < 0 \tag{10}$$

where subscript 0 denotes the initial impact effect. The increase in core inflation is more likely to lead to an immediate discrete appreciation in the real exchange rate. The initial jump in c have immediate repercussions on the short-run equilibrium variables of the system, e, p, Y and r. These can be obtained by taking the differential of (5a)–(5b) and substituting from (10). More specifically,

$$\frac{de_0}{d\pi} = \left(\frac{q_{11}}{\lambda_2} - a_2\lambda_1\right)\left(1 + \frac{q_{12}}{q_{11} - \lambda_1}\right) \tag{11a}$$

$$\frac{dp_0}{d\pi} = \left(\frac{q_{11}}{\lambda_2} - a_2\lambda_1\right) > 0 \tag{11b}$$

$$\frac{dY_0}{d\pi} = -\left(\theta a_2\lambda_1 + \frac{q_{12}q_{21}}{(q_{11} - \lambda_1)\lambda_2}\right) \tag{11c}$$

$$\frac{dr_0}{d\pi} = -\frac{a_1}{a_2}\left(\theta a_2\lambda_1 + \frac{q_{12}q_{21}}{(q_{11} - \lambda_1)\lambda_2}\right) \tag{11d}$$

where in all cases the subscript 0 is used to denote the initial impact effect. In addition, the above results imply,

$$\frac{d\dot{c}_0}{d\pi} = \frac{d(e_0 - p_0)}{d\pi} = \frac{q_{12}}{q_{11} - \lambda_1}\left(\frac{q_{11}}{\lambda_2} - a_2\lambda_1\right) < 0$$

$$\frac{d\dot{h}_0}{d\pi} = -\frac{dp_0}{d\pi} = -\left(\frac{q_{11}}{\lambda_2} - a_2\lambda_1\right) < 0, \tag{12}$$

which capture the adjustment process towards the long-run equilibrium. Figure 7.1 illustrates the impact of an increase in core inflation, where the original steady state is given by point A on the stable locus (line *SL*). The effect of the initial appreciation in the real exchange rate, as a result of the negative jump in the nominal exchange rate, leads to a shift in the stable locus to position *SL′* and point D reflects the short-run equilibrium. Then, both c and h begin to adjust and the system could converge to point B, which represent the new long run equilibrium.

In the short-run the increase in core inflation pushes up the inflation rate while it is more likely to lead to an immediate appreciation of the nominal exchange rate. Given that the price of domestic output adjusts sluggishly, which means that it is fixed at the time of the disturbance, the real exchange rate c_0 immediately falls. The increase in inflation reduces the real interest rate generating expansionary effects on output, while the real appreciation of the exchange rate has the opposite effect. As a result, output may increase in the short-run, while it certainly falls by less, and this, in turn, reduces the extent of real exchange rate appreciation. Note, however, that the fact that the increase in p affects only part of the product market, it lessens its overall influence on output. Moreover, in case of a short-run increase in output, there is even a possibility of real exchange rate depreciation.

That is, to the extent that the nominal interest rate rises for money market equilibrium, as a result of the output increase, it diminishes the expansionary impact of a lower real interest rate on aggregate demand. Thus, a real depreciation of the exchange rate may be required in order to maintain equilibrium in the product market. We postulate, however, that the interest elasticity of the demand for money function is quite small in the case of transition economies so that the possibility of initial exchange rate depreciation is rather ruled out. Finally, equilibrium in the external sector may require an increase or a decrease in the rate of exchange depreciation depending on the response of the nominal interest rate. It is certain, however, that in case of an increase in e, it will be by less than the corresponding increase in p.

As a result, the fact that the relations in (12) are negative means that the real exchange rate and the real money stock fall during the adjustment process until the new long run equilibrium is reached at point B. That is, the fact that the real exchange rate undershoots its long-run equilibrium, as it appreciates by less, gives rise to additional appreciation during the adjustment process as the system moves towards the new long run equilibrium.

7.5 Decrease in the demand for money

In this section we examine the impact of a liberalisation shock on the financial sector. More specifically, a fall in a_0 can be interpreted as a decrease in the demand for money reflecting the fact that the increasing liberalisation of the financial sector reduces the need for money holdings.

In the long run, a decrease in the demand for money leads to a proportional increase in the real money stock through a fall in the domestic price level. As a result, the rest of the economy remains unaffected. The effects of a fall in the demand for money in the short-run can be analysed in a manner similar to previous disturbance. Taking differentials of (9) with respect to a_0, the instantaneous effect on the real exchange rate is

$$\frac{dc_0}{da_0} = \frac{q_{12}}{q_{11} - \lambda_1} < 0, \tag{13}$$

while the impact effect on the short-run equilibrium variables of the system is given by:

$$\frac{de_0}{da_0} = \lambda_1\left(1 + \frac{q_{12}}{q_{11} - \lambda_1}\right) \tag{14a}$$

$$\frac{dp_0}{da_0} = \lambda_1 < 0 \tag{14b}$$

$$\frac{dY_0}{da_0} = \frac{\theta\lambda_1}{\gamma\delta} < 0 \tag{14c}$$

$$\frac{dr_0}{da_0} = \frac{1}{a_2}\left(1 + \frac{\theta a_1\lambda_1}{\gamma\delta}\right) \tag{14d}$$

from which it follows that

$$\frac{d\dot{c}_0}{da_0} = \frac{d(e_0 - p_0)}{da_0} = \frac{\lambda_1 q_{12}}{q_{11} - \lambda_1} > 0$$

$$\frac{d\dot{h}_0}{da_0} = -\frac{dp_0}{da_0} = -\lambda_1 > 0 \tag{15}$$

The response of the economy to a decline in the demand for money is illustrated in Figure 7.2. Now starting from the initial steady state at point A on the line *SL*, the initial real depreciation of the exchange rate leads to a shift in the stable locus to position *SL'* and point D represents the short-run equilibrium. Then, both *c* and *h* begin to fall and the system converges along this locus towards the new equilibrium at point B.

In the short-run the fall in the demand for money requires an increase in output or a fall in the nominal interest rate so that the equilibrium in the money market is maintained. Note, however, that the nominal interest rate may rise in case of a larger increase in output, which, in turn, is positively related to the size of the private sector. As a consequence of the output increase the real exchange rate immediately depreciates in order to stimulate demand and equilibrate the output market. The rise in output also leads to an increase in the inflation rate while, to the extent that the nominal interest rate rises, it is more likely to cause an increase in the rate of exchange depreciation in the external sector. It must be pointed out, however, that the increase in the inflation rate exceeds that of the exchange depreciation rate under this disturbance as well. During the adjustment, both the real exchange rate and the real money stock fall, as the relations reported in (15) indicate, until they get to the new long run equilibrium at point B.

The analysis indicates that the initial real exchange rate depreciation, reflecting the positive impact of financial liberalisation on output, gradually slides back following an appreciating trend until it returns to its original equilibrium value. The fact that the particular disturbance impacts more on the inflation rate than on the exchange depreciation rate in the short run generates the necessary adjustment mechanism that brings the system towards the new long run equilibrium.

7.6 Conclusions

In this paper we have developed and analysed a macroeconomic model of a small open transition economy operating under flexible exchange rates. The analysis embodies three basic features that normally characterise a typical transition economy: The co-existence of a state as well as a private sector in the product market; the long-run endogeneity of output; and the underdevelopment of the financial sector.

The scope of the paper has been to identify the role of liberalisation in the emergence of the stylised fact concerning the behavior of the real exchange rate at the early stages of transformation of the transition economies. Furthermore, we have incorporated the fact that these economies were experiencing conditions of generally secular inflation.

The analysis considered the impact of two specific shocks related to liberalisation. As pointed out, the first refers to price liberalisation and the second to financial liberalisation. Real exchange rate appreciation occurred under both disturbances during the adjustment process, as the economy moved towards the long run equilibrium following the initial impact effects, and this is in line with the actual experience of the transition economies.

The results were significantly affected by two basic assumptions, which reflect specific features of the transition economies. The first has to do with the existence of the state sector. More specifically, the fact that prices are determined by the market forces together with the observation that the private sector does not extend over the entire economy magnify the impact of the particular shocks on domestic inflation. The second concerns the underdevelopment of the domestic financial sector and the assumption of less than perfect capital mobility, which diminishes the impact of the two disturbances on the rate of exchange depreciation. As a result of these assumptions and given the nature of the disturbances, the possibility of real appreciation during the adjustment process is increased. That is, in the short-run, largely because of these specific features, the disturbances impact more on the inflation rate rather than on the rate of exchange depreciation. Consequently, the adjustment process of the economy is associated with real exchange rate appreciation.

Finally, we must point out that the analysis on real exchange rate appreciation primarily reflects the macroeconomic consequences of the particular disturbances under consideration. That is, the context of the analysis does not consider possible appreciation in the real equilibrium exchange rate due to substantial productivity gains resulting from the transformation process.

Appendix

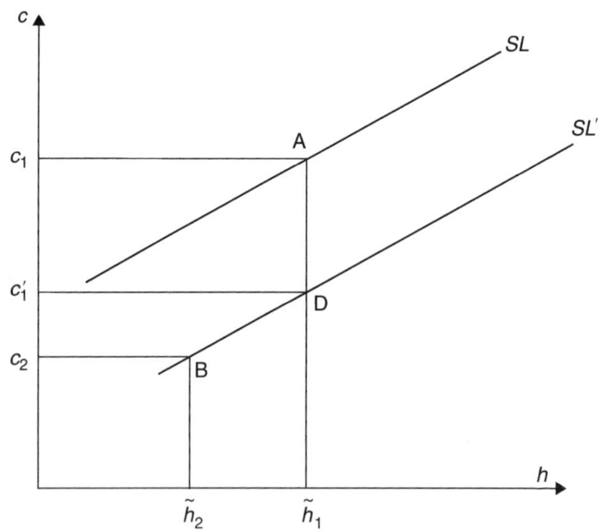

Figure 7.1 Response to increase in core inflation

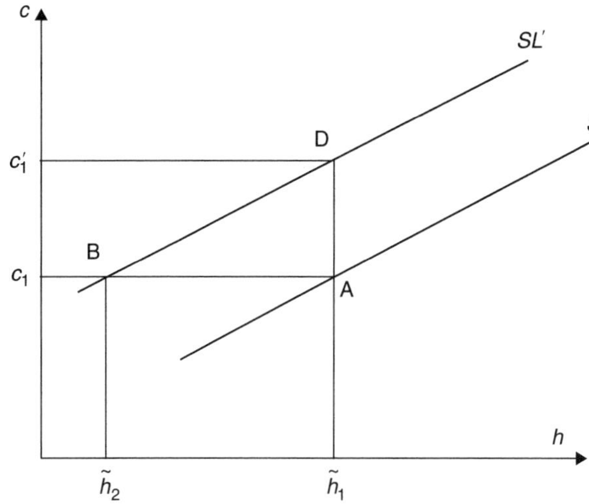

Figure 7.2 Response to decrease in the demand for money

Notes

1. Similar evidence is presented in L. Halpern and C. Wyplosz (1977) and K. Krajnyak and J. Zettelmeyer (1998).
2. For similar arguments see, N. Roubini and P. Wachtel (1999), L. Halpern and C. Wyplosz (1977) and K. Krajnyak and J. Zettelmeyer (1998). The latter two papers attempted to empirically estimate the changes in the equilibrium real exchange rate.
3. See also Turnovsky (1981) and Buiter and Miller (1982).
4. For a more detailed discussion on this, see Papazoglou (2005).
5. This assumption is rather strict. State goods are usually of low quality and thus cannot be considered as perfect substitutes with the ones produced by the private sector. It does, however, facilitate our analysis. The same assumption is also made by C. Grafe and C. Wyplosz (1999).

References

Buiter, W. and M. Miller (1982), 'Monetary Policy and International Competitiveness: The problem of Adjustment', *Oxford Economic Papers*, 33, pp. 143–75.

Grafe, C. and C. Wyplosz (1999), 'A Model of Real Exchange-Rate Determination in Transition Economies', in M. Blejer and M. Skreb (eds),

Balance of Payments, Exchange Rates, and Competitiveness in Transition Economies, London: Kluwer Academic Publishers.
Halpern, L. and C. Wyplosz (1997), 'Equilibrium Exchange Rates in Transition Economies', *IMF Staff Papers*, 44 (4), pp. 430–461.
Krajnyak, K. and J. Zettelmeyer (1998), 'Competitiveness in Transition Economies: What Scope for Real Appreciation?', *IMF Staff Papers*, Vol. 45, 2, pp. 310–362.
Papazoglou, C. (2005), 'Real Exchange Rate Dynamics and Output Contraction under Transition', Working Paper, Bank of Greece, No. 29, November.
Roubini, N. and P. Wachtel (1999), 'Current Account Sustainability in Transition Economies', in M. Blejer and M. Skreb (eds), *Balance of Payments, Exchange Rates, and Competitiveness in Transition Economies*, London: Kluwer Academic Publishers.
Turnovsky, S.J (1981), 'Secular Inflation and Dynamics of Exchange Rates under Perfect Myopic Foresight', *Scandinavian Journal of Economics*, 83, pp. 522–40.

Index